语言学丛书

# 汉语使动及其中介语表征
## Causativity in L2 Chinese Grammars

赵 杨 著

图书在版编目(CIP)数据

汉语使动及其中介语表征(Causativity in L2 Chinese Grammars)/赵杨著．
—北京：北京大学出版社，2006.3
（语言学丛书）
ISBN 7-301-10501-0

Ⅰ．汉… Ⅱ．赵… Ⅲ．汉语-语法-研究-英文 Ⅳ．H146

中国版本图书馆 CIP 数据核字(2006)第 003169 号

书　　　名：汉语使动及其中介语表征
著作责任者：赵杨　著
责任编辑：孙娴
标准书号：ISBN 7-301-10501-0/H·1652
出版发行：北京大学出版社
地　　　址：北京市海淀区成府路 205 号　100871
网　　　址：http://cbs.pku.edu.cn　电子信箱：zpup@pup.pku.edu.cn
电　　　话：邮购部 62752015　发行部 62750672　编辑部 62752028
印　　刷　者：世界知识印刷厂
发　　行　者：北京大学出版社
经　　销　者：新华书店
　　　　　　　890 毫米×1240 毫米　A5　11.25 印张　326 千字
　　　　　　　2006 年 3 月第 1 版　2006 年 11 月第 2 次印刷
定　　　价：23.00 元

未经许可，不得以任何方式复制或抄袭本书之部分或全部内容。
版权所有，翻版必究。

# Abstract

Chinese does not allow causative alternating unaccusative verbs or object-Experiencer psych verbs. It employs analytical causative (headed by *shi* 'make'), resultative (headed by *de*) and compound causative (with an activity predicate $V_1$ and a result predicate $V_2$ forming a $V_1$-$V_2$ compound) constructions to represent causativity. The present study explores syntactic and semantic properties of these verbs and constructions within the generative framework. It is proposed that Chinese unaccusative verbs and psych verbs involve a single VP and that Chinese resultative and compound causative constructions involve a functional category AspP (Aspect Phrase). An empirical study is conducted to look into the mental representations of these Chinese verbs and constructions in English-, Japanese- and Korean-speaking learners' L2 Chinese grammars. The aim of the research is to find out whether L1 transfer persists in L2 Chinese and whether L2 learners can acquire the functional AspP (Aspect Phrase) involved in Chinese resultative and compound causative constructions. The experiment consists of a cloze test, a production test, an acceptability judgment test and a comprehension test. It involves 55 English speakers, 56 Japanese speakers, 73 Korean speakers and 28 native Chinese as controls. Both developmental patterns and variations between different language groups are examined to see whether L2 Chinese learners can acquire native-like mental representations of the structures examined and whether L2 groups from different L1s show any variation in their L2 Chinese mental representations. The results suggest that L2 Chinese learners are more likely to make causative errors with Chinese unaccusative verbs than with psych verbs and that compound causative constructions are more difficult to acquire than resultative constructions in L2 acquisition of Chinese. It is concluded that L1 transfer does not happen everywhere and that functional categories unavailable in the learners' L1s can be properly represented in L2 Chinese grammars.

# 内容简介

汉语词汇使动已渐渐消失,因此,非宾格动词和心理动词不能用作使动动词,汉语使动通过分析型使动结构、结果补语结构和复合使动结构来表现。分析型使动结构和结果补语结构分别由"使"和"得"引导,复合使动结构由一个行为动词和一个表示结果的成分组成,两者构成 $V_1-V_2$ 复合结构。本书以生成语法理论为框架,探讨非宾格动词、心理动词和上述三种使动结构的语义和句法特征。作者认为,汉语的非宾格动词和心理动词投射到句法上的是动词短语(VP),而不是动词短语壳(VP shell);汉语的结果补语结构和复合使动结构含有一个功能范畴,即体短语(AspP)。作者对非宾格动词、心理动词和三种使动结构在中介语中的表征做了实证研究,主要目的有两个:一是考察第一语言迁移情况,二是考察学习者能否习得汉语结果补语结构和复合使动结构中包含的功能范畴。实证研究由完形填空和试验主体两部分构成,试验主体部分使用了产出测试、可接受性判断测试和理解测试三种测试工具,试验对象包括 55 名母语为英语的学习者、56 名母语为日语的学习者和 73 名母语为韩语的学习者,控制组由 28 名母语为汉语的成年人组成。为了发现以汉语为第二语言的学习者和以汉语为母语的学习者是否具有同样的句法表征以及英、日、韩不同母语背景的学习者在习得汉语过程中是否存在差异,作者对同一母语背景的学习者做了发展研究,对不同母语背景的学习者做了比较研究。研究结果显示,与心理动词的习得相比较,以汉语为第二语言的学习者更容易在非宾格动词上出现使动错误;在三个使动结构的习得上,复合使动结构对学习者来说最难掌握。作者的结论是,第一语言迁移现象并不是随处都出现,第二语言有而第一语言无的功能范畴可以在中介语中具有适当表征。

# Preface

As explicitly revealed by the title of this book *Causativity in L2 Chinese Grammars*, what is presented before us is a fruitful record of the writer's study of causativity in Chinese and its acquisition in CSL (Chinese as a second language). When the two come together, the writer clearly informs us that Chinese does not allow (causative alternating) unaccusative verbs or object-Experiencer psych verbs, but that it employs analytical causative, resultative, and compound resultative.

The above understanding results from the writer's years of persevering efforts in doing a syntactic, morphological, and semantic analysis of data collected from English, Japanese and Korean learners of Chinese within the generative approach, although, honestly speaking, I am an outsider myself. Nevertheless, I am still deeply impressed by the writer's logicality in reasoning, and sharp-witted mind in observation as well. Thus, the book is appreciated for its aim to solve practical problems of language acquisition and use. It is also highlighted by the writer's own creative postulation of Asp(ect) P(hrase), a functional category.

The writer's achievements in his research are also due to his patient and thorough review of literature, from which research questions were pinned down, and to his carefully worked out methodology, especially the employment of the production test, acceptability judgement test, and comprehension test. Throughout the procedure, the writer did not hesitate to explain why a question was raised and why an unexpected result turned up. In this sense, in spite of the fact that the study is confined to one aspect of Chinese grammar and mainly 3 non-Chinese languages are involved, one has to recognize that the book is the first ever study of the acquisition of causativity in L2 Chinese, and that it should be highly commended for its implications to general theories of second language acquisition.

As a friend of the writer Zhao Yang, once an MA student of the English department of Peking University and a colleague of mine after his graduation, I heartily congratulate all his achievements and share all his delights. I am confident that Zhao will scale a new height in his future work as he is now professionally devoting himself to the teaching of L2 Chinese to overseas students in Peking University.

Hu Zhuanglin<br>
Peking University<br>
February 8, 2006

# 序

正如标题《汉语使动及其中介语表征》所示，我们面前的这本书是作者对汉语使动及其在汉语作为第二语言习得的研究成果。当汉语本体问题和习得问题结合在一起的时候，作者清晰地告诉我们，汉语不允许非宾格动词转换为使动动词，也不允许以宾语为经验者的心理动词，但是汉语的使动则是通过分析型使动结构、结果补语结构和复合使动结构来表达的。

在过去的几年里，作者以生成语法为框架，研究母语为英语、日语、韩语的学习者对汉语使动的习得，并对搜集到的语料从句法、词法和语义等层面进行分析。本书所展示的研究成果正是源于作者这种锲而不舍的努力。老实讲，我对作者研究的课题是个门外汉，不过，作者推理的逻辑性和观察的敏锐性仍给我留下了深刻的印象。本书的研究目的是解决第二语言习得和应用中的实际问题，作者创造性地提出了"体短语"这一功能范畴，这些都成为本书的亮点。

作者的研究成就也源于他对相关文献的详细、全面的掌握，在回顾前人研究成果的同时，作者明确提出了自己的研究课题，周密设计了研究方法，在实证研究中采用了产出测试、可接受性判断测试和理解测试三种方法。在整个研究过程中，作者对出现的问题，逐一进行了解释，当结果与假设不一致时，也做出了说明。尽管作者把研究范围限制在汉语语法的一个方面，只涉及到三种母语背景的汉语学习者，但是我们应该承认，本书是研究使动在汉语中介语中的表征的第一部著作，对第二语言教学和理论有重要贡献。

本书作者赵杨曾在北京大学英语系攻读英语语言学硕士学位，毕业后留校任教。作为他的朋友和同事，我对他取得的学术成绩表示衷心的祝贺，并一同分享研究给他带来的快乐。赵杨现在北大致力于汉语作为第二语言习得的教学和研究,我坚信,他一定会在这一领域取得更大的成绩,在未来的研究中达到一个新的高度。

胡壮麟
2006年2月8日于北京大学

# Acknowledgments

This is my PhD thesis at the University of Cambridge, originally entitled *Causativity in Chinese and Its Representations In English, Japanese and Korean Speakers' L2 Chinese Grammars*.

This thesis would not have been possible without the help of many individuals and institutions. First of all, I would like to express my heartfelt thanks to my supervisor, Boping Yuan, for insightful discussions, constructive instructions and critical examinations throughout the project, and for the time that he spent reading drafts of the thesis.

I am also indebted to Jin Limin for helpful discussions and advice on my thesis; to Li Xiaoqi, Jiang Baohong, Rao Qin, Tian Yuan, Zhang Shiliu and Zheng Jie for helping me with the organization of some of the experiments; to David Carruthers, Katharine Carruthers, Roger Curtis, Paul Williams and Shan Chuan-Kuo for reading different chapters of the thesis and giving suggestions on the content and language; to Hou Yuli and Weng Jianqing for the illustrations used in the pilot study and the main study; to all the participants who took part in the experiment.

I owe my thanks to Professor Hu Zhuanglin for kindly writing the preface and to Miss Sun Xian of the Peking University Press for her patience and effort in editing this book.

I am grateful to the Cambridge Overseas Trust and Trinity Hall for their generous financial support throughout the project.

I would like to give my special thanks to my wife Yu Bin and my daughter Jingyi for their love, support and understanding.

# Contents

Figures ................................................................. i
Tables ................................................................. ii
Abbreviations ...................................................... v
1 **Introduction** ................................................. 1
2 **Unaccusative verbs and psych verbs** ............ 8
  2.1  Unaccusative verbs and causativity ............ 9
      2.1.1  Subclasses ............................................ 11
      2.1.2  Case ...................................................... 12
      2.1.3  Causative alternation ......................... 13
          2.1.3.1  Morphological formation ............. 14
          2.1.3.2  Semantic representations ............ 15
          2.1.3.3  Syntactic derivations .................... 20
      2.1.4  Unaccusative verbs in Chinese ............ 25
          2.1.4.1  Surface and deep unaccusativity .. 25
          2.1.4.2  Causative alternation ................... 27
              2.1.4.2.1  Non-accomplishment verbs ... 27
              2.1.4.2.2  Partitive case ......................... 30
              2.1.4.2.3  θ-roles .................................... 33
      2.1.5  Unaccusative verbs in Japanese ......... 34
      2.1.6  Unaccusative verbs in Korean ............. 36
      2.1.7  Summary ............................................. 37
  2.2  Psych verbs and causativity ...................... 39
      2.2.1  Semantic representations ................... 39
      2.2.2  Syntactic derivations .......................... 41
      2.2.3  Psych verbs in Chinese ...................... 44
          2.2.3.1  SE verbs and OE verbs .............. 44
          2.2.3.2  Decausativized psych verbs ....... 44

  2.2.3.3 Syntactic derivations ················· 46
  2.2.4 Psych verbs in Japanese ················ 49
  2.2.5 Psych verbs in Korean ················· 50
  2.2.6 Summary ································ 51
2.3 Summary ······································ 53

# 3 Resultative and compound causative constructions ················· 60

3.1 Resultative constructions in English ············ 62
  3.1.1 The result XP and DOR ················ 64
  3.1.2 Semantic and syntactic representations ······ 67
   3.1.2.1 The small-clause proposal ············ 67
   3.1.2.2 The ternary-analysis approach ········ 70
   3.1.2.3 A solution with VP shell ············· 71
3.2 Resultative and compound causative constructions in Chinese ································ 72
  3.2.1 Previous studies on resultatives and compound causatives ···························· 74
   3.2.1.1 Y. Li (1990, 1995, 1998) ············ 74
   3.2.1.2 C.-T. Huang (1992) ················ 78
   3.2.1.3 Tang (1997) ······················· 80
  3.2.2 A proposal of AspP ····················· 84
   3.2.2.1 The derivation of resultative constructions ······ 85
   3.2.2.2 The derivation of compound causative constructions ······················ 90
3.3 Resultative and compound causative constructions in Japanese ······························· 95
3.4 Resultative and compound causative constructions in Korean ································ 98
3.5 Summary ····································· 100

## 4　Second language acquisition and causativity ·················· 108

- 4.1　A brief review of SLA studies ······························· 109
  - 4.1.1　L1 transfer ···················································· 111
  - 4.1.2　Interlanguage ················································ 114
  - 4.1.3　Functional categories ······································ 116
  - 4.1.4　Learnability problems ····································· 118
- 4.2　SLA studies of causativity ···································· 121
  - 4.2.1　Previous studies ············································ 121
    - 4.2.1.1　Juffs (1996b) ·········································· 121
    - 4.2.1.2　White et al (1999) ···································· 123
    - 4.2.1.3　Montrul (1999) ········································ 124
    - 4.2.1.4　Montrul (2000) ········································ 127
    - 4.2.1.5　Montrul (2001a) ······································ 129
    - 4.2.1.6　Cabrera and Zubizarreta (2003) ················ 132
  - 4.2.2　Summary of the findings ································· 134
- 4.3　Summary ························································· 136

## 5　Research methodology of the present study ·················· 138

- 5.1　Causativity in Chinese, English, Japanese and Korean ··· 139
- 5.2　Research questions and hypotheses ······················· 146
  - 5.2.1　Unaccusative verbs and psych verbs ················ 146
  - 5.2.2　Resultative and compound causative constructions ··· 148
  - 5.2.3　The analytical causative construction ················ 152
- 5.3　Participants ······················································ 152
- 5.4　Procedures and Instruments ································· 156
  - 5.4.1　Data-collecting procedures ····························· 156
  - 5.4.2　Instruments ·················································· 157
    - 5.4.2.1　The production test ·································· 158
    - 5.4.2.2　The acceptability judgment test ················ 160

    5.4.2.2.1 Psych verbs and unaccusative verbs in the AJ test ................ 161
    5.4.2.2.2 Resultative and compound causative constructions in the AJ test ............ 164
   5.4.2.3 The comprehension test ............... 169
5.5 Summary ............... 174

# 6 Results and discussion: psych verbs and unaccusative verbs ............... 176

6.1 Psych verbs ............... 177
  6.1.1 Results of the AJ test ............... 178
   6.1.1.1 Psych verbs used in the analytical causative construction ............... 180
   6.1.1.2 Psych verbs misused as OE verbs ............... 181
  6.1.2 Results of the production test ............... 182
   6.1.2.1 Psych verbs used in the analytical causative construction ............... 183
   6.1.2.2 Psych verbs misused as OE verbs ............... 186
  6.1.3 Summary ............... 190
6.2 Unaccusative verbs ............... 192
  6.2.1 Results of the AJ test ............... 192
   6.2.1.1 L2 Chinese learners' judgments on the ungrammatical alternating unaccusative structures ............... 195
   6.2.1.2 Comparisons between judgments on unaccusative verbs and transitive verbs ............... 199
  6.2.2 Results of the production test ............... 201
  6.2.3 Summary ............... 204
6.3 Comparisons between psych verbs and unaccusative verbs in the group's judgments ............... 205
6.4 Discussion ............... 207

- 6.4.1 The acquisition of Chinese analytical causative construction ……………………………………… 208
- 6.4.2 Causative errors with unaccusative verbs ………… 209
- 6.4.3 Fossilized representations of unaccusative verbs … 211

# 7 Results and discussion: resultative and compound causative constructions ……………………………………… 218

- 7.1 Resultative constructions ……………………………………… 219
  - 7.1.1 Results of the AJ test ……………………………… 219
  - 7.1.2 Results of the comprehension test ………………… 224
    - 7.1.2.1 Resultative construction: Type A …………… 226
    - 7.1.2.2 Resultative construction: Type B …………… 229
  - 7.1.3 Summary ……………………………………………… 232
- 7.2 Compound causative constructions ……………………………… 233
  - 7.2.1 Results of the AJ test ……………………………… 233
    - 7.2.1.1 Comparisons between L2 proficiency groups and comparisons between L2 groups from different L1s ……………………………………… 236
    - 7.2.1.2 A closer examination of different types of compound causatives ……………………… 239
  - 7.2.2 Results of the comprehension test ………………… 242
  - 7.2.3 Summary ……………………………………………… 249
- 7.3 Comparisons between results on the resultative construction, the compound causative construction and the V – NP – XP structure ……………………………………………………… 249
- 7.4 Discussion ……………………………………………………… 254
  - 7.4.1 The acquisition of the resultative construction …… 254
  - 7.4.2 The acquisition of the compound causative construction ……………………………………………… 256
    - 7.4.2.1 L2 Chinese representations of compound causatives ……………………………………… 257

  7.4.2.2 L1 transfer ·················································· 264

# 8 Representations of causativity in L2 Chinese: summary, implication and conclusion ······················· 269

8.1 Summary of the empirical study ····························· 270
8.2 General discussion: theoretical issues in SLA revisited ··· 273
  8.2.1 L1 transfer ·················································· 273
  8.2.2 Functional categories ······································ 277
  8.2.3 Fossilization ················································ 279
8.3 Implications for future research ······························ 280
8.4 Conclusion ······················································ 282

**References** ······························································· 283

**Appendixes** ····························································· 308
1 General introductions and personal information ··················· 308
2 Cloze test ······························································ 309
3 The production test ··················································· 311
4 The acceptability judgment test ····································· 312
5 Pictures used in the comprehension test ··························· 320
6 Testing items used in the experiment ······························ 321
7 Descriptive statistics ·················································· 327
8 Pair-wise comparisons between judgments on compound causatives in the AJ test ············································ 335

# Figures

4.1　The subset condition for two grammars ················ 119
6.1　Psych-verb structures: mean scores in the AJ test ········· 179
6.2　Analytical causative construction: mean scores of the transformed data in the production test ······················ 185
6.3　Psych verbs: mean scores of the transformed data in the production test ··························································· 188
6.4　The unaccusative structure with the Theme argument as sentence subject: mean scores in the AJ test ················ 193
6.5　The incorrect alternating unaccusative structures and the correct transitive control structures: mean scores in the AJ test ······································································· 195
6.6　Unaccusative verbs: mean scores of the transformed data in the production test ················································· 203
6.7　The incorrect OE-verb structure and the incorrect alternating unaccusative structure: mean scores in the AJ test ········· 206
7.1　Resultative constructions: mean scores in the AJ test ······ 221
7.2　Compound causative constructions: mean scores in the AJ test ········································································· 235
7.3　Comparisons between the resultative construction, the compound causative construction and the V-NP-XP structure: mean scores in the AJ test ······················· 251

· i ·

# Tables

2.1 Summary: properties of unaccusative verbs in Chinese, English, Japanese and Korean in relation to causativity ··· 37

2.2 Summary: properties of psych verbs in Chinese, English, Japanese and Korean in relation to causativity ············· 51

3.1 Summary: resultative and compound causative constructions in Chinese, English, Japanese and Korean ················ 101

4.1 Previous studies on the acquisition of L2 alternating unaccusative verbs and psych verbs ·························· 135

5.1 Information of the subjects in the study ···················· 154

5.2 The mean score and standard deviation (SD) of each subject group in the cloze test ································ 154

6.1 The number and percentage of grammatical analytical causative sentences formed and consistent subjects who formed such sentences in the production test ············· 184

6.2 Psych verbs: the number and percentage of three types of structure formed and subjects who consistently formed such structures in the production test ······························ 186

6.3 Summary of results on the analytical causative construction and the incorrect OE-verb structure in the AJ test and the production test: pair-wise comparisons ······················ 191

6.4 Percentage of rejected and accepted tokens of each of the incorrect alternating unaccusative structures and percentage of subjects who consistently rejected or accepted the three tokens of each structure in the AJ test ······················ 198

6.5 Comparisons between judgments on the incorrect alternating unaccusative structures and the correct transitive control structures in paired-samples T tests ·························· 200

6.6  Unaccusative verbs: number and percentage of two types of structure formed and consistent subjects who formed such structures in the production test ·············· 202

6.7  Summary of results on the ungrammatical alternating unaccusative verbs in the AJ test and the production test: pair-wise comparisons ·············· 204

6.8  The OE-verb structure and the active unaccusative structure: percentage of accepted/rejected tokens and that of consistent subjects in the AJ test ·············· 207

7.1  Summary of the results on resultative constructions in the AJ test: pair-wise Bonferroni comparisons ·············· 222

7.2  Type A of the resultative construction in the comprehension test: frequency (in percentage) of each of the interpretations ·············· 227

7.3  Type A of the resultative construction in the comprehension test: percentage of subjects who consistently chose the same option (B, C or D) on the three tokens of the construction ·············· 228

7.4  Type B of the resultative construction in the comprehension test: frequency (in percentage) of each of the interpretations ·············· 230

7.5  Type B of the resultative construction in the comprehension test: percentage of subjects who consistently chose the same option (B, C or D) on the three tokens of the construction ·············· 231

7.6  Compound causative constructions: percentage of subjects who consistently accepted or rejected the three tokens of each type of structure in the AJ test ·············· 236

7.7  The compound causative construction in the comprehension test: frequency (in percentage) of each of the

|  | interpretations ............................................. 244 |
|---|---|
| 7.8 | The compound causative construction in the comprehension test: percentage of subjects who consistently chose the same option (B, C or D) on the three tokens of the construction ............................................. 244 |
| 7.9 | Percentage of subjects who consistently accepted or rejected the three tokens of the resultative construction, the compound causative construction and the V-NP-XP structure in the AJ test ............................................. 251 |
| 7.10 | Results of paired-samples T tests between the mean scores on the resultative construction, the compound causative construction and the V-NP-XP structure within each subject group in the AJ test ............................................. 253 |
| 7.11 | Summary: L2 Chinese groups' judgments of the six types of compound causative construction in terms of mean scores and native-like judgments ............................................. 256 |
| 7.12 | The six types of compound causative construction under study: hierarchy of acceptability in terms of mean scores and native-like judgments ............................................. 257 |

# Abbreviations

| | | | |
|---|---|---|---|
| ACC | accusative | A/Adj | adjective |
| ANIM | animate | ANTICAUS | anticausative |
| AP | adjective phrase | ASP | aspect marker |
| Asp | aspect | AspP | aspect phrase |
| C | complementizer | CAUS | causative |
| CL | classifier | COMP | complementizer |
| CP | complementizer phrase | DAT | dative case |
| DEC | declarative case | Exp | experiencer |
| F | function category | FP | functional phrase |
| GEN | genitive case | IL | interlanguage |
| INTR | intransitive | IP | inflectional phrase |
| L1 | first language | L2 | second language |
| N | noun | NOM | nominative case |
| NP | noun phrase | Obj | object |
| PASS | passive | PAST | past tense |
| PP | prepositional phrase | PRES | present tense |
| RC | result clause | REFL | reflexive pronoun |
| SC | small clause | Spec | specifier |
| Subj | subject | TOP | topic |
| TopP | topic phrase | TRANS | transitive |
| V | verb | VP | verb phrase |
| XP | X phrase | YP | Y phrase |

# 1 Introduction

　　本章首先简要阐述了"使动"的定义、论元结构和词汇语义结构,之后介绍了使动的三种原型,即分析型使动、形态使动和词汇使动。作者指出,汉语中没有真正意义上的形态使动和词汇使动,因此非宾格动词和心理动词不能用作使动,汉语使动由分析型使动结构、结果补语结构和复合使动结构来表现。随后作者指出了本书的三个主要研究目的:

　　(1) 在以汉语为第二语言的中介语中,使动具有怎样的表征?

　　(2) 在这样的表征中,有无第一语言迁移现象?

　　(3) 汉语结果补语结构和复合使动结构中包含的功能范畴能否在以汉语为第二语言的中介语中得到表现?

　　在本章最后,作者对本书各章的主要内容做了简要介绍。

# Introduction

Causativity reflects the notion of causality, "according to which agents are seen as the causes of the situations which, by their actions, they bring into existence" (Lyons 1977: 490). In this sense, causativity involves both causality and agency. In languages, causativity is represented by causative and resultative constructions.

According to Goddard (1998: 260), a causative is "an expression in which an event (the caused event) is depicted as taking place because someone does something or because something happens". This definition implies that at least two events are involved in a causative, a causing event and a caused event, and there is a 'causing' relation between them. According to Shibatani (1976a: 1-2), a causative situation is characterized as a relation between two events such that one occurs at $t_1$ and the other at $t_2$, after $t_1$, and the occurrence of the second event is dependent on the occurrence of the first, so that "the caused event would not have taken place at that particular time if the causing event had not taken place, provided that all else had remained the same".

In terms of argument structure, a causative construction involves (at least) two arguments, Causer and Causee, which are connected by a verb, as shown in (1):

(1)

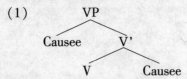

With regard to event structure, a causative construction expresses an event of transition, which involves two sub-events, action and state, or a causing event and an event that specifies the change associated with the verb (Pustejovsky 1991). In lexical semantics, a causative construction contains two semantic components, CAUSE and BECOME (Hale and Keyser 1993; Jackendoff 1990), and has a lexical semantic structure as shown in (2):

(2) [[x DO] CAUSE [x/y BECOME STATE]]

On the basis of morphological distinctions, causatives can be classified into three prototypes, syntactic (or analytical) causatives, morphological (or synthetic) causatives and lexical causatives (Comrie 1976, 1985), as exemplified in (3):

(3) a. John made the cleaner work 12 hours a day.
   (syntactic/analytical)
   b. The City Council widened the road.
   (morphological/synthetic)
   c. John killed a cat. (lexical)

Analytical causatives like (3a) contain a causative verb like *make* to represent the causative meaning. They use regular syntactic devices to form (usually) bi-predicate sentences without fusing the predicates together. *Make* and *have* are such verbs in English. Morphological causatives involve a productive process in which causatives are derived from non-causative words by adding causative affixes to these words. Sentence (3b) is an example of this kind of causative, which is derived from affixation of -(e)n to the adjective *wide*. Lexical causatives like (3c) differ from the other types of causative in that they do not have any formal indications such as causative verbs like *make* or causative suffixes like *-en* to represent the cause so that their causative meaning is not derived but inherent. A related property is that, unlike a morphological causative verb which is connected with its non-causative counterpart morphologically as shown in *wide* and *widen*, a lexical causative has no formal similarity between the causative verb like *kill* and its non-causative counterpart like *die*.

English has two types of lexical causative, one represented by words like *kill* and the other represented by words like *break* (Lemmens 1998). Words like *break* are unaccusative verbs which participate in causative/inchoative alternation, but words like *kill* cannot be used inchoatively.

In causatives, the cause element is predicated. If the result element is predicated, resultatives as shown in (4) are generated. In resultative constructions, causativity is represented by the result predicate like *flat* in (4a) and *hoarse* in (4b).

(4) a. John pounded the metal flat.
    b. John shouted himself hoarse.

Not all the three types of causative exist in every language. Chinese has analytical causatives but does not have morphological or lexical causatives. Due to lack of lexical causatives in Chinese, psych verbs which select Experiencer as object are not allowed, as shown in (5a); nor are unaccusative verbs allowed to participate in causative alternation, as shown in (5b). Causativity in Chinese is represented by analytical causatives, compound causatives and resultatives, as illustrated in (6).

(5) a. *Na ge xiaoxi xingfen le   Zhangsan.
       that CL news excite ASP Zhangsan
       'That news excited Zhangsan.'
    b. *Zhangsan sui   le   huaping.
       Zhangsan break ASP vase
       'Zhangsan broke the vase.'
(6) a. Analytical causative headed by *shi*
      Na ge xiaoxi shi Zhangsan hen xingfen.

      that CL news *shi* Zhangsan very excite
      'That news made Zhangsan very excited.'
  b. Compound causative composed of $V_1$ and $V_2$
      Zhangsan da- sui le    huaping.
      Zhangsan hit-break ASP vase
      'Zhangsan broke the vase.'
  c. Resultative headed by the resultative marker *de*
      Zhangsan pao de hen lei.
      Zhangsan run *de* very tire
      'Zhangsan ran and got very tired as a result.'

    The present study explores within the generative framework representations of causativity in native Chinese grammar and English-, Japanese- and Korean-speaking learners' L2 Chinese grammars, with particular attention to unaccusative verbs, psych verbs, analytical causatives, compound causatives and resultatives. It examines semantic structures and syntactic derivations of these verbs and constructions and addresses the following questions with regard to their representations in L2 Chinese grammars:
    a) How is causativity represented in L2 Chinese grammars?
    b) Is there L1 effect in L2 Chinese representations of causativity?
    c) Can functional categories involved in compound causatives and resultatives be projected in L2 Chinese grammars?

The organization of the dissertation is as follows. Representations of causativity in Chinese are examined in Chapters 2 and 3. Chapter 2 looks into the argument structure, the event structure and the syntactic structure of unaccusative verbs and psych verbs in Chinese, English, Japanese and Korean with a focus on causative alternation. It is argued that a VP shell is projected for these verbs in English but a single VP is projected in Chinese, Japanese and Korean. Chapter 3 examines the semantic and syntactic structures of resultative and compound causative constructions. It first introduces the small-clause proposal and the tertiary-analysis approach for English resultatives and posits a VP-shell solution. Then it describes resultatives and compound causatives in Chinese, arguing for a functional aspectual phrase (AspP) projected in the two constructions. Through comparisons between resultatives and compound causatives in Chinese, English, Japanese and Korean, it is argued that the functional AspP is present in Korean resultatives but absent in English and Japanese resultatives; it is also absent in Japanese and Korean compound causatives.

Chapters 4 and 5 provide a background for the following empirical study. Chapter 4 first gives a brief review of second language acquisition study, addressing such topics as first language (L1) transfer, interlanguage, functional categories and learnability. Then it introduces previous studies of causativity in relation to unaccusative verbs and psych verbs. These studies seem to indicate that the thematic hierarchy (Grimshaw 1990), the Uniformity of Theta Assignment Hypothesis (UTAH) (Baker 1988) and L1 morphological properties play roles in the acquisition of L2 argument structure. Chapter 5 introduces research methodology of the empirical study. It first summarizes representations of causativity in Chinese, English, Japanese and Korean, and, on the basis of these representations, proposes research questions and hypotheses. Then it describes participants, procedures and instruments of the study. The experiment involves 55 English-speaking learners, 56 Japanese-speaking learners, 73 Korean-speaking learners and 28 native Chinese speakers as controls. L2 Chinese learners of each of the three L1s are classified into low-intermediate, intermediate and high-intermediate groups according to their Chinese proficiency. The experiment employs three instruments, including a production test, an acceptability judgment test and a comprehension test.

Results of the present study are reported in Chapters 6 and 7. Chapter 6 reports and analyses results of the production test and the acceptability judgment test on Chinese unaccusative verbs and psych verbs. Chapter 7 presents and examines results of the acceptability judgment test and the comprehension test on Chinese resultatives and compound causatives.

Results of the three tasks are summarized in Chapter 8 with discussion of the findings. On the basis of the findings, theoretical issues regarding second language acquisition studies are revisited and directions for future research are suggested.

# 2  Unaccusative verbs and psych verbs

**导言**

　　本章主要探讨汉、英、日、韩四种语言中非宾格动词和心理动词的语义特征、句法表征以及使动转换能力。

　　作者从非宾格假说入手,介绍了非宾格动词的分类、赋格能力、使动转换特点等,着重介绍了能够转换为使动词的非宾格动词的形态构成、语义特征和句法推导式。随后,作者指出汉语非宾格动词不能用作使动,原因有二:在赋格能力上,这类动词能够赋予后面的名词以部分格,但不能赋予它们以宾格;在论元角色方面,这类动词只能够指派"受事"论元,而不能指派"施事"论元。由于不能用作使动,汉语非宾格动词投射到句法上的是动词短语,而不是动词短语壳。日语和韩语中的非宾格动词同汉语非宾格动词具有相似特征,也不能用作使动,投射到句法上的也是动词短语。与汉、日、韩不同,英语中表示状态转换的非宾格动词有赋予宾格的能力,能够同时指派"施事"和"受事"论元,因此可以用作使动。

　　心理动词方面,作者首先介绍了以主语为经验者和以宾语为经验者这两类心理动词,并且重点介绍了以宾语为经验者的心理动词的语义特征和句法表征。随后指出,汉语心理动词只能以主语为经验者,而不能以宾语为经验者,换言之,这类动词不能用作使动,投射到句法上的是动词短语,而不是动词短语壳。日语和韩语中的心理动词与汉语中的心理动词相似,只能以主语为经验者,不能用作使动。与汉、日、韩不同,英语允许以宾语为经验者的心理动词,这类动词在句法上的投射是动词短语壳。

# Unaccusative verbs and psych verbs

In this chapter I will examine unaccusative verbs and psych verbs in relation to causativity, in particular their properties in Chinese. The chapter is arranged as follows. Properties of unaccusative verbs and psych verbs will be addressed in § 2.1 and § 2.2 respectively. In § 2.1 I will discuss unaccusative verbs in general and alternating unaccusative verbs in particular in Chinese, English, Japanese and Korean. In § 2.2 I will discuss psych verbs, particularly object-Experiencer psych verbs, in the four languages. Properties of these two types of verb will be summarized in § 2.3.

## 2.1 Unaccusative verbs and causativity

Under the Unaccusative Hypothesis (Burzio 1986; Perlmutter 1978), intransitive verbs can be classified into two types, unaccusative verbs and unergative verbs. Their distinctions can be summarized in at least three aspects. The first aspect of distinction is the underlying syntactic position of the single argument they select: it is the direct object in the case of unaccusative verbs, but the subject in the case of unergative verbs. Put differently, an unaccusative verb selects an internal argument but does not select an external argument, whereas an unergative verb selects an external argument but does not select an internal argument. The underlying configurations of the two classes of intransitive verbs are schematized in (1) (from Levin and Rappaport Hovav 1995: 3). The second aspect of distinction is the θ-role of the single argument: while agentivity correlates with unergativity, patienthood correlates with unaccusativity (Dowty 1991). The third distinction is aspect and event structure:

unaccusative verbs denote a bounded event, i. e. an event with a specified endpoint or resulting state, while unergative verbs denote unbounded events, or activities (e. g. van Hout 2004). Because of these distinctions, unaccusativity and unergativity are argued to be both syntactically represented and semantically determined: on the one hand, they are semantically predictable; on the other hand, they are syntactically encoded (Levin and Rappaport Hovav 1995).

(1) a. Unergative verb: NP[$_{VP}$ V]
    b. Unaccusative verb: _____ [$_{VP}$ V NP/CP]

Such a strong claim of distinctions between unaccusative and unergative verbs is challenged by Sorace (1995, 2004), who argues that languages vary in the degree of surface differentiation between these two types of verbs and in the degree of internal consistency of their syntactic behaviours. Thus, systematic differences within the syntactic classes of unaccusative and unergative verbs may be captured by a hierarchy in which "core" monadic verbs are distinguished from progressively more "peripheral" verbs. Evidence found to support this claim is the auxiliary selection hierarchy in languages that have a choice of perfective auxiliaries. In these languages, unaccusative verbs tend to select the counterpart of the English auxiliary *be* and unergative verbs tend to select the counterpart of the auxiliary *have*. Native intuitions on auxiliaries are consistent for certain types of verb but are much less determinate for other types, which indicates that there may not be a clear dividing line between unaccusatives and unergatives and that some verbs may have properties of both. Therefore, distinctions between the two types of verbs are not absolute but statistical.

  The focus of the present study is unaccusative verbs or, to be more exact, causative alternating unaccusative verbs. In the next subsections, I will only discuss properties that are related to unaccusative verbs.

## 2.1.1 Subclasses

Unaccusative verbs can be divided into three subclasses, which are verbs of change of state, verbs of change of location and verbs of existence and appearance (Levin and Rappaport Hovav 1995). Change-of-state verbs like *break* in (2a) are externally caused verbs, which usually participate in causative alternation (see § 2.1.3); verbs of change of location like *arrive* in (2b) are inherently directed verbs, which specify a direction of motion; verbs of existence and appearance like *happen* in (2c) mainly occur in locative-inversion and *there*-insertion constructions.

(2) a. A vase *broke*. (change of state)
    b. Three men *arrived* at the school. (change of location)
    c. A terrible thing *happened*. (existence/appearance)

Levin and Rappaport Hovav (1995) make a distinction between deep unaccusativity and surface unaccusativity: the former refers to cases where the argument of an unaccusative verb is analysed as the object of the verb in the underlying structure but not in the surface structure, while the latter refers to cases where the argument of an unaccusative verb occurs at the object position in both the underlying structure and the surface structure. In English, the resultative construction qualifies as a diagnostic of deep unaccusativity as shown in (3), whereas surface unaccusativity is manifested only in the *there*-insertion and locative-inversion constructions as shown in (4) (examples in (3) and (4) quoted from Levin and Rappaport Hovav 1995: 39, 19).

(3) The bottle *broke* open.
(4) a. There *appeared* a ship on the horizon.
    b. Into the room *came* a man.

In English, verbs of change of location (e.g. *arrive*) and verbs of existence and appearance (e. g. *exist* and *happen*) are usually compatible with surface unaccusativity, whereas verbs of change of state (e. g. *break* and *sink*) are compatible with deep unaccusativity.

## 2.1.2 Case

According to Burzio (1986), a verb cannot case-mark an NP if it does not have an external argument; a verb cannot θ-mark an external argument if it cannot assign accusative case. This is usually referred to as Burzio's Generalization in the linguistic literature. Since an unaccusative verb does not have an external argument and consequently is not a case assigner, its internal argument is caseless. There are two ways in which the internal argument is case-marked: one is to move to the subject position to be assigned nominative case as illustrated in (5a) and (6a); the other is to form a chain with an expletive in the subject position as shown in (6b). According to Chomsky (1986: 135), "a chain is case-marked if it contains exactly one case-marked position; a position in a case-marked chain is visible for θ-marking". This is called "case transmission" (Lasnik 1992). In (6b), the expletive *there* transmits the nominative case to the otherwise caseless argument *a storm*, which thereby becomes visible for θ-marking.

(5) a. A vase broke.
    b. *There broke a vase.
(6) a. A storm arose here.
    b. There$_i$ arose [a storm]$_i$ here.
    c. *There arose the storm here.
    d. *There arose every terrible storm in that area.

With regard to the three subclasses of unaccusative verb in English illustrated in (2), the internal argument NP can be case-marked by the first means, i. e. by moving to the subject position, and this is the only means by which the internal argument of change-of-state verbs is case-marked, as can be seen from the ungrammatical sentence in (5b). For verbs of change of location and verbs of existence/ appearance, the internal argument NP can also be case-marked by forming a chain with the expletive in the subject position. In this case, however, the NP must be indefinite. Otherwise, ill-formed sentences as shown in (6c) and (6d) will result.

In contrast to Perlmutter (1978) and Burzio (1986), both of whom claim that unaccusative verbs are not case assigners, Belletti (1988) argues that unaccusative verbs can assign inherent partitive case[1] (cf. Wanner 2000) despite their inability to assign structural accusative case.[2] According to this proposal, a verb can assign two kinds of case to its internal argument, accusative case and partitive case. With respect to unaccusative verbs, their capability of assigning accusative case is suspended, but their ability to assign partitive case is maintained.[3] They can assign partitive case to an object NP on condition that this NP is indefinite and is part of a set (also see Kiparsky 1998). This proposal can account for the ungrammaticality of (6c) and (6d): *the storm* in (6c) is definite and thus fails to satisfy the indefiniteness requirement; *every terrible storm* in (6d) contains a universal quantifier *every*, which is intrinsically incompatible with partitive case.[4]

## 2.1.3 Causative alternation

In languages like English, change-of-state unaccusative verbs like *break* in (7) are externally caused verbs, which can usually be used transitively/causatively.

(7) a. The vase broke. (unaccusative/inchoative)
    b. Tom broke the vase. (causative/transitive)

These verbs are both transitive and intransitive, and V-transitive can be roughly paraphrased as "cause to V-intransitive" (Goddard 1998: 277).[5] The unaccusative verb and its causative counterpart form a causative/inchoative pair,[6] which express the same basic situation, generally a change of state, and differ only in that "the causative verb meaning includes an agent participant who causes the situation, whereas the inchoative verb meaning excludes a causing agent and presents the situation as occurring spontaneously" (Haspelmath 1993: 90). In terms of Haegeman (1994) and Radford (1997), this kind of verb is ergative.[7]

In English, the causative use of a verb is morphologically identical with its unaccusative/inchoative counterpart. The same verb can express change of state or motion when used intransitively, or, when used transitively, causation of the state of affairs expressed by the intransitive verb.

2.1.3.1 Morphological formation

Causative/inchoative verb pairs mainly have three types of morphological form, which are causative, anticausative and non-directed alternations (Haspelmath 1993), as illustrated in (8). Which type to use depends on individual languages.

(8) Three types of causative/inchoative alternation (Haspelmath 1993: 91)
 a. Causative alternation: French
  *fondre* 'melt' (inchoative)
  *faire fondre* 'melt' (causative)
 b. Anticausative alternation: Russian
  *katat'-sja* 'roll' (inchoative)
  *katat'* 'roll' (causative)

c. Non-directed alternation: Japanese
*atum-aru* 'gather' (inchoative)
*atum-eru* 'gather' (causative)

In the causative alternation, the inchoative verb is basic and the causative verb is derived by adding a causative affix or a causative auxiliary as in (8a), in which the causative auxiliary *faire* is added to causativize the verb *fondre*, the two words forming a "single complex verb" (Guasti 1997: 125). In the anticausative alternation, the causative verb is basic while the inchoative verb is derived and is marked with an anticausative affix or auxiliary as in (8b), in which the suffix *-sja* is used to decausativize *katat*'. In non-directed alternations, neither the inchoative verb nor the causative verb is derived from the other as in (8c), in which *atum-aru* (inchoative) and *atum-eru* (causative) are independent of each other, neither being derived from the other in spite of the same root *atum* they have.

English belongs to the 'non-directed alternation' type: inchoative verbs like *break* have the same morphological form as their causative counterparts and neither is derived from the other.

## 2.1.3.2 Semantic representations

Verbs can be classified into four types in terms of aspectual properties such as temporal duration, temporal termination and internal temporal structure (Dowty 1979; Vendler 1967). They can denote states, activities, achievements and accomplishments: states (e.g. *know*, *love*) have no change during a span of time; activities (e.g. *walk along the river*) are on-going events with duration but without necessary temporal endpoint; accomplishments (e.g. *draw a circle*) are events with an obligatory temporal endpoint as well as duration; achievements (e.g. *die*) are events with a temporal endpoint but without duration. According to Verkuyl (1972), the aspectual classification requires that one look not just at the verb but at VP at least. For the same verb *walk*, for example, *walk along the river* is an activity, while *walk to school* is an accomplishment. The internal argument of a verb, a prepositional phrase and a resultative small clause can all turn an activity into an accomplishment (Hoekstra 1992; Tenny 1994).

Of the four types of verb in Vendler's classification, accomplishments and achievements have a temporal endpoint, whereas states and activities do not. In the linguistic literature, events that have a temporal endpoint are referred to as "bounded", while those that do not are classed as "unbounded".[8] In an inchoative/causative pair, both the inchoative verb and its causative alternant express bounded events. In other words, a result is encoded in both the inchoative form and its causative counterpart.

In lexical semantics (Dowty 1979; Hale and Keyser 1993; Jackendoff 1990; Levin and Rappaport Hovav 1995), the lexical meaning of a verb can be represented by decomposed semantic primitives: an inchoative verb contains a semantic primitive BECOME, while its causative alternant contains CAUSE as well as BECOME. Accordingly, causative verbs have two verbal projections, an upper VP headed by CAUSE and a lower VP headed by BECOME. If argument structure is taken to be derived configurationally (Baker 1988; Hale and Keyser 1993), Agent occupies the specifier position of the upper VP projected by CAUSE and Theme occupies the specifier position of the lower VP projected by BECOME, as illustrated in (9):

(9)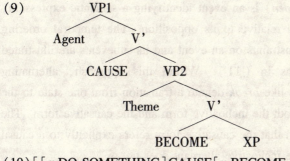

(10) [[ $x$ DO SOMETHING ] CAUSE [ $y$ BECOME STATE ]]

According to Levin and Rappaport Hovav (1995), whether an unaccusative verb participates in inchoative/causative alternation is determined by its meaning: CAUSE is implicated in the lexical decomposition of the transitive form of alternating verbs, whereas there is no CAUSE in non-alternating unaccusatives. It is further argued that alternating unaccusative verbs have a single lexical semantic representation as in (10) (from Levin and Rappaport Hovav 1995: 94) which is associated with both the unaccusative form and the causative form, meaning that change-of-state unaccusative verbs are semantically causative. The distinction between an unaccusative verb and its causative alternant lies, therefore, not in whether there is CAUSE or not in the lexical semantic representation, but in whether the Agent or Causer is explicitly represented or not: in the causative form, it is explicitly represented, whereas in its unaccusative alternant, it is not.

Pustejovsky (1991) extends the decompositional approach and posits syntax of event structure, which makes explicit reference to quantified events as part of the word meaning. According to this proposal, there are three basic event types, which are states, processes and transitions: a state (e.g. *love*) refers to a single event, which is evaluated relative to no other event; a process (e.g. *run*) is a sequence of events identifying the same semantic expression; a transition (e.g. *open*) is an event identifying a semantic expression, which is evaluated relative to its opposition. The temporal ordering and dominance constraints on an event and its subevents are illustrated with tree diagrams in (11). Within this approach, alternating unaccusative verbs like *break* denote a transition from one state to the opposite state in both the inchoative form and the causative form. The two forms differ in that the causative form refers explicitly to a causal agent, whereas the inchoative alternant does not.

(11) Three types of event structure (Pustejovsky 1991)

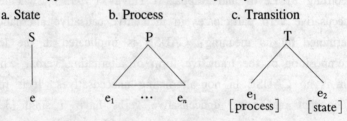

a. State      b. Process      c. Transition

Grimshaw (1990) proposes a similar approach, arguing that each verb has associated with it an event structure, which represents the aspectual analysis of the clause where the verb occurs. The event structure breaks down events into aspectual subparts. An accomplishment denotes a complex event which consists of an activity and a resulting state, as shown in (12). For *x breaks y*, the activity is the event in which *x* engages in breaking and the resulting state is one in which *y* is broken. The event structure of an unaccusative verb corresponds to the second subpart of an accomplishment, namely the part indicating the resulting state.

(12)

According to Grimshaw, the event template determines prominence, assigning the maximally prominent position in the aspectual dimension

only to the argument participating in the first subevent. This maximally prominent argument is the external argument. Since an unaccusative verb corresponds to the second subevent and lacks the first subevent, it does not have external argument.

Rapoport (1999: 656) describes the composition of event types structurally with an Aspectual Structural Model (cf. Slabakova 2001). This model distinguishes activity, accomplishment/causative and achievement/unaccusative, as shown in (13):

(13) a. Activity        b. Achievement/unaccusative

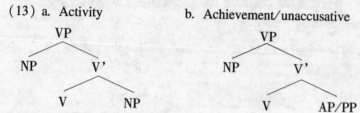

c. Accomplishment/causative

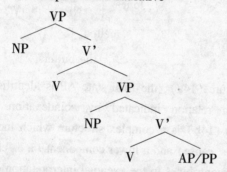

Structures in this model are composed of categories, each of which is related to a particular interpretation: N is "instance"; A is "state"; V is "dynamic"; P is an "interrelation/terminal coincidence" whose complement is a goal. Each category projection combines one of the following basic relations with the dynamic V-head to form a predicate: V-VP instantiates CAUSE; V-NP represents DO; V-AP/PP represents BECOME/GO. In terms of the relation of subject to the verb, subject of the DO predicate and that of the CAUSE predicate are interpreted as Agent or Causer ("actor" or "initiator" in Rapoport's terminology), while subject of the BECOME/GO predicate is interpreted as Theme or Event Measurer (cf. Tenny 1994).

In principle, a verb can be associated with any one of the structures above. In terms of alternating unaccusative verbs exemplified in (14) (adapted from Rapoport 1999: 658), the unaccusative reading results if it is associated with the achievement structure, whereas the causative reading results if it is associated with the accomplishment structure.[9]

(14) a. The butter melted.  b. Jones melted the butter.

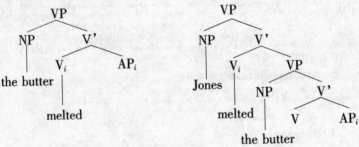

In the achievement structure (14a), the final state AP is identified by the state verb *melt*, a relation indicated by coindexation. The accomplishment structure (14b) is a complex structure which includes an upper component (i. e. cause) and a lower component (i. e. change of state), each of which contributes to the eventual interpretation of the sentence represented. The causative verb *melt* is an association of the two components. In relation to the NPs *Jones* and *the butter*, (14b) means that Jones caused the butter to go to a melted state.

2.1.3.3 Syntactic derivations

Let us examine in detail the examples in (7), which are repeated below:

(7) a. The vase broke. (inchoative/unaccusative)
   b. Tom broke the vase. (causative/transitive)

Different approaches are proposed on the syntactic representations of causative/unaccusative alternating verbs. Here, I mainly introduce two proposals, the VP-shell proposal (Chomsky 1995; Larson 1988) and the PrP-TrP proposal (Bowers 1993, 2002).

To accommodate properties of lexical verbs like *break*, Larson (1988) proposes a VP shell, which includes an upper *v*P and a lower VP. The lower VP is headed by the lexical verb, whereas the upper *v*P is headed by a causative light verb which selects the lower VP as complement. In a VP shell, the underlying position for the internal argument is Spec-VP, while that for the external argument is Spec-*v*P. Since the light verb *v* is affixal in nature and thus carries strong feature, it attracts the head of the lower VP to adjoin to it. Sentences like (7b) are thus derived as shown in (15b). With regard to unaccusative verbs like *break* in (7a), no upper *v*P is projected and the sentence is derived as illustrated in (15a). In this derivation, the internal argument *the vase* is base-generated at the complement position. It first moves to Spec-VP to satisfy the Extended Projection Principle, or EPP (Chomsky 1982), and further moves to Spec-IP to be assigned case.

Chomsky (1995: 352) adopts the VP-shell proposal and posits a construction for transitive verbs as illustrated in (16). In this construction, *v* has strong feature and attracts V to move; it also introduces Subj and licenses Obj. If *v* is absent, both accusative case and Subj will be absent.[10] In (15b), *v* introduces the external argument *Tom* and assigns accusative case to the NP *a vase*. There is no *v* in (15a), so there is no external argument, nor can accusative case be assigned, forcing the object NP to move to the subject position in search of case.

(15) a. The vase broke.    b. Tom broke the vase broke.

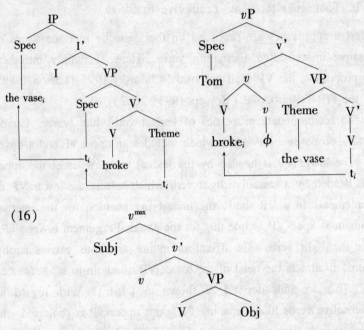

(16)

Bowers (1993) argues that the predication relation is represented by means of a functional category Pre, which is simply a mnemonic for either "predicate" or "predication" and is a generalization of the light verb $v$. Unlike $v$, which is assumed to be present only in transitive sentences, Pr is argued to be present in all sentences and small clauses (cf. Johnson 1991). In English, Pr is realized either as the light verb $v$ in the main clause or as *as* in the small-clause construction with a predicate nominal or adjective. Bowers (2002) further argues that the relation of transitivity is represented by another functional category Tr, which stands for "transitivity". TrP is optionally selected by Pr and occurs between PrP and VP, as illustrated in (17):

(17)

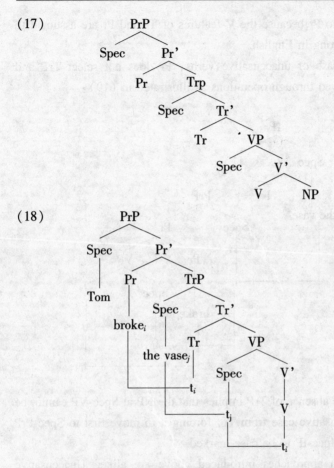

(18)

In English, Tr has no overt phonetic realization. It contains Φ-features and assigns accusative case to the NP at Spec-VP. Spec-TrP is the position to which the accusative-case-marked NP moves from Spec-VP, but all verbs end up in Pr. Within this approach, a causative construction like (7b) is derived through operations as illustrated in (18). In this derivation, the external argument *Tom* is base-generated at Spec-PrP; the internal argument *the vase* is base-generated at Spec-VP and moves to Spec-TrP to have its feature checked against the head Tr; the verb that heads VP moves in successive-cyclic fashion first to

Tr and then to Pr because the V-features of Tr and Pr are assumed to be always strong in English.

In the case of unaccusative verbs, Pr does not select TrP and (7a) is derived through operations as illustrated in (19):

(19)

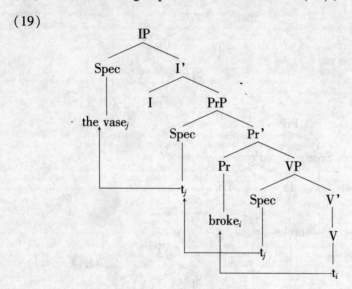

In (19), the absence of TrP implies that the NP at Spec-VP cannot be assigned accusative case from Tr, forcing it to move first to Spec-PrP and then to Spec-IP to be case-marked.

The two approaches introduced above are alike. Unaccusative verbs project a single VP in both approaches. While causative verbs project $v$P within the VP-shell proposal, they project TrP within the proposal of functional categories Pr and Tr. A difference between the two approaches is that a VP shell contains two categories, i. e. a functional category $v$ and a lexical category V, whereas Bowers' proposals (1993, 2002) contain two functional categories (i. e. Pr and Tr) and a lexical category (i. e. V). In a VP shell, the verb is base-generated at V but moves to $v$ to merge with the causative light verb when used causatively, but remains at V when used unaccusatively. In the structure containing Pr and Tr, both causative and unaccusative verbs land in Pr no matter where their base positions are. Although positing Pr can accommodate other structures like small clauses, it makes derivations less economical as far as causative/ unaccusative verbs are concerned. In contrast, the VP-shell proposal involves less movement and is thus more economical. In terms of applicability, however, Bowers' proposal is more appealing theoretically because all kinds of verbs end up in the same position (i.e. the head position of PrP), which may reveal derivational differences more clearly.

In the present study, the VP-shell proposal will be adopted in the analysis of unaccusative verbs.

### 2.1.4 Unaccusative verbs in Chinese

In this section, I will discuss unaccusative verbs in Chinese in terms of deep/surface unaccusativity, causative alternation and syntactic derivations.

### 2.1.4.1 Surface and deep unaccusativity

In languages like English, the internal argument of an unaccusative verb moves obligatorily to the subject position as in (20a) unless it is possible for the verb to occur in the there-insertion construction as in (20b) or in the locative-inversion construction as in (20c). Otherwise, ungrammatical sentences will result, as shown in (21).

(20) a. A ship sank yesterday.
     b. There appeared a ship on the horizon.
     c. Into the room came a man.
(21) a. *Sank a ship yesterday.
     b. *Appeared a ship on the horizon.

c. *Came a man into the room.

In Chinese, the internal argument of an unaccusative verb can either move to the subject position as in (22a) or remain in the object position in surface structure when it is indefinite as in (22b) (Y. -H. Li 1990; Yu 1995; Yuan 1999; see § 2.1.4.2). In other words, movement of the internal Theme argument to the subject position is obligatory only if it is definite, as shown in (22c) (examples in (22) quoted from Yuan 1999: 279-80). Otherwise, it may remain in situ. Thus, the distinction between deep and surface unaccusativity found in English is neutralized in Chinese.

(22) a. Shang ge yue, san sou chuan zai zhe ge hai yu chen le.
last CL month three CL ship in this CL sea area sink ASP
'Last month, three ships sank in this sea area.'
b. Shang ge yue, zai zhe ge hai yu chen le san sou chuan.
last CL month in this CL sea area sink ASP three CL ship
'Last month, three ships sank in this sea area.'
c. *Shang ge yue, zai zhe ge hai yu chen le na sou chuan.
last CL month in this CL sea area sink ASP that CL ship
'Last month, that ship sank in this sea area.'

In Chinese, the three subclasses of unaccusative verbs (i.e. verbs of change of state, verbs of change of location and verbs of existence/ appearance) can all take an indefinite NP in the surface object position, as shown in (23):

(23) a. Qu nian na chang hongshui *si* le bu shao ren.
last year that CL flood die ASP not few people
'Quite a few people died in last year's flood.'

b. Women xuexiao *lai* le liang ge xin laoshi.
our school come ASP two CL new teacher

'To our school came two new teachers.'
c. Zuotian  chu   le   yi qi  jiaotong shigu.
   yesterday occur ASP one CL traffic  accident
   'There happened a traffic accident yesterday.'
(24) *Zuotian  yi qi   jiaotong shigu  chu    le.
   yesterday one CL  traffic accident  occur  ASP
   'There happened a traffic accident yesterday.'

The predicates *si* 'die' in (23a), *lai* 'come' in (23b) and *chu* 'occur' in (23c) are verb of change of state, verb of change of location and verb of existence/appearance respectively, whose internal argument occurs in the object position. The internal argument of some unaccusative verbs like *chu* 'occur' in (23c) occurs obligatorily in the surface object position, as can be seen from the ungrammatical sentence in (24).

2.1.4.2  Causative alternation

Change-of-state unaccusative verbs can usually participate in causative alternation in English. In this section, I will examine whether alternating unaccusative verbs are allowed in Chinese.

2.1.4.2.1  Non-accomplishment verbs

Before discussion, first consider the Chinese sentences in (25):

(25) a. Men  kai  le.           b. Zhangsan  kai  le  men.
     door open ASP              Zhangsan  open ASP  door
     'The door opened'          'Zhangsan opened the door.'

The verb *kai* 'open' selects one argument in (25a) but two arguments in (25b). This seems to suggest that unaccusative verbs in Chinese participate in causative alternation, as in English. However, these verbs in Chinese have different properties from their counterparts in English, as we will see in the following discussion.

In English, an alternating unaccusative verb like *break* has two components, the activity and the accomplished outcome (Comrie 1989). It describes a delimited event and includes in its meaning the existence of a temporal terminus as well as an end state (Tenny 1994). This can be seen from its event structure and semantic representation introduced in § 2.1.3. In Chinese, however, such verbs do not entail a necessary outcome.

According to Juffs (1996a, 1996b, 2000), languages differ in conflation patterns (see Talmy 1985 for a definition of conflation; see Chapter 3 of Hale and Keyser 2002 for detailed discussion of conflation): while semantic primitives CAUSE and BECOME can be conflated into one verb in languages like English, they cannot in languages like Chinese. Regarding unaccusative verbs, this means that English verbs like *break* in (7) contain both the CAUSE and BECOME components, while their Chinese counterparts like *sui* 'break' contain only one semantic primitive, i.e. BECOME (cf. Tai 1984). In terms of event structure (Pustejovsky 1991), Chinese unaccusative verbs express transition but without an explicit agent. In lexical semantics, they involve BECOME but not CAUSE, as shown in (26):

(26)

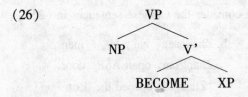

According to Tai (1984), Chinese has three categories of verb, which are state, activity and result; accomplishments and achievements cannot be expressed by single verbs but by resultative verb compounds (RVCs) like *da-sui* 'hit-break' which consist of an activity verb like *da* 'hit' and a result-denoting morpheme like *sui* 'break'. The difference in conflation patterns between Chinese and English can be seen from the discrepancy between a Chinese sentence and its English translation, as shown in (27):

(27) Zhangsan kai    men, keshi mei tui-kai.
　　　Zhangsan open door but   not   push-open
　　* 'Zhangsan opened the door, but didn't push it open.'

If *kai* 'open' is an accomplishment verb like its English counterpart, the clause *Zhangsan kai men* '(literally) Zhangsan open the door' will entail the necessary result, i.e. "the door was open". But such an interpretation is negated by the following clause *keshi mei tui-kai* 'but didn't push it open'. Comparing (27), in which *kai men* 'open the door' does not necessarily denote the result "the door was open", with (25b), in which *kai le men* 'open ASP door' does denote the result, one might conclude that the aspectual marker *le* is responsible for the accomplishment reading (see Sybesma 1997). While this claim can explain the difference between (27) and (25b), counter examples as shown in (28) indicate that such a generalization is superficial.

(28) Zhangsan zisha     le   san  ci, keshi dou mei si.
　　　Zhangsan self-kill ASP three times but  all   not die
　　* 'Zhangsan killed himself three times, but didn't die.'

With the aspectual marker *le*, the clause *Zhangsan zisha le san ci* 'Zhangsan self-killed three times' does not entail the result, i.e. "Zhangsan died", even if it is not followed by a clause of negation. A possible explanation is that the aspectual marker *le* may present events as bounded, but without information as to the termination or completion (Smith 1997). In other words, a bounded event is not necessarily a completed one. Without completive RVCs, Chinese verbs represent processes only.

From a historical point of view, verbs like *kai* 'open' entail an outcome in ancient Chinese. After Chinese verbs underwent a process of decausativization, single verbs in modern Chinese lost the inherent causative meaning that they used to have in ancient time and, as a result, RVCs are employed to express cause and effect (Li and Thompson 1976b, 1981). Consequently, unaccusative verbs in Chinese only denote change of state but cannot participate in causative/inchoative alternation, as can be seen from the contrast between sentences in (29) and (30).

(29) Lisi de tui duan le.
 Lisi *de* leg break ASP
 'Lisi's leg broke.'
(30) *Zhangsan duan le Lisi de tui.
 Zhangsan break ASP Lisi *de* leg
 'Zhangsan broke Lisi's leg.'

The verb *duan* 'break' can be used unaccusatively but cannot be used causatively, as shown in (29) and (30). In this sense, it is not equal to *break* in English, as can be seen from the discrepancy between the incorrect Chinese sentence and the correct English translation in (30).

2.1.4.2.2 Partitive case

Example (31) may pose a challenge to the claim that Chinese unaccusative verbs like *duan* 'break' do not participate in causative/inchoative alternation:

(31) Zhangsan duan le yi tiao tui.
 Zhangsan break ASP one CL leg
 'Zhangsan broke a leg.'

In both (30) and (31), the verb *duan* 'break' has two arguments, one in the subject position (*Zhangsan* in both sentences) and the other in the object position (*Lisi de tui* 'Lisi's leg' in (30) and *yi tiao tui* 'one leg' in (31)). A question arises from the contrast between these sentences: why is (31) allowed in Chinese, whereas (30) is not?

At first glance, *Lisi de tui* 'Lisi's leg' and *yi tiao tui* 'one leg' differ in definiteness: the former is definite while the latter is indefinite. Since definiteness plays a key role here and partitive case is subject to the definiteness restriction, it can be concluded that unaccusative verbs in Chinese can assign partitive case,[11] in line with Belletti (1988). Since the definite object NP in (30) cannot be assigned partitive case, it can only be assigned accusative case if possible. However, since unaccusative verbs in Chinese do not participate in causative alternation and therefore do not have a Causer argument, they consequently lack the ability to assign structural accusative case according to Burzio's Generalization (1986). The ungrammaticality of (30), therefore, can be attributed to the conflict between the verb that does not have the ability to assign accusative case and the definite internal argument NP the verb selects.

Indefiniteness is not the only requirement on the object NP of verbs like *duan* 'break', as can be seen from (32):

(32) *Zhangsan duan le    yi tiao zhuozi tui.
    *Zhangsan break ASP one CL table   leg
    'Zhangsan broke a table leg.'

Sentences (31) and (32) differ only in the internal argument NP. The contrast between (31) and (32) is also connected with partitive case that the NP is assigned. An NP that can be assigned partitive case must be indefinite and at the same time must be a part of a set of entities but not all. In other words, the postverbal NP must form a part-whole relation with a set which is usually denoted by the preverbal NP in the sentence (Li and Thompson 1981).[12] The NP *yi tiao tui* 'one leg' in (31) satisfies the two conditions for partitive case: it is indefinite and forms a part-whole relation with the subject NP *Zhangsan*, resulting in the reading that "it was one of Zhangsan's legs that was broken, not anyone else's". The NP *yi tiao zhuozi tui* 'a table leg' in (32) only satisfies the indefiniteness requirement; it cannot form part-whole relation with the other NP *Zhangsan* due to the fact that it is not a part of the set that constitutes *Zhangsan*. Thus, it cannot be assigned partitive case.

It is also possible to analyse (31) syntactically as illustrated in (33).

(33)

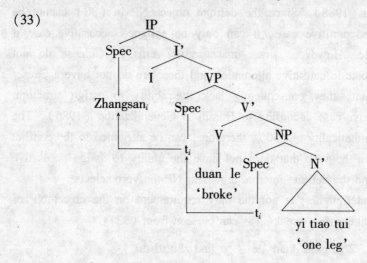

In this derivation, *Zhangsan yi tiao tui* 'one of Zhangsan's legs' as a whole is selected as the Theme argument by the verb *duan* 'break'; *Zhangsan* occurs at the specifier position of the Theme NP but raises to Spec-VP to satisfy the EPP (Chomsky 1982) and further to Spec-IP to get case-marked; *yi tiao tui* 'one leg' remains at the complement position and is assigned partitive case. If such an analysis is on the right track, the ill-formed sentence in (32) results from the semantic anomaly of the NP *Zhangsan yi tiao zhuozi tui* 'one of Zhangsan's table legs', which, if taken as whole, cannot be the Theme argument.

The non-causative nature of unaccusative verbs like *duan* 'break' can also be tested with the *ba*-construction.[13] A typical *ba*-construction is argued to be interchangeable with the SVO structure (see Bender 2000; Goodall 1987, 1989, 1990; Y.-H. Li 1990; L. Liu 1997; Sybesma 1992; Zou 1993), as illustrated in (34): the accusative-case-marked NP *zixingche* 'bicycle' in the object position in (34a) is preposed and occurs in the position between *ba* and the verb *mai* 'sell'; the VO structure in (34a) *mai le zixingche* 'sold the bicycle' changes into a *ba*-construction *ba zixingche mai le* '*ba* bicycle sold' in (34b). Such a transition,[14] however, does not apply to (31), as can be seen in (35).

(34) a. Zhangsan mai le zixingche.
       Zhangsan sell ASP bicycle
       'Zhangsan sold the bicycle.'
   b. Zhangsan ba zixingche mai le.
       Zhangsan *ba* bicycle sell ASP
       'Zhangsan sold the bicycle.'

(35) a. Zhangsan duan le yi tiao tui.
       Zhangsan break ASP one CL leg
       'Zhangsan broke a leg.'
   b. *Zhangsan ba yi tiao tui duan le.
       Zhangsan *ba* one CL leg break ASP
       'Zhangsan broke a leg.'

The contrast between (34) and (35) implies that the internal argument *yi tiao tui* 'one leg' in (31) cannot receive accusative case.

### 2.1.4.2.3 θ-roles

Let us now turn to the subject NP in these sentences. The subject NP is assigned Agent or Causer θ-role if the verb is causative.

However, the verb is not causative, so the subject NP is not the entity that initiates the action but is affected by the action. In (31), for example, the subject NP *Zhangsan* is a Patient/Theme rather than an Agent. Another example is presented in (36), which has only one reading that the three ships belong to the enemy and it is the enemy who suffers the loss. Again, the NP *san sou chuan* 'three ships' in (36) is assigned partitive case and forms a part-whole relation with the subject NP *diren* 'enemy'.

(36) Diren chen le    san sou chuan.
     enemy sink ASP three CL ship
     'Three of the enemy's ships sank.'

It can be concluded from the above discussion that Chinese unaccusative verbs such as *duan* 'break' and *chen* 'sink' cannot be used causatively, unlike their English counterparts, although they may have a subject NP and an object NP in the surface structure. Their non-causative nature can be seen in their incapability of assigning accusative case to the following NP and the Theme/Patient θ-role of the subject NP.

## 2.1.5 Unaccusative verbs in Japanese

According to Miyagawa (1989) and Tsujimura (1990), the Unaccusative Hypothesis holds in Japanese (cf. Harada 2000). It is claimed that the underlying object of an unaccusative verb stays in situ in its base position, as shown in (37) (from Hirakawa 1999: 90), due to the SOV order of Japanese:

(37) Tokei-ga     koware-ta.
     watch-NOM break-PAST
     'The watch broke.'

According to Harada (1999, 2000), there is no causative-inchoative alternation in Japanese. Transitive verbs of change of state like *sizume-* 'sink' in (38a) (from Miyagawa 1984: 191) cannot be used as intransitive verbs[15] as in (38b) (from Harada 2000: 85). In order to express the inchoative meaning, a morphologically related but distinct word must be used as shown in (39) (from Hirakawa 1995: 294), in which the transitive form *kowa-si* differs from the intransitive form *kowa-re*, the two words having the same root *kowa*.

(38) a. Taroo-ga    hune-o    sizume-ta.
Taroo-NOM boat-ACC sink-PAST
'Taro sank the boat.'
b. *Hune-ga    sizume-ta.
ship-NOM sink-PAST
'Ships sank.'
(39) a. John-ga    kabin-o    kowa-si-ta.
John-NOM vase-ACC break-TRANS-PAST
'John broke the vase.'
b. Kabin-ga    kowa-re-ta.
vase-NOM break-INTR-PAST
'The vase broke.'

According to Fukui and Takano (1998) and Takano (2004), Japanese verbs and their inflectional morphemes are not fully inflected when entering syntactic derivation, but are separated in syntax and are merged on phonological component. As a result, the light verb *v* in Japanese, being an affix in nature, is inert and cannot trigger syntactic operations (Harada 2002; cf. Matsumoto 1996b). The contrast between the two sentences in (38) indicates that (38a) is not derived from verb raising. The marking of transitive and intransitive verbs in Japanese is therefore lexical rather than syntactic, as shown in (39), in which transitivity and intransitivity are expressed with different lexical verbs.

Although unaccusative verbs cannot be causativized syntactically through movement to *v*, some can be causativized with the help of the causative marker (*s*)*ase*, as shown in (40) (from M. Kim 1999: 125-6), in which the intransitive verb *toke* 'melt' in (40a) is causativized through the morpheme *-ase* in (40c).

(40) a. Yuki-ga    toke-ta.
       snow-NOM melt-PAST
       'The snow melted.'
    b. *Taiyo-ga   yuki-o   toke-ta.
       sun-NOM snow-ACC melt-PAST
       'The sun melted the snow.'
    c. Taiyo-ga   yuki-o   tok-ase-ta.
       sun-NOM snow-ACC melt-CAUS-PAST
       'The sun melted the snow.'

The examples above indicate that Japanese does not allow alternating unaccusative verbs. Transitive verbs of change of state are not derived from verb raising. Unaccusative verbs cannot be used causatively without the help of the causative suffix -(*s*)*ase*.

## 2.1.6 Unaccusative verbs in Korean

According to M. Kim (1999), unaccusative verbs in Korean do not participate in causative alternation, as illustrated in (41) (from M. Kim 1999: 136). The unaccusative verb *nok* 'melt' in (41a) cannot be used causatively, as shown in (41b). It can only be causativized through the causative morpheme *-i* as in (41c). However, some unaccusative verbs and their corresponding transitive/causative verbs are morphologically the same, as in (42) (from Sohn 1994: 311).

(41) a. elum-i   nok-ass-ta.
       ice-NOM melt-PAST-DEC
       'The ice melted.'

b. *theyang-i elum-ul   nok-ass-ta.
      sun-NOM ice-ACC melt-PAST-DEC
      'The sun melted the ice.'
   c. theyang-i elum-ul   nok-i-ass-ta.
      sun-NOM ice-ACC melt-CAUS-PAST-DEC
      'The sun melted the ice.'
(42) a. kicha-ka   wumciki-ess-ta.
       train-NOM move-PAST-DEC
       'The train moved.'
    b. kikwansa-ka   kicha-lul wumciki-ess-ta.
       engineer-NOM train-ACC move-PAST-DEC
       'The engineer moved the train.'

Korean is a typical agglutinative language, in which syntactic functions such as case relation, relativization, verbal complementation, passivization and causativization are indicated by particles or suffixes (Sohn 1994). In light of this, the transitivity of verbs like *wumciki* 'move' in (42b) is lexical rather than syntactically derived because no transitive/causative particle or suffix is involved in this sentence.

## 2.1.7 Summary

The properties of unaccusative verbs in Chinese, English, Japanese and Korean in relation to causativity are summarized in Table 2.1.

*Table 2.1 Summary: properties of unaccusative verbs in Chinese, English, Japanese and Korean in relation to causativity*

| Language | Causative alternation | Causative affixes[16] | Assigning partitive case |
|---|---|---|---|
| Chinese | × | × | √ |
| English | √ | × | × |
| Japanese | × | √ | × |
| Korean | × | √ | × |

Of the four languages, English is the only one that allows alternating unaccusative verbs. Root unaccusative verbs cannot be used causatively in the other three languages. In Japanese and Korean, explicit causative affixes are used to causativize an unaccusative verb. Chinese unaccusative verbs can assign partitive case. A consequence is that movement of an indefinite internal argument to the subject position is not obligatory in Chinese.

If unaccusative verbs in the four languages are represented with VP or VP shell, their syntactic structures will be such as illustrated in (43):

(43) a. Chinese        b. English

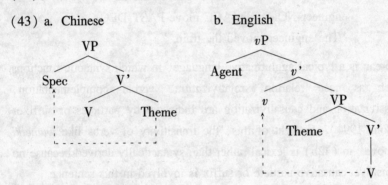

c. Japanese and Korean

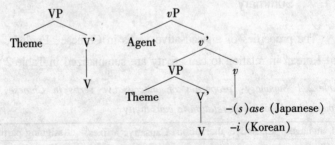

As shown in (43a), unaccusative verbs in Chinese project a single VP; when the Theme argument is definite, it moves to the subject position obligatorily; when it is indefinite, it can remain in situ and is assigned abstract partitive case. Change-of-state unaccusative verbs in

English participate in causative alternation. The unaccusative verb heads the VP but its causative alternant projects a VP shell with the upper *v*P headed by an abstract causative light verb. Causative alternation is derived from verb raising from head position of the lower VP to that of the upper *v*P, as shown in (43b). As seen in (43c), unaccusative verbs in Japanese and Korean project a single VP, but they can be causativized by means of causative affixes, which project and head the upper *v*P.

## 2.2 Psych verbs and causativity

Psychological verbs, or psych verbs, like *please*, *enjoy* in English, express psychological state. Generally speaking, a psych verb selects two arguments: one is the individual experiencing the mental state; the other is the content or object of the mental state.

### 2.2.1 Semantic representations

Belletti and Rizzi (1988: 291-2) distinguish three primitive lexical classes of psych verbs in Italian, which are verbs with subject Experiencer as in (44a), verbs with object Experiencer as in (44b), and verbs involving a dative Experiencer and a nominative Theme with both orderings allowed, as in (44c):

(44) a. Subject Experiencer    b. Object Experiencer
      Gianni teme questo.    Questo preoccupa Gianni.
      Gianni fears this       this  worries  Gianni
    c. Dative Experiencer and nominative Theme
      (i) A Gianni piace questo.
         to Gianni pleases this
      (ii) Questo piace a Gianni.
         this pleases to Gianni

In this section, the discussion will focus on subject-Experiencer (like *teme* 'fear') and object-Experiencer (like *preoccupa* 'worry'/'frighten') psych verbs, henceforth SE verbs and OE verbs respectively.

English has both SE verbs and OE verbs. Verbs like *fear* in (45a) allow Experiencer to appear in the subject position and are therefore SE verbs, whereas verbs like *frighten* in (45b) have Experiencer occurring in the object position and are therefore OE verbs (examples in (45) quoted from Pesetsky 1995: 18).

(45) a. Bill fears/is afraid of ghosts.
　　 b. Ghosts frighten Bill.

In Dowty's (1979: 67) term, OE verbs are verbs of "psychological movement", which have a propositional subject and a human object. The propositional subject is termed Stimulus (Dowty 1991; Talmy 1985), Target of Emotion (Pesetsky 1995) or Theme (Belletti and Rizzi 1988). In this thesis, it is called Theme.

In terms of lexical semantics, SE verbs are generally classed as statives (Grimshaw 1990; Tenny 1994), whereas OE verbs are classified as inchoatives or causatives, which denote a change in the psychological state (Croft 1998; Levin 1993; Pesetsky 1995; Tenny 1994).[17] In terms of event structure, an SE verb denotes a single event, which is evaluated relative to no other event, while an OE verb denotes a transition from one state to the opposite state (Pustejovsky 1991). According to Van Valin and LaPolla (1997), an SE verb like *fear* denotes a state, whereas an OE verb like *frighten* denotes a causative state. In other words, OE verbs are the causative counterparts of SE verbs.

Pesetsky (1995) posits a "bimorphemic" analysis and take OE verbs like *frighten* as containing a morphologically null causative morpheme and a root $\sqrt{}$ *frighten*. In other words, OE verbs are inherently causative. This proposal is in line with Levin and Rappaport Hovav's (1995) treatment of alternating unaccusative verbs: both OE verbs and alternating unaccusative verbs are taken as inherently causative and involve two semantic primitives, CAUSE and BECOME.

### 2.2.2 Syntactic derivations

Although SE verbs and OE verbs differ sharply in the surface representations, their underlying representations are identical in most respects (Belletti and Rizzi 1988). For example, (44a) and (44b) have underlying configurations as illustrated in (46a) and (46b) respectively (adapted from Belletti and Rizzi 1988: 293):

(46) a. Gianni teme questo.        b. Questo preoccupa Gianni.
     Gianni fears this             this    worries  Gianni

```
        IP                              IP
       /  \                            /  \
     NP    VP                        NP    VP
     |    /  \                       |    /  \
   Gianni V   NP                     e   V'   NP
          |    |                        /  \   |
        teme questo                    V   NP Gianni
                                       |    |
                                  preoccupa questo
```

As shown in (46a) and (46b), a main difference between an SE verb and an OE verb is that the former has a base-generated subject while the latter has a derived subject. An OE verb is treated as an unaccusative, which has a base-generated Theme as internal argument. Since an unaccusative verb cannot assign case, its internal Theme argument is forced to move to the subject position in search of case, resulting in a surface representation as in (47).[18] In the underlying structure, the Experiencer has a position higher than the

Theme. The Theme always occupies the underlying direct object position, the most embedded position. To illustrate the relation between the surface structure and the underlying structure, Belletti and Rizzi (1988: 344) propose a linking principle as in (48), through which the thematic hierarchy is maintained in the underlying structure in spite of the difference in the surface structure.

(47) Theme$_i$ [ $_{VP}$ [ $_{V'}$ V e$_i$ ] Experiencer ]
(48) Given a θ-grid [ Experiencer, Theme ], the Experiencer is projected to a higher position than the Theme.

Belletti and Rizzi's treatment of OE verbs as unaccusatives is not unproblematic. A characteristic of unaccusative verbs in many languages is their incompatibility with passive morphology. OE verbs in English, however, can be passivized, as illustrated in (49) (from Pesetsky 1995: 22), which indicates that they are not unaccusatives.

(49) a. John was worried by my remarks.
　　　b. Bill was frightened by strange noises.

To solve this problem, Pesetsky (1995) introduces the Causer argument and argues that the NP at the subject position of OE verbs is not Theme but Causer. Psych verbs assign two θ-roles: one is Experiencer; the other is either Causer (when it is assigned to the subject) or Theme (when it is assigned to the object). Causer, Experiencer and Theme form a thematic hierarchy as in (50) (adapted from Pesetsky 1995: 59). Such a hierarchy, when projected onto syntax, can be represented with a VP shell, as in (51).

(50) Causer > Experiencer > Theme

(51)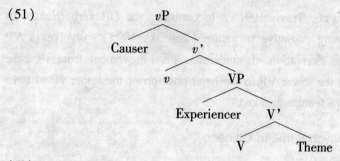

(52) a. Bill fears ghosts.

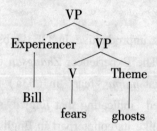

b. Ghosts frighten Bill.

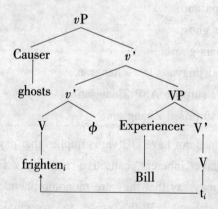

In (51), the Causer is base-generated at Spec-$v$P and the Experiencer at Spec-VP; the Theme is base-generated at the complement position of V. Both SE verbs and OE verbs head the lower VP in the underlying structure. The syntactic operations of both types of verbs are illustrated in (52). The SE verb *fear*, being stative, projects a single VP (cf. Travis 1991). In contrast, the OE verb *frighten* in (52b), being causative in nature (Pesetsky 1995), involves a VP shell in the derivation. It undergoes head-movement from its base position in the lower VP to the head position of the upper *v*P to have its causative feature checked.

### 2.2.3 Psych verbs in Chinese

#### 2.2.3.1 SE verbs and OE verbs

Chinese has SE verbs but is unproductive in OE verbs (Chen 1995),[19] as illustrated in (53). The Experiencer *Zhangsan* occurs at the subject position, indicating that *haipa* 'fear' in (53a) is an SE verb. Sentence (53b) is ill-formed, indicating that *jingya* 'surprise' is not an OE verb in Chinese, unlike its counterpart in English.

(53) a. Zhangsan haipa gui.
　　　　Zhangsan fear ghost
　　　　'Zhangsan fears ghosts.'
　　 b. *Zhe ge xiaoxi jingya　le　Zhangsan.
　　　　this CL news surprise ASP Zhangsan
　　　　'This news surprised Zhangsan.'

The fact that Chinese does not have OE verbs implies that psych verbs in Chinese do not have inherent causative meaning. Following Pesetsky (1995), we may say that they are monomorphemic without the null causative morpheme. With regard to aspectual features (Tenny 1994), they are not accomplishment verbs but statives, which do not involve change of psychological state.

#### 2.2.3.2 Decausativized psych verbs

In Chinese, some monosyllabic psych verbs like *lei* 'tire' and *fan* 'bore' can be used causatively in restricted contexts, as illustrated in (54): both *fan* 'bore' and *lei* 'tire' seem to have Experiencer as object, which may suggest that they are OE verbs. Under scrutiny, however, the causative use of these verbs has been greatly reduced, as shown in (55).

(54) a. Bie fan wo.
   not bore me
   'Don't bore me (with nuisances).'
   b. Zhe zhong shi zhen lei ren.
   this sort matter really tire people
   'This sort of thing is really tiring.'
(55) a. *Zhangsan zuotian fan le wo.
   Zhangsan yesterday bore ASP me
   'Zhangsan bored me yesterday.'
   b. *Zhe zhong shi lei le ren.
   this kind matter tire ASP people
   'This sort of thing tired people.'

Neither of the sentences in (55) is acceptable, suggesting that psych verbs like *fan* 'bore' and *lei* 'tire' can be used in imperative sentences as in (54a) or as a set phrase like *lei ren* 'tire people (tiring)' as in (54b), but cannot be used with *le*, a perfective aspectual marker indicating a bounded event (Li and Thompson 1981). This implies that such verbs can be used causatively only in a very restricted way. In fact, they are not contradictory with the aspectual marker *le* if the Experiencer occurs at the subject position, as illustrated in (56). The contrast indicates that sentences in (55) are unacceptable not because of *le*, but because of the Experiencer argument at the object position.

(56) a. Zhangsan fan le.     b. Zhangsan lei le.
       Zhangsan bore ASP       Zhangsan tire ASP
       'Zhangsan was bored.'   'Zhangsan was tired.'

In ancient Chinese, monosyllabic verbs like *fan* 'bore' and *lei* 'tire' can be used causatively. The threat of too many homophonous syllables has forced the language to increase dramatically the proportion of polysyllabic words, principally by means of compounding (Li and Thompson 1976b, 1981). A consequence is that disyllabic compound causatives, which are composed of an activity predicate and a result predicate, are dominant in modern Chinese, as illustrated in (57):

(57) a. Zhangsan ting-fan le.
        Zhangsan listen-bore ASP
        'Zhangsan listened (time and again) and got bored as a result.'
     b. Zhangsan pao-lei le.
        Zhangsan run-tire ASP
        'Zhangsan ran (a long way) and got tired as a result.'

In (57), psych verbs *fan* 'bore' and *lei* 'tire' form verb compounds with activity verbs *ting* 'listen' and *pao* 'run'. Although psych verbs alone cannot express transition of psychological state, the compounds can, as indicated in the translation (see § 3.2).

2.2.3.3 Syntactic derivations

In Chinese, psych verbs are all SE verbs, which can be classified into two types: transitive and intransitive, as illustrated in (58) and (59):

(58) a. Zhangsan hen jingya.
        Zhangsan very surprise
        'Zhangsan was very surprised.'

b. *Zhangsan jingya le zhe ge xiaoxi.
   Zhangsan surprise ASP this CL news
   *'Zhangsan surprised the news.'

(59) a. Zhangsan hen haipa.
   Zhangsan very fear
   'Zhangsan fears.'

b. Zhangsan (hen) haipa gui.
   Zhangsan (very) fear ghost
   'Zhangsan fears ghosts (very much).'

The verb *jingya* 'surprise' in (58) is intransitive and cannot take a Theme argument, whereas *haipa* 'fear' in (59) is transitive and can select an internal argument. Whether a psych verb is transitive or intransitive, it expresses the psychological state of the Experiencer. It is stative rather than dynamic and functions more like an adjective. Both transitive and intransitive psych verbs can be modified by *hen* 'very', an adverb considered to be a modifier of adjectives (Zhu 1982). There is no clear-cut distinction between verb and adjective in Chinese.[20]

In terms of syntactic representations, Chinese psych verbs, being stative, project a single VP, with Experiencer at Spec-VP and Theme, in the case of transitive psych verbs, at the complement position of V, as shown in (60):

(60)
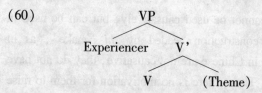

(61) a. *Zhe ge xiaoxi jingya le Zhangsan.
   this CL news surprise ASP Zhangsan
   'This news surprised Zhangsan.'

b. Zhe ge xiaoxi shi Zhangsan hen jingya.

this CL news *shi* Zhangsan very surprise
'The news made Zhangsan surprised.'

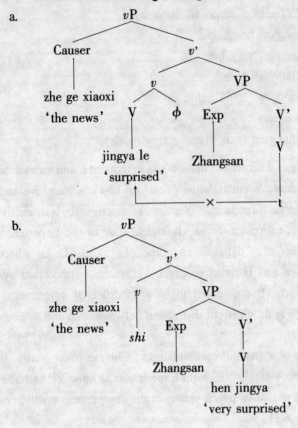

Psych verbs in Chinese cannot be used causatively, but can be used in the analytical causative construction headed by *shi* 'make', as in (61). Since psych verbs in Chinese are not causative, they do not have a cause feature to check. Thus, there is no motivation for them to raise from their base position, i.e. the head position of the lower VP, to the head position of the upper *v*P. The derivation crashes if they do move, as shown in (61a). An explicit causative morpheme like *shi* is used obligatorily as in (61b) if causation is to be expressed.

## 2.2.4 Psych verbs in Japanese

Japanese has SE verbs: the Experiencer argument is marked with nominative case -*ga* or topic morpheme -*wa*, while the Theme argument is marked with accusative case -*o* as in (62a) or with dative case -*ni* as in (62b). Some psych verbs allow both accusative case and dative case to be assigned to the Theme argument as in (62c). The Theme argument may also occur as sentence subject. In this case, however, the causative affix -(*s*)*ase* is added to the psych verb obligatorily as in (63a). Otherwise, ungrammatical sentences would result, as shown in (63b) (examples in (62) and (63) are adapted from Sato 2003: 126-30)

(62) a. John-ga   eiga-o      tanoshin-da.
       John-NOM movie-ACC  enjoy-PAST
       'John enjoyed the movie.'
    b. John-wa  sono shirase-ni  odoroi-ta.
       John-TOP the news-DAT surprise-PAST
       'John was surprised at the news.'
    c. John-ga    sono shirase-o/ni   yorokon-da.
       John-NOM the news-ACC/DAT be pleased-PAST
       'John was pleased with the news.'

(63) a. Sono sirase-ga  John-o   yorokob-ase-ta.
       the news-NOM John-ACC be pleased-CAUS-PAST
       'The news pleased John.'
    b. *Sono sirase-ga  John-o   yorokob-ta.
       the news-NOM John-ACC be pleased-PAST
       'The news pleased John.'

These examples indicate that Japanese has SE verbs but does not have root OE verbs. Causation can be expressed only with the help of the causative morpheme -(s)ase. Sentences where psych verbs are used with the causative affix -(s)ase exhibit the same property as causatives with other types of verbs, as shown in (64) (adapted from Harada 2002: 86-87), in which the transitive verb *katazuke* 'clean' and the intransitive verb *hatarak* 'work' are both causativized by the causative affix -(s)ase.

(64) a. Mary-ga John-ni sono heya-o katazuke-sase-ta.
Mary-NOM John-DAT that room-ACC clean-CAUS-PAST
'Mary made John clean the room.'
b. Mary-ga John-ni/o hatarak-ase-ta.
Mary-NOM John-DAT/ACC work-CAUS-PAST
'Mary made John work.'

The examples above indicate that psych verbs in Japanese are all SE verbs in their root form. Whether they are causative or not depends on the (non) existence of the morpheme -(s)ase attached to them. When a psych verb is thus causativized, the Experiencer is marked accusative case. Otherwise, it is assigned nominative case or marked as topic.

2.2.5 Psych verbs in Korean

As in Japanese, psych verbs in Korean do not have a distinction between SE verbs and OE verbs in their root form. They can only be causativized through the causative affix -i (-hi in (65c)), taking an accusative-case-marked Experiencer. Without the causative morpheme, however, they are SE verbs as in (65a) and cannot take Experiencer as object as in (65b) (examples in (65) quoted from M. Kim 1999: 137).

(65) a. Yumi-un ku chaek-e silmang-ha-yess-ta.
Yumi-TOP that book-GEN disappoint-PAST-DEC
'Yumi was disappointed at that book.'

b. *ku chaek-i    Yumi-lul    silmang-ha-yess-ta.
   that book-NOM Yumi-ACC disappoint-PAST-DEC
   'That book disappointed Yumi.'
c. ku chaek-i    Yumi-lul    silmangsik-hi-ess-ta.
   that book-NOM Yumi-ACC disappoint-CAUS-PAST-DEC
   'That book disappointed Yumi.'

As in Japanese, when a psych verb in Korean is causativized through an explicit causative marker, the Experiencer argument is marked with accusative case.

### 2.2.6 Summary

The properties of psych verbs in Chinese, English, Japanese and Korean are summarized in Table 2.2. Of the four languages, only English allows OE verbs. While Japanese and Korean only allow SE verbs, they can express causation with these psych verbs by means of causative affixes ( -(s)ase in Japanese and -i in Korean). Although Chinese lacks causative affixes, it can express causation with psych verbs with causative morphemes like *shi* 'make'.

*Table 2.2 Summary: properties of psych verbs in Chinese, English, Japanese and Korean in relation to causativity*

| Language | SE verb | OE verb | Causative affixes |
|---|---|---|---|
| Chinese | √ | × | × |
| English | √ | √ | × |
| Japanese | √ | × | √ |
| Korean | √ | × | √ |

In fact, an OE verb in English, in addition to its ability to express causation with the root form, can be used with the causative verb *make* to express causation, as shown in (66) (from Juffs 1996b: 181):

(66) a. John disappointed Mary.
　　　b. John made Mary disappointed.

If we follow Pesetsky (1995) and represent psych verbs with VP or VP shell, SE verbs in the four languages have the same syntactic structure as illustrated in (67):

(67) The structure of SE verbs in Chinese, English, Japanese and Korean

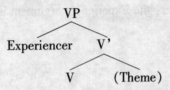

Causation with psych verbs is expressed in different ways in the four languages, as shown in (68):

(68) Causativity of psych verbs in Chinese, English, Japanese and Korean

　　　a. Chinese

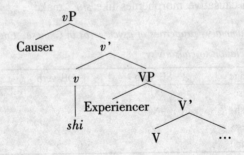

b. English

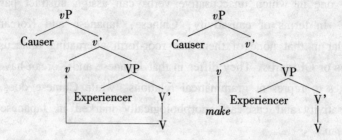

c. Japanese and Korean

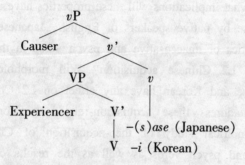

Syntactically, OE verbs in English project a VP shell with an abstract light verb heading the upper $v$P, as in (68b). They raise to the head position of the upper $v$P to have their causative feature checked. In the other three languages, psych verbs are not causative themselves. As a result, they remain in the head position of VP. Causative morphemes or affixes must be used if causation is expressed. Causative morphemes like *make* can also be used in English to express causation.

## 2.3 Summary

In this chapter, I discussed behaviours of unaccusative and psych verbs in Chinese, English, Japanese and Korean in relation to causativity. Of the four languages, English is the only one that allows alternating unaccusative verbs and OE verbs, whereas Chinese is the only one in which unaccusative verbs can assign abstract partitive case. In terms of causativity, Chinese, Japanese and Korean are similar in that none of them has root-form alternating unaccusative verbs or OE verbs. They differ in that Japanese and Korean have rich affixes to represent grammatical relations, while Chinese does not. Causativity and case are morphologically marked in Japanese and Korean.

Given different properties of unaccusative verbs and psych verbs in these languages, what implications will these properties have in the acquisition of Chinese by native speakers of English, Japanese and Korean? Will properties of unaccusative and psych verbs in the L1 impede or facilitate L2 Chinese acquisition? Will morphological properties in Japanese and Korean have any effect on L2 Chinese acquisition? I will address these acquisition-related questions in Chapter 5. The empirical study of the acquisition of Chinese unaccusative verbs and psych verbs as well as the results of the empirical study will be presented in Chapter 6.

## Notes

[1] According to Blake (2001: 203), partitive case is a case "that indicates an entity partly affected".

[2] Chomsky (1986) makes a distinction between structural case and inherent case: the former is assigned in terms of the surface position, whereas the latter is assigned in the underlying structure. According to Minimalism (Chomsky 1995), structural case assignment takes place in two distinct configurations: agreement is responsible for nominative case assignment, which can be regarded as an instantiation of Spec-head agreement; accusative case assignment is viewed as arising from government relation between a verb and an accusative NP, which

can also be reduced to Spec-head agreement if there is an object agreement (AgrO) projection, but this time holding between Spec and head of AgrO. Unlike structural case, inherent case is associated with θ-marking and necessitates thematic dependence of the NP receiving the case upon its case assigner (see Blake 2001, Webelhuth 1995, for detailed discussion).

[3] Belletti (1988) extends her proposal to passive verbs in Italian, claiming that they still retain the ability to assign inherent case because assignment of inherent case is not suspended under passive morphology. Lasnik (1992) supports this proposal and makes a parametric distinction between Italian and English: in Italian passiveness blocks only the assignment of accusative case, whereas in English it blocks the assignment of both accusative and partitive case.

Belletti's proposal seems to find supporting evidence in Chinese, in which passive verbs are able to assign case, as shown in (i) and (ii) (from Goodall 1999: 4):

(i) Taizi bei    ta da    le    la.
    table PASS he apply ASP wax
    'He applied wax to the table.'

(ii) Wu ge mantou bei ta chi   le   liang ge.
    five CL roll PASS he eat ASP two CL
    'He ate two out of the five rolls.'

In contrast to Belletti, Goodall (1999) argues that *la* 'wax' in (i) and *liang ge* 'two' in (ii) are assigned accusative case. In other words, accusative case is available in passive clauses in Chinese.

[4] Vainikka and Maling (1996) agree with Belletti (1988) on the ability of unaccusative verbs to assign case but disagree on the nature of partitive case. They argue that partitive case is not inherent but structural, which is assigned by default to obligatory complements of verbs, prepositions, comparative adjectives, caseless numerals and certain quantifiers. Kiparsky (1998: 265), citing examples from Finnish, argues that partitive case is a "hybrid category of semantically conditioned structural case".

[5] According to Parsons (1990: 120), such causative verbs are derived from related adjectives with the "cause to become adjective" meaning. In English, they may have a causative-inchoative-adjective pattern, as illustrated below:

(i) a. The door is close. (adjective)
    b. The door closed. (inchoative)
    c. John closed the door. (causative)
(ii) a. The road is wide. (adjective)
    b. The road widened. (inchoative)

c. The workers widened the road. (causative)

Verbs like *close* in (i) have the same form as the corresponding adjectives and are thus said to be "zero-derived" (Goddard 1998: 278). Verbs like *widen* in (ii) are morphologically derived from the corresponding adjectives by adding the suffix *-en*.

In English there may not be an inchoative verb between an adjective and the corresponding causative verb, like *random* and *randomize*.

[6] In this thesis, an inchoative verb refers to an unaccusative verb that denotes a change of state. The two terms are used interchangeably.

[7] Haegeman (1994) and Radford (1997) make a distinction between unaccusative verbs and ergative verbs: the former refer to verbs like *arrive* and *happen*, whereas the latter refer to verbs like *break* which have causative alternant. The two subclasses of verbs are both called ergative verbs in Burzio (1986). In this thesis, they are both called 'unaccusative' in line with Levin and Rappaport Hovav (1995).

[8] The bounded/unbounded distinction (Jackendoff 1990; Verkuyl 1972) is also expressed as telic/atelic distinction (Smith 1997), or delimited/non-delimited distinction (Tenny 1994).

[9] According to Ritter and Rosen (1998), arguments can determine events and alternations. The semantic content of the arguments can narrow the possible interpretation of the verb and the possible syntactic structures in which it may occur. Therefore, whether an unaccusative verb has a causative alternant or not depends on the arguments as much as on the verb itself, as shown in the following sentences (from Ritter and Rosen 1998: 142-3):

(i) a. The storm broke.
   b. *The gods broke the storm.
(ii) a. *Our agreement broke.
   b. She broke our agreement.

The verb *break* in these sentences cannot alternate freely, indicating that the lexically listed meaning of the verb cannot by itself determine its syntactic realization.

[10] Unlike Chomsky (1995), who claims that both subject and object form nontrivial chains to check their formal features with a functional category, López (2001) argues that object and exceptional-case-marking subjects check their formal features with lexical verbs.

[11] Since Chinese is a topic-prominent language (Li and Thompson 1976a), *Zhangsan* in (31) may be taken as the topic rather than the subject. Such an analysis does not affect the case status of the indefinite NP *yi tiao tui* 'one leg'. Under Case Filter (Chomsky 1981), every overt NP must be assigned case. Since (31) is a well-formed sentence, the indefinite NP must have already been assigned case. Otherwise, the sentence would collapse. Since it

has already been case-marked, it need not move to the subject position to search for case although the subject position is empty. So, whether the sentence-initial NP *Zhangsan* is treated as topic or subject is irrelevant to the conclusion.

[12] The picture is more complicated when we look at semantic connections between the postverbal NP and the preverbal NP with regard to other unaccusative verbs, as illustrated in the following sentences:

    (i) Zhangsan qunian si le fuqin.
        Zhangsan last year die ASP father
        'Zhangsan's father died last year.'
    (ii) Zhangsan zuotian fasheng le yiwai.
        Zhangsan yesterday happen ASP accident
        'Zhangsan had an accident yesterday.'
    (iii) Xuexiao jintian lai le henduo keren.
        school today come ASP many guest
        'There came many guests to school today.'

In (i), *Zhangsan* and *fuqin* 'father' have a kinship relationship; in (ii), *yiwai* 'accident' is the event in which *Zhangsan* is involved; in (iii), *xuexiao* 'school' is the location for *xuduo keren* 'many guests'.

[13] There are mainly two issues connected with the *ba*-construction. The first is the part of speech of *ba* and the second is the post-*ba* part. On the first issue, *ba* is taken as a preposition (e.g. Chao 1968; Y.-H. Li 1990), as a verb (e.g. Sybesma 1992), or as a particle which functions purely as a case-assigner (Goodall 1987). On the second issue, some linguists take the post-*ba* NP as the object which is assigned accusative case (e.g. Chao 1968; Y.-H. Li 1990), while others take it simply as a phrase headed by *ba* (e.g. Sybesma 1992).

[14] The *ba*-construction has other syntactic forms as well, as illustrated in (ia) and (iia) (adapted from Thompson 1973), which cannot be expressed with sentences in SVO order, as shown in (ib) and (iib).

    (i) a. Zhangsan ba taizi da le la.
        Zhangsan *ba* table apply ASP wax.
      b. *Zhangsan da le la taizi.
        Zhangsan apply ASP wax table
        'Zhangsan applied wax to the table.'
    (ii) a. Zhangsan ba wu ge mantou chi le liang ge.
        Zhangsan *ba* five CL rolls eat ASP two CL
      b. *Zhangsan chi le liang ge mantou wu ge.

Zhangsan eat ASP two CL rolls five CL
'Zhangsan ate two out of the five rolls.'
See Thompson (1973) and Y. -H. Li (1990) for detailed discussion.

[15] Some verbs are morphologically the same in both transitive and intransitive forms, as shown in (i) (from Shibatani 1976b: 241):

(i) a. Taroo-ga    mado-o      hirak-u.
    Taroo-NOM window-ACC open
    'Taro opens the window.'
    b. Mado-ga      hirak-u.
    window-NOM open
    'The window opens.'

If (ia) is not taken as derived from verb-raising (Harada 2002), *hirak* 'open' is lexically both transitive and intransitive.

[16] English has affixes like *-en* and *-ize* to turn adjectives (e.g. *short*, *modern*) into causative verbs (e.g. *shorten*, *modernize*). But it does not have affixes to turn an unaccusative verb into a causative verb.

[17] van Voorst (1992: 66-7) distinguishes four types of psych verb, as shown in (i):

(i) a. *From action verb to psych verb*
    He *struck* me as rather odd.
    b. *Psych verbs with an intentional subject*
    The clown tried to *amuse* me.
    c. *Psych verbs with a non-intentional subject*
    These experiences *amused* me tremendously.
    d. *Psych verbs of the dislike-type*
    We all *detested* the dirty streets in that area.

van Voorst argues that the four types of psych verbs behave similarly with respect to aspectual tests although they are often distinguished by using various semantic primitives. Constructions with these psych verbs are all achievements because they express moods, which are less permanent and cannot be manipulated.

[18] Belletti and Rizzi (1988) do not explain what case the Experiencer *Gianni* in (46b) receives and how it is assigned the case.

[19] Chen (1995: 16) gives two examples of OE verbs in Chinese, as shown in (i):

(i) a. gui    xia    wo.
       ghost frighten me

'The ghost frightens me.'
b. Fangfang de chenggong zhenfen le    ziji.
   Fangfang's success    excite  ASP  self
   'Fangfang's success excited herself.'

My intuition judges (ia) as marginally acceptable and (ib) as completely unacceptable. If used with an aspect marker *le*, (ia) would be completely unacceptable as well, which indicates that *xia* 'frighten' is not an OE verb:

(ii) *gu   xia    le   wo.
     ghost frighten ASP me

OE verbs are rare in Chinese. The only one that I can find is *gandong* 'move', as in (iii):

(iii) zhe ge gushi gandong le    wo.
      this CL story move ASP me
      'This story moved me.'

A possible reason is that *gandong* 'move' is a resultative verb compound: the first element *gan* 'move' indicates the activity or process and the second element *dong* 'act' indicates the result.

[20] Chao (1968: 88) treats adjectives as "a species of verbs", which can be used as full predicates. Li and Thompson (1981) use the term "adjective verbs" because the vast majority of adjectives may function as verbs in Chinese.

· 59 ·

# 3 Resultative and compound causative constructions

**导言**

本章作者首先介绍了英语结果补语结构和"直接宾语限制条件"以及两种不同的句法分析方法,即"小句法"和"三分法"。随后他提出了"动词短语壳"分析法,从而解决了这类结构中"直接宾语"位置、行为动词和结果补语的关系等问题。

本章的重点是汉语的结果补语结构和复合使动结构。作者首先对 Li(1990,1995,1998)、Huang(1992)和 Tang(1997)的观点做了详细介绍,在 Tang(1997)的基础上,提出了体短语(AspP)这一功能范畴,指出汉语的结果补语结构和复合使动结构中都包含这个功能范畴,其作用是指明行为动词产生的结果并对其进行限定。在结果补语中,体短语的中心词是"得";在复合使动结构中,体短语的中心词没有语音词汇形式。在此基础上,作者推导出具有不同构成形式的结果补语和复合使动结构,赋予这些结构以统一的句法表征。跟汉语相比,英语的结果补语结构中没有像体短语这样的功能范畴。

同汉语一样,日语和韩语中也有结果补语结构和复合使动结构。作者经过分析后认为,日语的结果补语结构和复合使动结构中都不包含类似汉语中体短语的功能范畴,在其复合使动结构中,行为动词和结果成分的论元指派也与汉语有别,不允许歧义。韩语中的复合使动结构中也没有像汉语体短语一样的功能范畴,但其结果补语结构有类似的功能范畴。跟汉语不同的是,韩语结果补语结构允许歧义,即结果成分可以为不同的名词指派论元。

# Resultative and compound causative constructions

Resultative and causative constructions share some properties in semantics, event structure and aspectuality. In semantics, both involve two elements, cause and effect; in event structure, both involve an event type of transition from one state to another (Pustejovsky 1991); in aspectuality, the predicates are intimately connected with the temporal structure of the event described by the verb and impose delimitedness to the event (Tenny 1994). Despite these common properties, however, resultative and causative constructions differ fundamentally in predication: while a causative contains a cause predicate as in (1a), a resultative contains a result predicate as in (1b). Without the result predicate, the sentence denotes an activity that does not entail a change of state, as shown in (1c).

(1) a. Tom *broke* the vase. (causative)
    b. Tom pounded the metal *flat*. (resultative)
    c. Tom pounded the metal. (activity)

As mentioned in Chapter 2, CAUSE and BECOME can be conflated into one word like *break* in English. In Chinese, however, conflation of these two semantic primitives is impossible (Juffs 1996a, 1996b, 2000). As a result, CAUSE and BECOME are expressed with separate predicates like *da* 'hit' and *sui* 'break' in (2a), which are fused together to form a verb compound like *da-sui* 'hit-break'. Following Li and Thompson (1976b), I will refer to such verb compounds as compound causatives. In Chinese, the cause predicate and the result predicate can also stand separately like *pao* 'run' and *lei* 'tire' in (2b). Since (2b) contains *de*, a morpheme leading a result phrase, I will refer to such constructions as resultative constructions.

(2) a. Zhangsan da-sui le huaping.
   Zhangsan hit-break ASP vase
   'Zhangsan broke a/the vase.'
   b. Zhangsan pao de hen lei.
   Zhangsan run *de* very tire
   'Zhangsan ran and got very tired.'

Of the four languages under discussion in this thesis, Chinese, Japanese and Korean have both resultative and compound causative constructions, whereas English allows the resultative construction only.

In this chapter, I will discuss properties and derivations of resultative constructions in English in § 3.1. Properties and derivations of Chinese, Japanese and Korean resultative and compound causative constructions will be discussed in § 3.2, § 3.3 and § 3.4 respectively. A summary will be given in § 3.5. The purpose of this chapter is to provide a theoretical framework for the empirical study on the acquisition of Chinese resultative and compound causative constructions by native speakers of English, Japanese and Korean.

## 3.1 Resultative constructions in English

Resultative constructions contain two predicates: the activity predicate, which represents the CAUSE component, and the result predicate, which represents the BECOME component. In English, the former is the main predicate while the latter is the secondary predicate. In this thesis, phrase projected by the secondary predicate is termed XP. Thus the result phrase forms an XP in the resultative construction.

Resultatives in English can be divided into different types under different criteria. According to Carrier and Randall (1992), there is a distinction between transitive and intransitive resultatives with regard to transitivity of the activity predicate, as shown in (3) and (4) (from Carrier and Randall 1992: 173):

(3) Transitive resultatives
   a. The gardener watered the tulips flat.
   b. The grocer ground the coffee beans into a fine powder.
   c. They painted their house a hideous shade of green.

(4) Intransitive resultatives
   a. The joggers ran their Nikes threadbare.
   b. The kids laughed themselves into a frenzy.
   c. He sneezed his handkerchief completely soggy.

With respect to the relation between the activity verb and the postverbal NP, resultatives can also be classified into two types: those with subcategorized NPs and those with nonsubcategorized NPs. The transitive verbs in (3) subcategorize the postverbal NPs, so leaving the result predicate out will not result in ungrammatical sentences, as shown in (5). Without the result predicate that denotes "a bounded scale" (Wyngaerd 2001: 64), these sentences do not express accomplishments but activities. The activity predicates in (4) are unergative verbs, which do not subcategorize NPs as internal argument. In this case, the result predicate is indispensable to the grammaticality of these sentences, as shown in (6).

(5) a. The gardener watered the tulips.
   b. The grocer ground the coffee beans.
   c. They painted their house.

(6) a. *The joggers ran their Nikes.
   b. *The kids laughed themselves.
   c. *He sneezed his handkerchief.

Transitive verbs may also have non-subcategorized NPs in resultative constructions. Despite transitivity, these verbs, when used in isolation as in (8), cannot select the postverbal NPs that occur in resultatives in (7) ((7a) from Rappaport Hovav and Levin 2001: 794 and (7b-d) from Hoekstra 1988: 116). In this case, the postverbal NP forms a closer relation with the result predicate than with the activity predicate.

(7) a. They drank the pub dry.
    b. He rubbed the tiredness out of his eyes.
    c. They wrung a confession out of him.
    d. The sopranos sang us sleepy.
(8) a. *They drank the pub.
    b. *He rubbed the tiredness.
    c. *They wrung a confession.
    d. *The sopranos sang us.

In the next section, I will discuss the relations between the activity predicate, the result predicate and the NPs.

### 3.1.1 The result XP and DOR

Whether the activity predicate is transitive or unergative, or whether it is followed by a subcategorised or nonsubcategorized NP, a resultative in English has a linear structure as shown in (9):

(9) Activity predicate + NP + result predicate

As first observed by Simpson (1983), the controller of the result predicate is the object, whether the object is a surface object as in transitive verbs or an underlying object as in passive and unaccusative verbs, or whether the object is a fake reflexive as in unergative verbs. The main idea of this proposal is that the result phrase or XP appears invariably to be predicated of the NP in the object position, no matter whether it is an argument of the activity verb or not. This is called the

Direct Object Restriction, or DOR. According to Levin and Rappaport Hovav (1995: 34), a result XP is "an XP that denotes the state achieved by the referent of the NP it is predicated of as a result of the action denoted by the verb". Because a resultative denotes a state achieved by the NP it is predicated of, the XP acts as delimiter of an event.

The DOR is motivated by both transitive and intransitive resultative constructions (Rappoport Hovav and Levin 2001). In transitive resultatives, the result XP is predicated of the object of the verb but never of its subject, as shown in (10a). In intransitive resultatives, the result XP may be predicated of the underlying object of a passive verb as in (10b) or the underlying object of an unaccusative verb as in (10c). In the case of unergative verbs as in (10d), a fake reflexive which is coindexed with the subject fills in the object position obligatorily as a syntactic device that allows the result XP to be predicated of the object.

(10) a. Tom$_j$ pounded [the *metal*$_i$ flat$_{i/*j}$]. (transitive verb)
    b. The ice-cream$_i$ was frozen [$e_i$ solid$_i$]. (passive verb)
    c. The bottle$_i$ broke [$e_i$ open$_i$]. (unaccusative verb)
    d. The kids$_i$ laughed [ [*themselves*$_i$ [into a frenzy]$_i$].
      (unergative verb)
(11) a. The joggers ran *their Nikes* threadbare.
    b. They drank *the pub* dry.

Such an analysis, however, is problematic with unergative verbs whose postverbal NPs are not fake reflexives as in (11a) and with transitive verbs which have nonsubcategorised NPs as in (11b). To explain adequately the relation between the activity verb and the postverbal NP in resultative constructions, Levin and Rappaport Hovav (1995) posit the Change-of-State Linking Rule as in (12) (see Sorace 2004 for a review of such linking rules):

(12) The Change-of-State Linking Rule (Levin and Rappaport Hovav 1995: 51)

Version (a): An NP that refers to the entity that undergoes the change of state in the eventuality described in the VP must be governed by the verb heading the VP.

Version (b): An NP that refers to the entity that undergoes the change of state in the eventuality described in the VP must be the direct object of the verb heading the VP.

The two versions of the linking rule are complementary: Version (b) is applicable to transitive verbs with subcategorised NPs, whereas Version (a) applies if the NP is not the direct object of the verb. In both cases, the verb governs the NP and assigns case to it. A difference between the DOR and the Change-of-State Linking Rule is that the former explains resultatives in terms of configuration, whereas the latter combines configuration with event structure.

Wechsler and Noh (2001) distinguish between predicative resultatives and Exceptional-Case-Marking (ECM) resultatives. In an ECM construction the verb assigns case to the following NP but does not bear a thematic relation with it. In (15a), for example, the postverbal NP *Mary* receives case from the verb *consider*, but it is thematically related to the predicate *intelligent* in the embedded clause and is assigned a θ-role by this predicate. Without the embedded predicate, no θ-role is assigned to this NP and the θ-Criterion is thus violated, resulting in an ill-formed sentence (15b). In an ECM resultative like (14a), the verb behaves similarly to an ECM verb like *consider* and does not semantically select the postverbal NP. Since the postverbal NP is thematically related to the result predicate, leaving out the result predicate will generate ungrammatical sentences like (14b). In contrast, the verb in predicative resultatives like (13a) subcategorises an NP as the internal argument, as it does in non-resultatives like (13b).

(13) Predicative resultatives
    a. The gardener watered the tulips flat.
    b. The gardener watered the tulips.

(14) ECM resultatives
    a. The joggers ran their Nikes threadbare.
    b. *The joggers ran their Nikes.

(15) ECM construction
    a. We consider Mary intelligent.
    b. *We consider Mary.

According to Wechsler and Noh, predicative resultatives involve argument sharing: the postverbal NP is an argument of both the activity predicate and the result predicate. ECM resultatives, however, do not involve argument sharing: the postverbal NP is an argument of the result predicate but it is not an argument of the activity predicate. Since it is not the object of the acitivity predicate, DOR is not observed. In other words, DOR can only accommodate predicative resultatives.

### 3.1.2 Semantic and syntactic representations

There are several proposals on the argument and syntactic structures of resultative constructions. In the following sections, I will introduce the small-clause proposal and the ternary-analysis approach.

### 3.1.2.1 The small-clause proposal

Hoekstra (1988) posits a unified syntactic structure for resultative constructions irrespective of verb types. In this proposal, the postverbal NP and the result predicate form a small clause (SC),[1] which denotes a state of affairs that is presented as a consequence of the activity or process denoted by the verb; the postverbal NP and the result predicate form a predication relation in the sense of Williams (1980) that a semantic subject c-commands its predicate; the SC is a syntactic constituent which functions as an argument of the verb (cf. Baltin 1998), whether the verb is transitive or intransitive. Thus, transitive resultatives like *the gardeners watered the tulips flat* in (3a) and intransitive resultatives like *the joggers ran their Nikes threadbare* in (4a) have the same structure, as illustrated in (16):

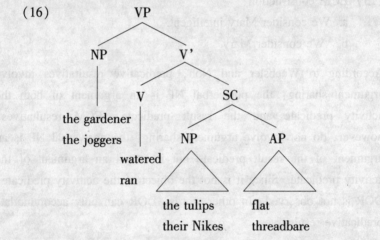

(16)

A problem arises with this structure: since unergative verbs like *run* can only select an external argument, how can they select SC as an internal argument? To solve this problem, Hoekstra (1988: 129) classifies verbs into two types, which are stative verbs and non-stative verbs as in (17), arguing that only non-stative verbs can select a result-denoting SC. In other words, both transitive and intransitive verbs can select SC as the result complement as long as they are semantically classified as non-statives.

(17)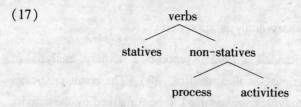

By postulating the result SC, Hoekstra intends to provide a unified structure for all types of resultatives. However, this proposal leaves some questions unanswered. Within this approach, any non-stative verb can select a result-denoting SC. In the case of transitive verbs like *water* in (18), the argument structure in resultatives will be different from that in non-resultatives. In the case of unergative verbs like *run* in (19), the resultative will have one more argument (i. e. the SC) than the non-resultative.

(18) a. The gardener watered the tulips flat.
     < Agent, result SC >
   b. The gardener watered the tulips this morning.
     < Agent, Theme >
(19) a. The joggers ran their Nikes threadbare.
     < Agent, result SC >
   b. The joggers ran every morning.
     < Agent >

Since the Theme argument of a transitive verb is suppressed in the resultative construction (cf. Goldberg 2001), the argument structure of a transitive verb and that of an unergative verb are identical in resultatives, both taking a result SC as complement. The difference between these two types of verb is thus neutralized. This may bring about problems in interpretation (Carrier and Randall 1992): since the activity verb *water* is disconnected with its potential Theme, i. e. *the tulips*, (18a) may be interpreted in a way that the tulips became flat because the gardeners watered something else rather than the tulips.

## 3.1.2.2 The ternary-analysis approach

Carrier and Randall (1992) propose a ternary analysis of resultative constructions, as illustrated in (20). The result predicates (i.e. *flat* and *threadbare*) are assumed to be θ-marked by the activity verbs (i.e. *water* and *run*) and are taken to be arguments of these verbs. The activity verb (transitive and intransitive), the postverbal NP and the result predicate are all sisters in a ternary-branching VP.

(20)

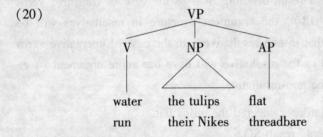

According to Carrier and Randall, although the result predicate can be NP, AP or PP, not all potential result predicates within these categories are allowed. The result predicate is semantically constrained and is s-selected by the verb. This requires that it be an argument and a sister of the verb irrespective of its transitivity. Another reason for the ternary analysis is that the argument structure of a verb must be satisfied in the syntax in accordance with the EPP (Chomsky 1982). Verbs in resultatives inherit the argument structure that they have in non-resultatives. The only difference is that one argument, i.e. the XP denoting the result state (R-state), is added in resultatives. Thus, transitive verbs like *water* in (18a) and unergative verbs like *run* in (19a) have θ-grids as shown in (21) (from Carrier and Randall 1992: 179):

(21) θ-grids under the ternary analysis
    basic verb               resultative verb

| | | | | |
|---|---|---|---|---|
| *water* | Agent | [Theme] | Agent | [Theme R-state] |
| *run* | Agent | [ ] | Agent | [ R-state] |

In this proposal, a transitive verb assigns a θ-role to the postverbal NP as in non-resultatives. The θ-role assignment guarantees the correct interpretation of transitive resultatives: in (18a), the tulips became flat as a consequence of the gardener watering the tulips, not as a consequence of the gardener engaging in the activity of watering, as might be in the SC proposal (Hoekstra 1988). In the ternary analysis, the postverbal NP is an argument of the verb and is closely related to the verb both syntactically and semantically.

If the postverbal NP in transitive resultatives receives its θ-role from the verb, how does the postverbal NP in an intransitive resultative receive its θ-role? Under the ternary analysis, it is assigned a θ-role not by the intransitive activity verb but by the result predicate, thus satisfying the θ-Criterion that "each argument bears one and only one θ-role, and each θ-role is assigned to one and only one argument" (Chomsky 1981: 36). However, if the result predicate can assign a θ-role to the postverbal NP in intransitive resultatives, why cannot it in transitive resultatives? If it can as well, the postverbal NP in a transitive resultative will receive two θ-roles, one from the transitive verb and the other from the result predicate. The θ-Criterion is thus violated.

### 3.1.2.3  A solution with VP shell

A common problem with the two proposals introduced in § 3.1.2.1 and § 3.1.2.2 lies in the argument structure of the activity verb. Here I propose a new solution, as shown in (22), on the basis of VP shell (cf. Embick 2004). In this proposal, all activity verbs can take a result XP as complement. The activity verb is base-generated at the head position of the lower VP. Spec-*v*P is the position for the Agent, and Spec-VP is the position for the Theme of a transitive verb. In the case of intransitive verbs, the postverbal NP occurs at Spec-XP. When the Theme occurs at Spec-VP, there is a coindexed PRO at Spec-XP. This structure can derive both transitive and intransitive resultatives, as illustrated in (23).

(22)
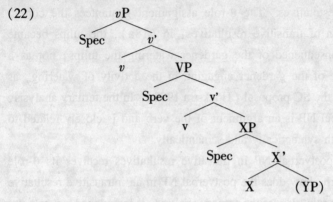

(23) a. Transitive resultative

[ $_{vP}$ The gardener [ $_{v'}$ watered$_i$ [ $_{VP}$ the tulips$_j$ [ $_{v'}$ t$_i$ [ $_{XP}$ PRO$_j$ [ $_{X'}$ flat ]]]]]].

b. Intransitive resultative

[ $_{vP}$ The joggers [ $_{v'}$ ran$_i$ [ $_{VP}$ [ $_{v'}$ t$_i$ [ $_{XP}$ their Nikes [ $_{X'}$ threadbare ]]]]]].

This proposal has at least two advantages. First, the argument structure of the activity verb is fully projected. Thus, transitive verbs differ from intransitive verbs in resultatives as in non-resultatives. Second, resultatives are derived in a binary fashion along the same line as non-resultatives are.

## 3.2 Resultative and compound causative constructions in Chinese

As pointed out at the beginning of this chapter, Chinese employs both resultative and compound causative constructions to represent causativity. Two more examples are given in (24). Both resultatives and compound causatives contain two predicates, the activity/cause predicate (underlined, henceforth $V_1$) and the result/state predicate (italicised, henceforth $V_2$).[2] As mentioned in Chapter 2, Chinese does not have accomplishment verbs (Chu 1976; Smith 1997; Sybesma 1997; Tai 1984). Since all predicates, except states, are activities, which are dynamic and have an open range, an accomplishment that denotes a bounded event is always a complex consisting of an activity/cause predicate and a result/state predicate.

(24) a. Resultative construction
   Zhangsan <u>ku</u> de shoujuan    dou  *shi* le.
   Zhangsan cry *de* handkerchief even wet ASP
   'Zhangsan cried the handkerchief soggy.'
   b. Compound causative construction
   Zhangsan <u>ku</u>-*shi*  le   shoujuan.
   Zhangsan cry-wet ASP handkerchief
   'Zhangsan cried the handkerchief soggy.'

As shown in (24a), resultatives in Chinese are introduced by a bound morpheme *de*,[3] which is invariably attached to the activity predicate $V_1$. English resultatives do not have resultative markers. This is a main difference between resultatives in the two languages. In Chinese, a resultative may have a linear "$V_1$-*de*-NP-$V_2$" order, as in (24a), or a "$V_1$-*de*-$V_2$" order, as we will see in the following discussion. In English, resultatives have the same surface structure as "$V_1$-NP-$V_2$". This is another distinction between resultatives in the two languages.

The basic formation of Chinese compound causatives is $V_1$-$V_2$. A difference between resultatives and compound causatives is that the former have a marker *de* while the latter have no explicit marker. In compound causatives, the activity predicate and the result predicate form a compound with nothing in-between in the surface structure.

As noted in Chapter 1, Chinese does not have lexical causatives.

Causative verbs in English, when translated into Chinese, can be expressed with compound causatives, as in (25). Resultatives in English, when translated into Chinese, can be expressed with resultatives or compound causatives, as in (26).

(25) a. Tom broke the vase. (English causative)
   b. Tom da-*sui*   le  huaping. (Chinese compound causative)
      Tom hit-break ASP vase
(26) a. Tom cried the handkerchief soggy. (English resultative)
   b. Tom ku-*shi*  le  shoujuan. (Chinese compound causative)
      Tom cry-wet ASP handkerchief
   c. Tom ku de shoujuan   dou  shi le. (Chinese resultative)
      Tom cry *de* handkerchief even wet ASP

Chinese resultatives and compound causatives contain two NPs. In the following discussion, the subject NP, i.e. the NP preceding $V_1$ (in resultatives) or $V_1$-$V_2$ compound (in compound causatives) will be called $NP_1$ and the other, $NP_2$. In (25b), $NP_1$ is *Tom* and $NP_2$ *huaping* 'vase'. In (26b) and (26c), $NP_1$ is *Tom* and $NP_2$ *shoujuan* 'handkerchief'. In some cases, $NP_2$ is null in the surface structure, as we will see in the following discussion.

### 3.2.1 Previous studies on resultatives and compound causatives

In this section, I will review previous studies on resultatives and compound causatives conducted by Y. Li (1990, 1995, 1998), C.-T. Huang (1992) and Tang (1997).

#### 3.2.1.1 Y. Li (1990, 1995, 1998)

Y. Li posits a lexical approach to resultatives and compound causatives. He makes a distinction between transitive resultatives and intransitive resultatives as in (27), in line with Carrier and Randall (1992) in their analysis of English resultatives: (27a) contains a transitive $V_1$ *zhui* 'chase', whereas (27b) contains an intransitive, or, to be more exact, an unergative $V_1$ *ku* 'cry'.

(27) a. Transitive resultative

   Zhangsan zhui de Lisi dou   *lei*   le.
   Zhangsan chased *de* Lisi even tire ASP
   'Zhangsan chased Lisi and Lisi got tired as a result.'

   b. Intransitive resultative

   Zhangsan ku de shoujuan      dou *shi*  le.
   Zhangsan cry *de* handkerchief even wet ASP
   'Zhangsan cried the handkerchief soggy.'

Y. Li (1998) argues that the activity predicate $V_1$ (i.e. *zhui* 'chase' in (27a) and *ku* 'cry' in (27b)) and the bound morpheme *de* form one word, namely V-*de*. However, the status of the postverbal NP, or $NP_2$, is decided by $V_1$ alone: if $V_1$ is intransitive as in (27b), $NP_2$ (i.e. *shoujuan* 'handkerchief') is the subject of the result predicate (i.e. *shi* 'wet'); if $V_1$ is transitive as in (27a), $NP_2$ (i.e. *Lisi*) is the complement of V-*de* and the subject of the result XP is a *pro* which is coindexed with $NP_2$. Thus, transitive and intransitive resultatives have two different structures, as illustrated in (28). In this derivation, the resultative marker *de* enters into syntax simply as a bound morpheme. Its syntactic function is ignored.

(28) a. Transitive resultative

   $[_{VP} NP1 [_{V'} V1\text{-}de\ NP2_i\ [_{XP} pro_i\ V2]]]$

   b. Intransitive resultative:

   $[_{VP} NP1 [_{V'} V1\text{-}de\ [_{XP} NP2\ V2]]]$

According to Y. Li, compound causatives enter syntax directly from the lexicon (cf. Gao 1997). His argument is based on Grimshaw

(1990) and Higginbotham (1985). Grimshaw (1990) argues that the assignment of θ-roles is strictly and consistently ordered, observing the thematic hierarchy shown in (29a). The θ-roles of a verb are assigned to its arguments in accordance with their relative prominence: the Agent θ-role is the most prominent, whereas the Theme/Location θ-role is the least prominent. The least prominent θ-role is assigned first and the most prominent θ-role is assigned last. The prominence order aligns with structural prominence of the arguments, for example (subject (object)). However, the thematic hierarchy is not the only factor that determines the link between θ-roles and syntactic arguments. It interacts with causative hierarchy shown in (29b) and, when in conflict, can be overridden by the latter. In other words, the θ-roles of a verb can be assigned to its arguments against the thematic hierarchy only if these arguments observe the causative hierarchy.

(29) a. Thematic hierarchy

(Agent(Experiencer(Goal/Source $V_1$(Theme/Location))))

b. Causative hierarchy

(Causer (Causee))

According to Higginbotham's (1985) theta-identification and head-feature percolation proposal, θ-role is not the only thematic operation to guarantee that θ-Criterion is satisfied. In a modifier-modifiee construction like (30), the θ-roles of the AP must be identified with that of the head N so that the NP as a whole is assigned one θ-role at some derivational stage. The head of a compound word determines the fundamental properties of the compound and the θ-role prominence of the head must be strictly maintained in the theta-grid of the compound. In terms of Chinese compound causatives, Higginbotham's proposal implies that θ-roles from $V_1$ and $V_2$ can be identified and assigned to one argument NP (i.e. $NP_1$ or $NP_2$); if $V_1$ is taken to be the head of the compound, its relevant features must be maintained throughout its derivational projection.

(30)

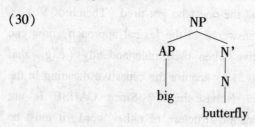

Applying the structured theta-grid and causative-hierarchy proposal (Grimshaw 1990) and the theta-identification and head-feature percolation proposal (Higginbotham 1985) to Chinese compound causatives, Y. Li (1990, 1995) argues that readings (i), (ii) and (iii) can be derived from (31), but (iv) cannot.[4]

(31) Zhangsan zhui-*lei*   le Lisi.
   Zhangsan chase-tired ASP Lisi
   (i) 'Zhangsan chased Lisi and Lisi got tired as a result.'
   (ii) 'Zhangsan chased Lisi and got tired as a result.'
   (iii) 'Lisi chased Zhangsan and got tired as a result.'
   (iv) *'Lisi chased Zhangsan and as a result Zhangsan got tired.'

(32) The thematic structures of $V_1$ and $V_2$
   $V_1$ *zhui* 'chase'   < Agent, Theme >
   $V_2$ *lei* 'tire'   < Theme >

Y. Li takes compound causatives as having a monoclausal structure in which $NP_1$ is the subject and $NP_2$ object. The thematic structures of $V_1$ and $V_2$ are given in (32). Reading (31i) is derived if the Theme θ-role of $V_2$ is identified with the Theme θ-role of $V_1$ and the identified θ-role is assigned to the object (i.e. *Lisi*). Thus, *Lisi* is interpreted as both the one who was chased (Theme of $V_1$) and the one who got tired (Theme of $V_2$) as the result of chasing. Reading (31ii) is derived if the Theme θ-role of $V_2$ is identified with the Agent θ-role of $V_1$ and the identified θ-role is assigned to the subject (i.e.

Zhangsan). In this case, Zhangsan is both the one who did the chasing (Agent of $V_1$) and the one who got tired (Theme of $V_2$).

A question is left unanswered in the lexical approach: how can verbs that are non-causative when used independently (e.g. *zhui* 'chase' and *lei* 'tire' in (31)) acquire the causative meaning in the compound (e.g. *zhui-lei* 'chase-tire')? Since CAUSE is not included in the lexical semantic structure of either word, it must be derived in syntactic operations.

### 3.2.1.2 C.-T. Huang (1992)

C.-T. Huang (1992) takes a syntactic approach, arguing that resultatives and compound causatives are derived in the same way syntactically, as illustrated in (33a) and (33b). A VP shell is involved in both (33a) and (33b) with $V_1$ (i.e. *ku* 'cry') heading the lower VP and $NP_2$ (i.e. *shoujuan* 'handkerchief') at Spec-VP. In the resultative (33a), the activity predicate $V_1$ (i.e. *ku* 'cry') and the resultative morpheme *de* is treated as one verb, which raises from the head position of the lower VP to the head position of the upper *v*P, where it assigns $NP_2$ (i.e. *shoujuan* 'handkerchief') accusative case (also see C.-T. Huang 1988). In the result clause (RC) in (33a), there is a *pro*, which is controlled by $NP_2$ (i.e. *shoujuan* 'handkerchief') under the Generalized Control Theory (C.-T. Huang 1984, 1989). As to the compound causative (33b), it is argued that the compound (i.e. *ku-shi* 'cry-wet') is short enough to be treated as one verb heading the lower VP. It raises to the head position of the upper *v*P and assigns accusative case to $NP_2$ (i.e. *shoujuan* 'handkerchief') at Spec-VP.

(33) a. resultative construction

    Zhangsan <u>ku</u> de shoujuan     dou *shi* le.
    Zhangsan cry *de* handkerchief even wet ASP

## 3 Resultative and compound causative constructions

'Zhangsan cried the handkerchief soggy.'

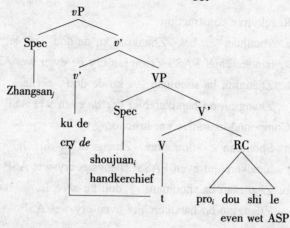

b. compound causative construction

Zhangsan <u>ku</u>-*shi*   le   shoujuan.
Zhangsan cry-wet ASP handkerchief
'Zhangsan cried the handkerchief soggy.'

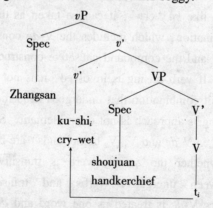

Evidence that C.-T. Huang finds to support his proposal is that NP$_2$ in (33a) and (33b) (e.g. *shoujuan* 'handkerchief') can be the subject of a passive sentence headed by *bei* as in (34a) and (35a) or the preverbal object preposed by *ba* (see notes 13 and 14 of Chapter 2) as in (34b) and (35b). This indicates that the θ-role of the NP does not change in these structures.

(34) Resultative construction
  a. Shoujuan    bei Zhangsan ku de dou   shi le.
     handkerchief PASS Zhangsan cry *de* even wet ASP
  b. Zhangsan ba shoujuan    ku de dou   shi le.
     Zhangsan *ba* handkerchief cry *de* even wet ASP

(35) Compound causative construction
  a. Shoujuan    dou bei Zhangsan ku-*shi* le.
     handkerchief even PASS Zhangsan cry-wet ASP
  b. Zhangsan ba shoujuan    dou ku-*shi* le.
     Zhangsan *ba* handkerchief even cry-wet ASP

The resultatives in (34) and the compound causatives in (35) are identical in meaning. According to C. -T. Huang, there is a constant semantic relationship between $NP_2$ like *shoujuan* 'handkerchief' and the rest of the sentence. Although it cannot be considered as the object of the main verb like *ku* 'cry', it can be taken as the object of the verb-result combination, which includes the V-*de* construction (e. g. *ku-de* 'cry-*de*') and the compound causative construction (e. g. *ku-shi* 'cry-wet'). If verb raising is involved, it is not the single verb but the verb-result combination that undergoes head movement.

C. -T. Huang's approach is not unproblematic. Since verb-result combinations (i. e. V-*de* and $V_1$-$V_2$ compounds) are both transitive in this approach whether the activity verb is transitive or not, the distinction between unergative verbs and transitive verbs is neutralized. Since V-*de* is treated as one word and *de* as part of the word, the status of *de* as a resultative marker is ignored.

3. 2. 1. 3   Tang (1997)

Tang (1997) treats resultatives and compound causatives as derived in the same way illustrated in (36) (adapted from Tang

1997: 209). Unlike C.-T. Huang, who treats verb compound as a lexical category, Tang argues for the presence of a functional category F, which acts as a kind of closure to the open range of the activity predicate and denotes the culmination in temporal extension. In other words, F is responsible for the bounded reading of a resultative or a compound causative.

(36)

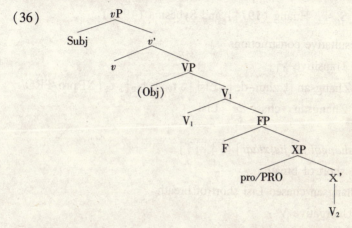

Within this approach, resultatives and compound causatives consist of a VP shell and a functional phrase (FP). The sentence subject is generated at Spec-$v$P and the object of transitive verbs at Spec-VP headed by the activity predicate $V_1$. $V_1$ selects the functional category FP as complement. F selects a result XP as complement, which is headed by the result predicate $V_2$ with an empty pronominal (*pro* or PRO) as specifier. According to the Generalized Control Theory (C.-T. Huang 1984, 1989), *pro* and PRO are instances of the same category, which is controlled in its domain (if it has one) by the closest nominal element. Since the empty pronominal is free in its governing category FP, Binding Principle B is not violated whether it is controlled by the subject or the object.

In resultatives, F is the position where the morpheme *de* is located. Due to the affixal nature of *de*, it undergoes movement to attach to the activity predicate $V_1$ to form a V-*de* complex. Then the V-*de* complex raises to the head position of the upper $v$P, generating resultative sentences, as shown in (37a) and (37b). If $V_1$ is transitive, the light verb $v$ can be phonetically realized as the morpheme *ba* and the word order shown in (37c) is derived. In this case, *ba* is treated as a causative morpheme in line with C.-T. Huang (1992), S.-F. Huang (1974) and Sybesma (1992).

(37) Resultative constructions

    a. Transitive $V_1$:

[$_{vP}$Zhangsan$_j$ [$_{v'}$ zhui–de [$_{VP}$Lisi$_i$ [$_{V'}$ t$_{V1}$-t$_{de}$ [$_{FP}$ [$_{F'}$ t$_{de}$ [XP pro/PRO$_i$

    Zhangsan  chase *de*  Lisi

[$_{X'}$ *shangqi bu jie xiaqi*]]]]]]]]

    short of breath

'Zhangsan chased Lisi short of breath.'

    b. Unergative $V_1$:

[$_{vP}$Zhangsan$_j$ [$_{v'}$ ku–de [$_{VP}$[$_{V'}$ t$_{V1}$-t$_{de}$ [$_{FP}$ [$_{F'}$ t$_{de}$ [XP pro/PRO$_i$

    Zhangsan  cry *de*

[$_{X'}$ *hen shangxin*]]]]]]]]

    very hurt-heart

'Zhangsan cried and became very sad as a result.'

    c. *Ba* as causative marker:

[$_{vP}$Zhangsan$_j$ [$_{v'}$ ba [$_{VP}$ Lisi$_i$ [$_{V'}$ zhui– de[$_{FP}$ [$_{F'}$ t$_{de}$ [XP pro/PRO$_i$

    Zhangsan  *ba*  Lisi  chase *de*

[$_{X'}$ *shangqi bu jie xiaqi*]]]]]]]]

    short of breath

'Zhangsan chased Lisi short of breath.'

In compound causatives, F does not have lexical realization in the surface structure. As illustrated in (38), due to its strong aspectual feature, F attracts the result predicate $V_2$ (i.e. *sui* 'break') to check its strong feature. From the head position of FP, $V_2$ (i.e. *sui* 'break') moves further and attaches to $V_1$ (i.e. *da* 'hit') for morphological reasons, forming a $V_1$-$V_2$ compound (i.e. *da-sui* 'hit-break'). The compound then raises to the head position of the upper *v*P, generating the compound causative. In this derivation, NP1 (i.e. *Zhangsan*) occurs at Spec-*v*P, while $NP_2$ (i.e. *huaping* 'vase') occurs at Spec-VP.

(38) Zhangsan da-*sui* le huaping.

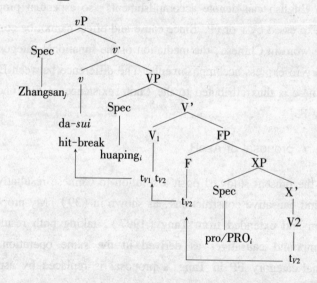

Tang's proposal of a functional category FP involved in Chinese resultatives and compound causatives seems to be on the right track. First, the introduction of the functional category F explains why resultatives and compound causatives denote accomplishments while single verbs cannot: it is F that is responsible for the bounded reading. Second, the resultative marker *de* is argued to be head of the functional FP rather than simply a bound morpheme. Different from treating V-*de* as one word as in the proposals by C.-T. Huang (1992) and Y. Li (1998), *de* is granted independent syntactic status in Tang's proposal and is argued to attach to $V_1$ through movement. This seems to be reasonable because although *de* is affixal in nature and must attach to a verb, its properties cannot be assimilated by the verb, nor can V-*de* behave in the same way as single verbs. *De* is a resultative morpheme, which can delimit the activity predicate. Thus a V-*de* complex is different from a single verb.

According to Tang, there is a parametric variation between Chinese and English with respect to the (non)existence of FP. Single verbs in English can denote accomplishments, so aspectual properties can be expressed by *v* or *v*P. Since cause and effect cannot be conflated into one word in Chinese, the mediation of the functional category F is obligatory to express accomplishments. The difference between English and Chinese is thus attributed to the (non)existence of the functional category F.[5]

### 3.2.2 A proposal of AspP

In the present study, I posit a solution to Chinese resultative and compound causative constructions, as shown in (39). My proposal is based on and extended from Tang (1997), taking both resultatives and compound causatives as derived in the same operation. The functional category FP in Tang's proposal is replaced by aspectual phrase (AspP)[6] in my proposal. Thus the derivation involves a VP shell and an AspP.

(39)
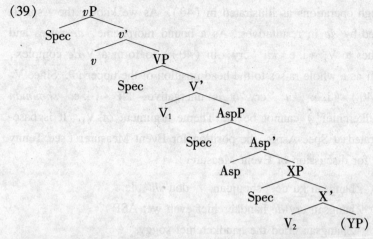

In this proposal, the activity predicate $V_1$ heads the lower VP, while the result predicate $V_2$ heads the result XP. Between VP and XP occurs AspP, which is responsible for the accomplishment reading of an event introduced by the activity predicate $V_1$. The AspP is headed by *de* in the case of resultatives or a phonetically unrealized morpheme in the case of compound causatives. The Agent NP (i.e. $NP_1$) is generated at Spec-*v*P and the Theme NP (i.e. $NP_2$) of a transitive verb at Spec-VP.

According to Travis (2003), Spec-AspP is the position for the element that measures the event (see Tenny 1994 for discussion of Measure), or, put differently, the element which helps to delimit the event. In the derivation shown in (39), an NP or an empty pronominal occurs at this position.

In the present study, it is argued that resultatives and compound causatives have the same structure as in (39). In the next two subsections, I will demonstrate how they are derived from this structure.

### 3.2.2.1 The derivation of resultative constructions

Based on (39), Chinese resultative constructions are derived through operations as illustrated in (40). As we know, the AspP is headed by *de* in resultatives. As a bound morpheme, *de* raises and attaches to $V_1$ (i.e. *ku* 'cry' in (40)) to form a V-*de* complex, which as a whole raises to the head position of the upper *v*P. Since $V_1$ in (40) (i.e. *ku* 'cry') is unergative, $NP_2$ (i.e. *shoujuan* 'handkerchief') cannot be the Theme argument of $V_1$. It is base-generated at Spec-AspP, the position for Event Measurer (see Tenny 1994 for discussion of Event Measurer).

(40) Zhangsan <u>ku</u> de shoujuan dou *shi* le.
Zhangsan cry *de* handkerchief even wet ASP
'Zhangsan cried the handkerchief soggy.'

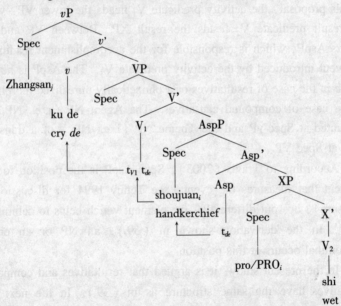

Let us now find out how the structure in (39) derives resultatives with a transitive $V_1$ like *zhui* 'chase' in (41). Of the three sentences in (41), (41a) contains V1 (i.e. *zhui* 'chase'), $V_2$ (i.e. *lei* 'tire'), $NP_1$ (i.e. *Zhangsan*) and $NP_2$ (i.e. *Lisi*); in (41b), the

Theme of $V_1$ is phonetically unrealized; in (41c), $V_1$ (i. e. *zhui* 'chase') is reduplicated.

(41) a. Zhangsan zhui de Lisi dou *lei* le.
   Zhangsan chase *de* Lisi even tire ASP
   'Zhangsan chased Lisi and Lisi got tired as a result.'
   b. Zhangsan zhui de dou *lei* le
   Zhangsan chase *de* even tire ASP
   'Zhangsan chased and got tired.'
   c. Zhangsan zhui Lisi zhui de dou *lei* le.
   Zhangsan chase Lisi chase *de* even tire ASP
   'Zhangsan chased Lisi and got tired as a result.'

In (41a), $NP_2$ (i. e. *Lisi*) is both the Theme argument of $V_1$ (i. e. *zhui* 'chase') occurring at Spec-VP and the event-measuring element occurring at Spec-AspP. After *de* attaches to $V_1$ (i. e. *zhui* 'chase'), one of them (i. e. *Lisi* at Spec-VP and Spec-AspP) is deleted due to haplology. At Spec-XP is a pro/PRO, which is coindexed with $NP_2$ (i. e. *Lisi*). The NP *Lisi* at Spec-VP is assigned a Theme θ-role by the transitive $V_1$ (i. e. *zhui* 'chase'); at Spec-AspP, it is assigned an Experiencer θ-role by $V_2$ (i. e. *lei* 'tire'). The syntactic operation of (41a) is briefly illustrated in (42):

(42) $[_{vP}$Zhangsan$_j$ $[_{v'}$zhui-de $[_{VP}$Lisi$_i$ $[_{V'}$ t$_{V1}$-t$_{de}$$[_{AspP}$Lisi$_i$$[_{Asp'}$t$_{de}$$[_{XP}$pro/PRO$_i$
   Zhangsan chase *de* Lisi

$[_{X'}$dou *lei* le]]]]]]]]
even tire ASP
'Zhangsan chased Lisi and Lisi got tired as a result.'

In (41b), the Theme of $V_1$ is phonetically null. Following C.-T. Huang (1984), we may assume an empty pronominal at this position which is coindexed with an empty topic heading the topic phrase

(TopP) at the sentence-initial position (see Gasde and Paul 1996, Jiang 1990, Shi 2000, Xu and Langendoen 1985, for discussion of topic structure in Chinese). At Spec-AspP, there is a PRO/pro, which is subject-oriented (Lin 1999) and is thus coindexed with $NP_1$ at Spec-$v$P. The pro/PRO at Spec-XP has the same coindexation with the pro/PRO at Spec-AspP. The derivation of the sentence is illustrated briefly in (43):

(43) [$_{TopP}$ $e_j$ [$_{vP}$ Zhangsan$_i$ [$_{v'}$ zhui-de [$_{VP}$ $e_j$ [$_{V'}$ $t_{V1}$-$t_{de}$ [$_{AspP}$ pro/PRO$_i$ [$_{Asp'}$ $t_{de}$
　　　　Zhangsan　chase de

[$_{XP}$ pro/PRO$_i$ [$_{X'}$ dou lei le]]]]]]]]]
　　　　　　　even tire ASP
'Zhangsan chased and got tired.'

In (41c), $V_1$ (i.e. *zhui* 'chase') is reduplicated so that one is followed by the Theme NP (i.e. *Lisi*) and the other by *de*. As we know, *de* is affixal in nature and must attach to a verb or adjective. Otherwise, it will be stranded and an ill-formed sentence as shown in (44) will result. Therefore, the reduplicated $V_1$ is to save an otherwise crashed derivation. The operation that derives (41c) is illustrated in (45). In this derivation, $V_1$ (i.e. *zhui* 'chase') moves from the head position of the lower VP to the head position of the upper $v$P, leaving a phonetically realized copy.[7] The resultative marker *de* raises and attaches to $V_1$ (i.e. *zhui* 'chase'), forming a V-*de* complex (i.e. *zhui-de* 'chase-*de*'). A resultative with reduplicated $V_1$ is thus generated. The pro/PRO at Spec-AspP is subject-oriented, coindexed with $NP_1$ (i.e. *Zhangsan*) at Spec-$v$P. The pro/PRO at Spec-XP is coindexed with the pro/PRO at Spec-AspP and is further coindexed with $NP_1$ (i.e. *Zhangsan*) at Spec-$v$P, generating the reading as indicated.

(44) *Zhangsan zhui  Lisi de dou lei  le.
Zhangsan chase Lisi *de* even tire ASP

(45) [$_{vP}$ Zhangsan$_i$ [$_{v'}$ zhui [$_{VP}$ Lisi$_j$ [$_{V'}$ zhui-de [$_{AspP}$ pro/PRO$_i$ [$_{Asp'}$ t$_{de}$
Zhangsan    chase    Lisi    chase *de*

[$_{XP}$ pro/PRO$_i$ [$_{X'}$ dou  lei  le]]]]]]]]
even tire ASP

'Zhangsan chased Lisi and got tired as a result.'

In resultatives, the activity predicate can be transitive or unergative. It can also be a psych verb as in (46). In this case, NP$_1$ (i.e. *Zhangsan* in (46)) is Experiencer, which is generated at Spec-VP (see Pesetsky 1995). Since psych verbs in Chinese are all SE verbs, V$_1$ (i.e. *xingfen* 'excite' in (46)) projects a single VP rather than a VP shell. The head of AspP *de* raises and attaches to the psych verb, generating the word order as appears in the surface structure.

(46)
[$_{VP}$ Zhangsan$_i$ [$_{v'}$ xingfen-de [$_{AspP}$ pro/PRO$_i$ [$_{Asp'}$ t$_{de}$ [$_{XP}$ shuibuzhaojiao]]]]]
Zhangsan    excite *de*                        cannot go to sleep

'Zhangsan was too excited to go to sleep.'

When a Causer argument occurs, sentences like (47) can be generated. The Causer NP (i.e. *zhe ge xiaoxi* 'this news' in (47)) is generated at Spec-vP headed by the causative marker *shi* 'make'.

(47)
[$_{vP}$ Zhe ge xiaoxi [$_{v'}$ shi [$_{VP}$ Zhangsan$_i$ [$_{v'}$ xingfen-de [$_{AspP}$ pro/PRO$_i$ [$_{Asp'}$ t$_{de}$
this CL news    *shi*    Zhangsan    excite    *de*

[$_{XP}$ pro/PRO$_i$ [$_{X'}$ shuibuzhaojiao]]]]]]]]
cannot go to sleep

'This news made Zhangsan too excited to go to sleep.'

So, the structure in (39) can derive all kinds of resultatives in Chinese, whether $V_1$ is a transitive verb, an unergative verb or a psych verb.

### 3.2.2.2 The derivation of compound causative constructions

Compound causatives have a basic $V_1$-$V_2$ structure. However, if we choose different types of $V_1$, $V_2$, $NP_1$, $NP_2$ and make different combinations, we will find a large variety of compound causatives. For example, $V_1$ can be a transitive verb or an unergative verb; $V_2$ can be an unaccusative verb, an unergative verb or a psych verb; $NP_1$ and $NP_2$ can be animate or inanimate.

In the present study, compound causatives are assumed to be derived from the same structure shown in (39) as resultatives. I will use three examples in (48) to illustrate how they are derived. These compound causatives are all agentive constructions, i.e. compound causatives with an animate Agent $NP_1$.[8]

(48) a. Zhangsan da-*sui*   le  Lisi de huaping.
     Zhangsan hit-break ASP Lisi's vase
     'Zhangsan broke Lisi's vase.'
   b. Zhangsan ku-*shi*  le  shoujuan.
     Zhangsan cry-wet ASP handkerchief
     'Zhangsan cried the handkerchief soggy.'
   c. Zhangsan zhui-*lei*  le  Lisi.
     Zhangsan chase-tire ASP Lisi
     (i) 'Zhangsan chased Lisi and Lisi got tired as a result.'
     (ii) 'Zhangsan chased Lisi and got tired as a result.'

In terms of $V_1$, *da* 'hit' in (48a) and *zhui* 'chase' in (48c) are transitive, while *ku* 'cry' in (48b) is unergative; as to $V_2$, *sui* 'break' in (48a) is unaccusative, while *shi* 'wet' in (48b) is adjective and *lei* 'tire' in (48c) is a psych verb; with respect to $NP_2$, while *Lisi de huaping* 'Lisi's vase' in (48a) and *shoujuan* 'handkerchief' in (48b) are inanimate, *Lisi* in (48c) is animate or, to be exact, human. With regard to interpretations, (48c) is ambiguous, whereas (48a) and (48b) are not.

In compound causatives, the AspP has an abstract head with strong feature. In deriving (48a), it attracts $V_2$ (i.e. *sui* 'break') to have its strong aspectual feature checked. Then $V_2$ undergoes head movement to attach to $V_1$ (i.e. *da* 'hit'). The compound (i.e. *da-sui* 'hit-break') moves together to the head position of the upper *v*P. $NP_1$ (i.e. *Zhangsan*) is Agent and is base-generated at Spec-*v*P. $NP_2$ (i.e. *Lisi de huaping* 'Lisi's vase') is the Theme of the transitive $V_1$ and is base-generated at Spec-VP. It is also the event-measuring NP which occurs at Spec-AspP. Due to haplology, one of them is deleted in the surface structure. The derivation is illustrated in (49). It should be noted that $V_2$ in (48a) (i.e. *sui* 'break') is an unaccusative verb, which selects an internal argument. Therefore, the pro/PRO coindexed with $NP_2$ (i.e. *Lisi de huaping* 'Lisi's vase') at Spec-AspP occurs at the complement position of the XP.

(49) Zhangsan <u>da</u>-*sui* le Lisi de huaping.
    Zhangsan hit-break ASP Lisi's vase
    'Zhangsan broke Lisi's vase.'

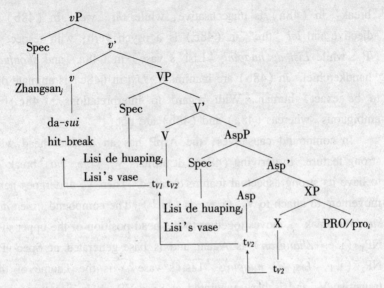

In (48b), $V_1$ (i.e. *ku* 'cry') is an unergative verb, which cannot select a Theme argument. Therefore, $NP_2$ (i.e. *shoujuan* 'handkerchief') cannot be generated at Spec-VP as the Theme argument. It is the event-measuring element base-generated at Spec-AspP.

Sentence (48c) has ambiguous readings, which are derived through syntactic operations as illustrated in (50). To derive reading (i), $NP_2$ (i.e. *Lisi*) is both the Theme of $V_1$ and the Event Measurer that forms a predication relation with the result predicate $V_2$ (i.e. *lei* 'tire'). One of them is deleted due to haplology in the surface structure. To derive reading (ii), a pro/PRO occurs at Spec-AspP. This pro/PRO is subject-oriented (Lin 1999), thus generating the reading as indicated.[9]

(50) Zhangsan zhui-*lei*　le　Lisi.
　　　Zhangsan chase-tire ASP Lisi
　　　(i) 'Zhangsan chased Lisi and Lisi got tired as a result.'
　　　(ii) 'Zhangsan chased Lisi and got tired as a result.'

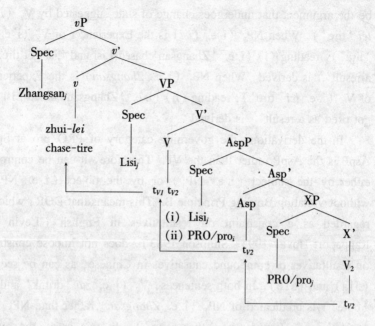

Comparison between (48a) and (48c) raises a question: why is (48c) ambiguous but (48a) is not? Semantic constraints may be responsible for the difference in interpretations: the result predicate of a compound causative must be applied to arguments that potentially undergo a change of state as a result of the action denoted by the activity predicate (cf. Goldberg 1995). In (48a), $NP_2$ (i. e. *Lisi de huaping* 'Lisi's vase') is both the Theme of the activity predicate $V_1$ (i. e. *da* 'hit') and the argument that undergoes change of state that the result predicate $V_2$ (i. e. *sui* 'break') suggests. $NP_1$ (i. e. *Zhangsan*) is the Agent of $V_1$ (i. e. *da* 'hit') but cannot be the Theme of $V_2$ (i. e. *sui* 'break'). Otherwise, the reading that "Zhangsan hit Lisi's vase and Zhangsan was broken" would result. In (48c), $V_2$ (i. e. *lei* 'tire') is a psych verb, which may select any animate NP as the Experiencer argument. Since $NP_1$ (i. e. *Zhangsan*) and $NP_2$ (i. e. *Lisi*) are both human, either of them can be the argument that undergoes change of state suggested by $V_2$ (i. e. *lei* 'tire'). When $NP_2$ (i. e. *Lisi*) is the Experiencer of $V_2$ (i. e. *lei* 'tire'), reading (i) (i. e. 'Zhangsan chased Lisi and Lisi got tired as a result') is derived. When $NP_1$ (i. e. *Zhangsan*) is the Experiencer of $V_2$ (i. e. *lei* 'tire'), reading (ii) (i. e. 'Zhangsan chased Lisi and got tired as a result') is derived.

In the derivation, the governing category of PRO/pro at Spec-AspP is the AspP rather than the VP. Therefore, it can be controlled either by the subject (i. e. $NP_1$) or by the object (i. e. $NP_2$), without violating Binding Principle B. This means that DOR, which is regarded as a constraint on resultatives in English (Levin and Rappaport Hovav 1995; Simpson 1983), does not impose constraint on resultatives or compound causatives in Chinese, as can be seen in (51a) and (51b). In both sentences, $V_2$ (i. e. *zui* 'drunk' and *fan* 'bore') is predicated of $NP_1$ (i. e. *Zhangsan*) rather than $NP_2$ (*jiu* 'wine' and *na shou ge* 'that song'). In this case, the event-measuring element is not $NP_2$ but $NP_1$.

(51) a. Zhangsan he-*zui*　　le　　jiu.
　　　　Zhangsan drink-drunk ASP wine
　　　　'Zhangsan drank wine and got drunk as a result.'
　　b. Zhangsan ting-*fan*　　le　na　shou ge.
　　　　Zhangsan listen-bore ASP that CL song
　　　　'Zhangsan listened to that song (time and again) and got bored as a result.'

Compared with previous proposals (e. g. C.-T. Huang 1988, 1992; Y. Li 1990, 1995, 1998; Tang 1997), the present approach has two advantages: first, the argument structures of different types of verb are maintained in the derivation so that compound causatives with transitive $V_1$ and those with unergative $V_1$ differ in the underlying structure; second, all types of compound causatives can be derived from the proposed structure.

## 3.3 Resultative and compound causative constructions in Japanese

According to Washio (1997), resultatives in Japanese have two distinct constructions, both of which are represented with verb compounds as shown in (52) (from Washio 1997: 2). The two constructions differ in the formation of the compounds: it is "adjective-verb" (A-V) in one construction as seen in (52a) but "$V_1$-$V_2$" in the other as illustrated in (52b). In the following discussion I will refer to the former as resultative construction and the latter as compound causative construction. In resultatives, A is the result predicate while V is the activity predicate. In compound causatives, $V_1$ is the activity predicate and $V_2$ the result predicate.

(52) a. John-ga    kabe-o    aoku nut-ta. (resultative)
        John-NOM wall-ACC blue paint-PAST
        'John painted the wall blue.'
    b. John-ga    Mary-o    uti-korosi-ta. (compound causative)
        John-NOM Mary-ACC shoot-kill-PAST
        'John shot Mary dead.'

Washio (1997) makes a distinction between strong resultatives and weak resultatives in Japanese. Resultatives in which the meaning of the verb and the meaning of the adjective are completely independent of each other are referred to as strong resultatives. In this type of resultative, it is impossible to predict from the meaning of the verb what result it can bring about. In weak resultatives, however, the verb does imply purpose of the activity or direction of the change it may bring about. According to Washio, English allows strong resultatives, while Japanese allows weak resultatives only. Their distinction is illustrated in (53): the verb *tatak-u* 'pound' in (53a) does not imply any state of the Theme that might result from the activity, so it cannot be used in the resultative; the verb *migak-u* 'polish' in (53b) does imply some change of state, therefore the resultative is grammatical. While the meaning of the activity predicate does not impose any constraint on English resultatives, as we can see from the English translations, it does on Japanese resultatives. In Washio's analysis, intransitive resultatives are instances of strong resultatives and therefore are disallowed in Japanese, as shown in (54). In Japanese resultatives, the result element A is predicated of the NP that is assigned accusative case marked with *-o* (examples in (53) and (54) quoted from Washio 1997: 9, 20).

(53) a. \* John-wa kinzoku-o pikapika-ni tatai-ta.
John-TOP metal-ACC shiny　　pound-PAST
'John pounded the metal shiny.'
　　b. John-wa　kinzoku-o　pikapika-ni migai-ta.
John-TOP metal-ACC shiny　　polish-PAST
'John polished the metal shiny.'
(54) a. \* karera-wa kutu-no　soko-o　boroboro-ni hasit-ta.
they-TOP　shoe-GEN sole-ACC threadbare　pull-PAST
'They ran the soles of their shoes threadbare.'
　　b. \* boku-wa zibun-o　kutakuta-ni odot-ta.
I-TOP　　self-ACC　tired　　　dance-PAST
'I danced myself tired.'

Compound causative constructions in Japanese have different formations as shown in (55) ((55a) from Nishiyama 1998: 175 and (55b) from Matsumoto 1996a: 213). Because Japanese is an SOV language, the result predicate $V_2$ is taken as the main predicate while the activity predicate $V_1$ is the secondary predicate (Nishiyama 1998), different from Chinese in which the activity predicate $V_1$ is taken as the main predicate while the result predicate is the secondary predicate (e. g.

C. -T. Huang 1992).

(55) a. $NP_1 + NP_2$ + transitive $V_1$ + transitive $V_2$
John-ga    niwatori-o    naguri-korosi-ta.
John-NOM chicken-ACC beat-kill-PAST
'John beat and killed a chicken.'
b. $NP_1 + NP_2$ + unaccusative $V_1$ + transitive $V_2$
kaze-ga    konoha-o    mai-age-ta.
wind-NOM leaves-ACC whirl-raise-PAST
'The wind whirled up the leaves.'

Japanese compound causatives have some other combinations. In (56a) (from Y. Li 1993: 481), for example, $V_1$ (i.e. *karakai* 'tease') is a transitive verb, $V_2$ (i.e. *akiru* 'bore') is a psych verb, and both NPs (i.e. *John* and *Mary*) are animate. However, it does not have ambiguous readings as found in its Chinese counterpart in (56b).

(56) a. John-ga    Mary-o    karakai-akiru-ta.
John-NOM Mary-ACC tease-bore-PAST
(i) 'John teased Mary and as a result John got tired.'
(ii) *'John teased Mary and as a result Mary got tired.'
b. John dou-*lei* le Mary.
John tease-tire ASP Mary.
(i) 'John teased Mary and as a result John got tired.'
(ii) 'John teased Mary and as a result Mary got tired.'

In Chinese, the result psych verb can be predicated of either $NP_1$ or $NP_2$ as long as both NPs are animate and $V_1$ is transitive. Compound causatives in Japanese are unambiguous because both $V_1$ and $V_2$ are obligatorily predicated of the sentence subject (i.e. $NP_1$), which is marked nominative case (*-ga*) or marked as Topic (*-wa*), as shown in (57) (from Y. Li 1993: 493):

(57) a. *John-ga    Mary-o    naguri-shinu-ta.
   John-NOM Mary-ACC hit-die-PAST
b. John-ga    Mary-o    naguri-korosu-ta.
   John-NOM Mary-ACC hit-kill-PAST
   'John hit Mary and as a result killed her.'
(58) John da-si le Mary.
   John hit-die ASP Mary
   (i) 'John hit Mary and Mary died as a result.'
   (ii) *'John hit Mary and died as a result.'

Example (57b) is well-formed because both $V_1$ (i.e. *naguri* 'hit') and $V_2$ (i.e. *korosu* 'kill') are predicated of the subject *John*. In (57a), however, $V_2$ (i.e. *shinu* 'die') is predicated of the object (i.e. *Mary*) instead of the subject (i.e. *John*). Therefore, it is an ill-formed sentence. In contrast, $V_2$ in its Chinese counterpart shown in (58) must be predicated of the object.

## 3.4 Resultative and compound causative constructions in Korean

According to M. Kim (1999), Korean does not allow Chinese-type compound causatives, as can be seen in (59a). Such a construction is allowed only when an overt causative morpheme *-i* is marked on the second verb of the compound as shown in (59b) (examples in (59) quoted from M. Kim 1999: 109).

(59) a. *John-i    Bill-ul    sswa-a-cwuk-ess-ta.
        John-NOM Bill-ACC shoot-die-PAST-DEC
    b. John-i    Bill-ul    sswa-a-cwuk-i-ess-ta.
        John-NOM Bill-ACC shoot-die-CAUS-PAST-DEC
        'John shot Bill dead.'

Given that Korean is an SOV language, the result predicate is the main predicate while the activity predicate is the secondary predicate, as in Japanese. In (59), the main predicate is *cwuk* 'die' while the secondary predicate is *sswa* 'shoot'.

Korean has two types of resultatives, predicative resultative and clausal resultative, with the result phrase marked with a complementizer *-key* (Wechsler and Noh 2001). Their crucial difference is that in predicative resultatives like (60a), the result element (i. e. *napcakha* 'flat') is predicated of the accusative-case-marked NP (i. e. *kumsok* 'metal'), while in clausal resultatives like (60b), the result element (i. e. *talh* 'threadbare') is predicated of the subject of the embedded clause (i. e. *sinpal* 'shoes') (examples in (60) quoted from Wechsler and Noh 2001: 404).

(60) a. Mary-nun kumsok-ul napcakha-key twutulki-ess-ta.
 Mary-TOP metal-ACC flat-COMP hammer-PAST-DEC
 'Mary hammered the metal flat. '
 b. ku-nun [sinpal-i talh-key] talli-ess-ta.
 he-TOP shoes-NOM threadbare-COMP run-PAST-DEC
 'He ran (his) shoes threadbare. '

When the main predicate is an unergative verb (e. g. *wul* 'cry'), the result element (e. g. *ces* 'soggy') cannot be predicated of the subject (e. g. *ku* 'he'), as shown in (61a). In this case, another NP (e. g. *sonswuken* 'handkerchief') can save this construction, as shown in (61b). However, unlike English, which observes DOR (Levin and Rappaport Hovav 1995; Simpson 1983), the NP (i. e. *sonswuken* 'handkerchief' in (61b)) is marked nominative case and functions as the subject of the embedded clause (examples in (61) quoted from J. -B. Kim 1999: 139).

(61) a. \*Ku-nun ces-key wul-ess-ta.
 He-TOP soggy-*key* cry-PAST-DEC

*'He cried soggy.'

b. Ku-nun [ (casin-uy) sonswuken-i ces-key ] wul-ess-ta.
 he-TOP self-GEN handkerchief-NOM soggy-*key* cry-PAST-DEC
 'He cried the handkerchief soggy.'

When the activity predicate is a transitive verb like *talli* 'run' in (62) (from J. -B. Kim 1999: 146), the result element can be predicated either of the Agent (i. e. *John*) or of the Theme (i. e. *mal* 'horse') if semantic constraints are not violated. Thus, ambiguous readings arise.

(62) John-i mal-ul cichi-key talli-ess-ta.
 John-NOM horse-ACC tired-*key* run-PAST-DEC
 (i) 'John ran (his) horse tired.'
 (ii) 'John ran his horse, and he became tired.'

As shown in the above discussion, compound causatives in Korean have a linear order XP-VP-$i$: the result predicate is the main predicate with the causative suffix -$i$ marked on it; the activity predicate is the secondary predicate heading the XP. In resultatives, XP is headed by the result predicate and is explicitly marked with -*key*; the result element can be predicated of an accusative-case-marked NP as in predicative resultatives or of a nominative-case-marked NP in an embedded clause as in clausal resultatives; when the activity predicate is transitive, ambiguous readings may arise as the result element can be predicated either of the Agent or of the Theme.

## 3.5 Summary

In this chapter, I mainly discussed properties of Chinese resultatives and compound causatives in terms of argument structure and syntactic structure. Since both compound causatives and resultatives are representations of causativity, a unified solution is theoretically more appealing. In the present study, I posit a proposal applicable to both on the basis of previous studies. In this proposal, resultatives and compound causatives involve a functional category AspP, whose function is to delimit an activity. Apart from Chinese, I also discussed resultatives and compound causatives in English, Japanese and Korean. Properties of the two constructions in the four languages are summarized in Table 3.1.

Table 3.1. Summary: resultative and compound causative constructions in Chinese, English, Japanese and Korean

| Language | Construction | Formation | Main predicate | Marker | Semantic relation | Ambiguity |
|---|---|---|---|---|---|---|
| Chinese | resultative | V-*de* | V | *de* | activity-result | × |
|  | CC | $V_1$-$V_2$ | $V_1$ | none |  | √ |
| English | resultative | V-NP-XP | V | none | activity-result | × |
| Japanese | resultative | A-V | V | none | result-activity | × |
|  | CC | $V_1$-$V_2$ | $V_2$ | none | activity-result | × |
| Korean | resultative | A-V | V | -*key* | result-activity | √ |
|  | CC | $V_1$-$V_2$ | $V_2$ | -*i* | activity-result | × |

CC = Compound causative

Of the four languages under study, English has resultatives but does not have compound causatives, while Chinese, Japanese and Korean have both constructions. Functional categories are not involved in English or Japanese resultatives or compound causatives, but involved in their Chinese and Korean counterparts.

Now let us summarize the syntactic representations of resultatives and compound causatives in the four languages. Chinese resultatives and compound causatives have a derivation shown in (39), repeated in (63). This derivation involves a functional category AspP occurring between VP headed by the activity predicate $V_1$ and XP headed by the result predicate $V_2$. The AspP has an explicit marker *de* in resultatives but a phonetically unrealized marker in compound causatives. To derive a resultative, *de* first attaches to $V_1$ to form a V-*de* complex, which raises as a whole to the head position of the upper *v*P. To derive a compound causative, the result predicate $V_2$ first raises and adjoins to the phonetically unrealized head of the AspP. It further raises and adjoins to the activity predicate $V_1$ to form a compound and finally the compound raises to the head position of the upper *v*P.

(63) Resultative and compound causative constructions in Chinese

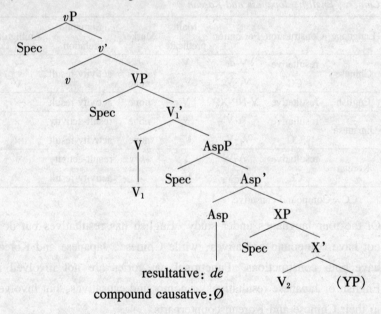

English resultatives have a linear order of V-NP-XP and involve no functional categories between the activity predicate and the result phrase. The activity predicate heads the VP and the result predicate heads the XP. The NP occurs either at Spec-VP if it is the Theme argument of V or Spec-XP if it is not. English resultatives can be represented with a VP shell, as shown in (22), repeated in (64).

(64) Resultative construction in English

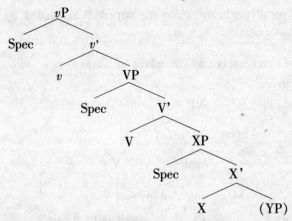

Japanese has both resultatives and compound causatives, but neither involves functional categories. Due to the SOV order in Japanese, the main predicate in the resultative construction (i.e. the A-V compound) is V, while in the compound causative construction (i.e. the $V_1$-$V_2$ compound), it is $V_2$. The derivations of Japanese resultatives and compound causatives are illustrated in (65):

(65) Resultative and compound causative constructions in Japanese

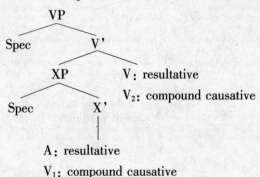

Korean resultatives involve an AspP[10] headed by the complementizer -*key*, which occurs between the activity predicate and the result XP, as shown in (66a). Compound causatives in Korean can be

represented with a VP shell, as shown in (66b): the lower VP is headed by the result predicate while the upper-vP is headed by the causative marker -*i*.

(66) Resultatives and compound causatives in Korean
    a. Resultatives

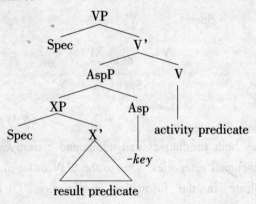

    b. Compound causatives

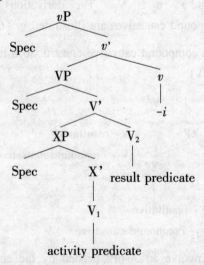

Comparing derivations of resultatives and compound causatives in Chinese, English, Japanese and Korean, we may find that Korean resultatives have the same underlying structure as Chinese resultatives: both involve a functional category AspP headed by an explicit marker. Although both Chinese and Korean involve a functional category in the compound causative construction, the positions of the functional categories are different in the two languages. They also differ morphologically: while the functional head has an explicit marker (i. e. -*i*) in Korean, it is phonetically unrealized in Chinese. English and Japanese do not involve functional categories in resultatives or compound causatives.

Given different properties in resultatives and compound causatives in Chinese, English, Japanese and Korean, questions in relation to L2 acquisition of Chinese arise: can English- and Japanese-speaking learners of Chinese acquire the functional category AspP which is present in Chinese but unavailable in English and Japanese? Will Chinese resultatives be easier for Korean-speaking learners to acquire, considering that resultative constructions have the same structure in the two languages? Given that Chinese resultatives and compound causatives have the same underlying structure, will L2 Chinese learners acquire them at the same pace? I will address these acquisition problems in an empirical study. The research questions and hypotheses of the empirical study will be proposed in Chapter 5 and results of the experiment will be presented in Chapter 7.

## Notes

[1] A small clause refers to "a string of XP YP constituents that enter into a predication relation, but where the predicate, YP, rather than containing a fully inflected verb, contains an adjective phrase, noun phrase, prepositional phrase, or uninflected verb phrase" (Basilico 2003: 1), as illustrated in (i):

(i) a. We consider [$_{SC}$ *the guard intelligent*].

b. We saw [$_{SC}$ *the guards leave*].

Chomsky (1981: 107) defines small clause as 'a clausal structure lacking INFL and the copula'.

[2] As we learned from Chapter 2, Chinese does not have a clear-cut distinction between adjectives and verbs. Therefore, the activity predicate and the result predicate are termed $V_1$ and $V_2$ respectively in this thesis for the convenience of discussion, whether they are verbs or adjectives.

[3] Most linguists (e.g. Chao 1968; Z. Liu 2003; Zhu 1982) treat *de*-phrase as a result-denoting construction, whereas some (e.g. Zhao 2002) take *de* as a causative marker which is further grammaticalized from the resultative meaning.

Apart from resultative constructions, *de* can introduce an expression of manner, as in (i):

(i) Zhangsan pao de hen kuai.

Zhangsan run *de* very fast

'Zhangsan ran very fast.'

In the present study, we will not deal with the manner-*de* and will focus our discussion on the result-*de*.

[4] According to Y. Li, the causative hierarchy overrides the thematic hierarchy in deriving reading (iii), while both the thematic hierarchy and the causative hierarchy are violated in deriving reading (iv. Readers are referred to Y. Li's works for detailed discussion of these two readings.

[5] Tang's (1997) proposal is similar to that of Slabakova (2001) and that of Travis (2003), both of which posit an AspP, which occurs embedded within *v*P, as illustrated briefly in (i):

(i) [$_{vP}$ *v*' [$_{AspP}$ Asp' [$_{VP}$ V' [$_{XP}$ X]]]]

According to Travis (2003), there are three possible positions to mark telicity. They are *v*, Asp and X. Telicity markers can pick out natural endpoints from all these positions, but elements in X can only describe the natural endpoints of events. Elements in Asp or *v* can in addition pick out beginning points of events, but only elements in *v*, as they have access to the whole event, can designate arbitrary endpoints of events. Different languages may vary as to which to employ to mark telicity.

[6] It should be pointed out that the AspP I proposed for Chinese resultative and compound causative constructions is an *ad hoc* category whose function is to delimit an otherwise unbounded activity (cf. Travis 2003). Readers are reminded of any possible distinction between the AspP in this proposal and the AspP in the literature of generative grammar.

[7] I will leave this multiple spell-out question for future research.

[8] According to Cheng et al (1997), compound causatives in Chinese can be classified into two types, which are agentive constructions and causative constructions. The former have an Agent subject as in (i), whereas the latter have a Causer subject as in (ii):

   (i) Zhangsan he-*zui*     le   jiu.
       Zhangsan drink-drunk ASP wine
       'Zhangsan drank wine and became drunk as a result.'
   (ii) Na ping jiu   he-*zui*     le   Zhangsan.
       that bottle wine drink-drunk ASP Zhangsan
       'That bottle of wine caused Zhangsan to be drunk.'

Both (i) and (ii) contain a compound causative *he-zui* 'drink-drunk'. Their difference lies in $NP_1$: while it is an Agent like *Zhangsan* in (i), it is a Causer like *na ping jiu* 'that bottle of wine' in (ii).

[9] A question remains unanswered: if resultatives and compound causatives are derived from the same structure, why are ambiguous readings allowed in compound causatives but not in resultatives? I will leave this question open for future research.

[10] In Korean, *-key* is a complementizer, which functions as head of the resultative phrase. In this thesis, the Korean resultative phrase headed by *-key* is called an AspP rather than a CP because it has the same function as AspP in Chinese resultatives headed by *de*.

# 4 Second language acquisition and causativity

导言

　　本章简要回顾了生成语法框架内的第二语言习得研究,对前人进行的使动习得研究做了介绍。

　　在本章第一节,作者首先介绍普遍语法在语言习得特别是第二语言习得中的扮演的角色,随后从四个方面介绍了目前第二语言习得研究的现状,同时提出包括"第一语言迁移现象为什么发生、何时发生"、"中介语产生僵化现象的原因是什么"、"第二语言中有而第一语言中没有的功能范畴在中介语中能否有适当表征"、"如果第一语言和第二语言的某一语法现象构成'超集－子集'关系,学习者在缺乏正面证据的情况下能否习得第二语言中的语法现象"等一些问题,作者介绍了前人在这些问题上的论述,同时要通过实证研究对这些问题做进一步探讨。

　　在本章第二节,作者介绍了第二语言习得领域对使动习得的研究,这些研究包括母语为汉语的学习者对英语心理动词的习得(Juffs 1996b),母语分别为日语、法语、马达加斯加语和西班牙语的学习者对英语心理动词的习得(White et al 1999),不同母语背景的学习者对西班牙语、英语和土耳其语中使动转换动词和心理动词的习得(Montrul 1999,2000,2001a;Cabrera and Zubizarreta 2003)。

　　本章的目的是把作者的研究放在第二语言习得研究的大框架内,把前人研究的终点作为自己研究的起点,以使自己的研究对整个第二语言习得研究领域有所贡献。

# Second language acquisition and causativity

In this chapter, I will give a general review of second language acquisition (SLA) studies within the generative framework, particularly in relation to the acquisition of causativity. The chapter is organized as follows. Section 4.1 provides a brief review, addressing such topics as first language (L1) transfer (§ 4.1.1), interlanguage (§ 4.1.2), functional categories (§ 4.1.3) and learnability problems (§ 4.1.4); Section 4.2 reviews L2 acquisition studies on causativity, including previous researches (§ 4.2.1) and a summary of the findings (§ 4.2.2).

## 4.1  A brief review of SLA studies

Linguistic research concerns three basic questions as listed in (1) (Chomsky 1986: 3):

(1) a. What constitutes knowledge of language?
  b. How is such knowledge acquired?
  c. How is such knowledge put to use?

The first question concerns native speakers' linguistic competence, of which the Universal Grammar (UG) forms a fundamental part; the second question concerns acquisition of a language through the interaction of UG and linguistic input; the third question concerns performance of individual speakers.

In generative linguistics, UG is taken to be a "set of properties, conditions, or whatever that constitutes the 'initial' state of the language learner, hence the basis on which knowledge of language develops" (Chomsky 1980: 69). UG forms the language faculty, or part of the language faculty (Hilles 1991; Radford 1997).

An argument for the existence of language faculty or UG is the underdetermination of syntactic knowledge by the input, which is stated as the "poverty of the stimulus" hypothesis (Lightfoot 1991; White 1989a; cf. Hawkins 2001b) or the logical problem of language acquisition (e.g. Hornstein and Lightfoot 1981; cf. Carroll 2001). It poses a basic but challenging question: how can speakers come to know more than is present in the input in so short a time? One way in which the input underdetermines the steady-state grammar is that it does not provide information about ungrammaticality. Nevertheless, native speakers of a language know which sentence is grammatical and which is not. Such knowledge is too abstract and complex to be acquired on the basis of limited input, and therefore must be innate.

In first language acquisition, "UG provides a genetic blueprint, determining in advance what grammars can (and cannot) be like" (White 2003a: 2). It not only provides an inventory of possible grammatical categories and features, but also constrains the functioning of grammars by determining the nature of the computational system. UG forms the initial state of a child's linguistic knowledge of his language. The primary linguistic data help the child to determine the form of the grammar and trigger the parameters of UG to be set to values appropriate to the language in question.

It is widely accepted that UG plays a role in second language acquisition (e.g. Bennett 1994; Epstein et al 1996; Flynn 1987, 1996; Slabakova 2000; Thomas 1989, 1991; Tsimpli and Roussou 1991; Uziel 1993; White 1989a, 1990; Yuan 1998, 2001; Zobl 1986, 1992; see Bley-Vroman 1986, Clahsen 1990, Clahsen and Muysken 1986, Meisel 1997, for different views). However, there are disagreements on what role UG plays in second language acquisition. Some linguists argue that L2 learners have full access to

UG: it either operates independently of the L1 representation (e. g. Epstein et al 1996; Platzack 1996) or functions via L1 but not restricted to L1 (e. g. Schwartz and Sprouse 1996; White 1985). Others argue for a partial access of UG principles to L2 learners (e. g. Beck 1997, 1998), claiming that certain functional features never become specified in the course of L2 development and consequently L2 grammars are permanently impaired in a local domain.

Apart from the debate about the extent to which UG operates in L2 acquisition, there are also disagreements on the role of L1 in the L2 grammar, on the characteristics of interlanguage and on L2 functional projections. In the following subsections, I will review briefly some of the proposals and hypotheses on these issues.

### 4. 1. 1 L1 transfer

The problem of transfer concerns "the influence resulting from similarities and differences between the target language and any other language that has been previously (and perhaps imperfectly) acquired" (Odlin 1989: 27; see Odlin 2003 for a general review of language transfer) or, more restrictively, "those processes that lead to incorporation of elements from one language to another" (Sharwood Smith and Kellerman 1986: 1). In SLA studies, the first question concerning transfer is whether L1 transfer occurs at all. If it does, what transfers and to what extent do L1 properties determine the L2 grammar? Does transfer occur at the initial stage of L2 acquisition only or happen at later stages as well?

There is little consensus on these issues. Some researchers posit full-transfer proposals. One of them is the Full Transfer/Full Access Hypothesis (Schwartz 1998; Schwartz and Sprouse 1994, 1996; see Mazurkewich 1984, White 1985, 1986, for an early version of the hypothesis), which states that the entirety of the L1 grammar forms the L2 initial state and that failure to assign a representation to L2 input data forces subsequent restructurings, drawing from options of UG. Thus, L1 and L2 acquisition are different fundamentally with regard to the initial state: L1 acquisition starts from UG, but L2 acquisition starts from L1. When learners come across aspects of the L2 input that cannot be accommodated by the L1 grammar, they have recourse to UG options. Therefore, the course of L2 development is determined partly by the initial state, partly by the L2 input, partly by the apparatus of UG and partly by learnability considerations.

Another full-transfer proposal is the Full Transfer/No Access Hypothesis (Clahsen and Hong 1995; Schachter 1988, 1990). This hypothesis shares the assumption of the Full Transfer/Full Access Hypothesis in that the L1 grammar constitutes the initial state of the L2 grammar. However, it claims that L2 acquisition is constrained by UG only via the L1 instantiations.

Different from proponents of the full-transfer proposals, some researchers believe that the L1 grammar only partially transfers into L2. A version of the partial-transfer proposal is the Valueless Features Hypothesis (Eubank 1993/1994, 1994a, 1994b, 1996), which holds that both lexical and functional properties of L1 transfer into the initial state of L2. However, L2 functional features encoding tense and agreement do not take on L1 values but are initially unspecified, or inert. Another version of the partial-transfer proposal is the Minimal Trees Hypothesis (Vainikka and Young-Scholten 1994, 1996a, 1996b). It takes a more restrictive view, arguing that only lexical categories of L1 are found in the initial L2 grammar and that functional categories are not transferred. According to this hypothesis, the initial stage of L2 acquisition is the VP stage (cf. Pierce 1992, Radford 1990, on L1 acquisition) and the development of functional projections is driven solely by the interaction of X'-theory with the target-language input.

In contrast to the "transfer" models, some linguists propose that L1 grammar does not transfer into L2. One of such proposals is the No Transfer/Full Access Hypothesis (Epstein et al 1996; Flynn 1987, 1996; Platzack 1996), which argues that L1 grammar does not constitute the initial state for L2 learners and that L2 grammar is acquired on the basis of UG principles and parameters interacting with L2 input directly. According to Platzack (1996), both L1 learners and L2 learners assume weak functional features in the initial state of grammar because strong features trigger movement, which is costly according to the Minimalist Program (Chomsky 1995). Only after learners have sufficient evidence for movement can they set the parameterized features to the strong value in accordance with the target grammar. This hypothesis predicts that L1 acquisition and L2 acquisition are essentially alike and that L2 learners can acquire the L2 grammar. Another no-transfer proposal is the No Transfer/No Access Hypothesis (Bley-Vroman 1986, 1989, 1990; Clahsen and Muysken 1986; Meisel 1997). According to this proposal, L2 acquisition neither starts from L1 grammar nor has access to UG, but proceeds by exploiting general problem-solving skills.

L1 transfer may be more complex than is claimed in these hypotheses. The first question that needs to be answered is: why does L1 transfer happen, or what decides L1 transfer? Research findings indicate that L1 transfer can be influenced by learners' L2 proficiency level (Kellerman 1983; Odlin 1989), the degree of markedness of the structure (Gass 1984; Kellerman 1983), language typology (Jin 1994) or the orthography of the two languages (Chikamatsu 1996), but not by the surface word order (Sasaki 1994). Kellerman (1983: 117) raises the problem of transferability, namely "the probability with which a structure will be transferred relative to other structures in the L1", arguing that L2 learner's perception of the distance, i. e. degree of typological relatedness between L1 and L2, will strongly influence the extent to which he or she attempts to transfer from one to the other (also see Andersen 1983; Kellerman 1977, 1979; Singleton 1987). If two languages are perceived as similar with regard to a particular structure, transfer is more likely to occur. If a particular L1 item is perceived by the learner to be irregular, infrequent, semantically or structurally opaque, it is less likely to transfer[1]. This implies that not everything is transferred and that L1 transfer is selective (cf. Zobl 1980) and relative (cf. Yuan 2001, 2003).

Another problem that needs further exploration is the timing when L1 transfer occurs. In the hypotheses mentioned above, it is argued to occur at the initial stage of L2 acquisition if it happens at all. It is also suggested in other researches that L1 transfer or cross-linguistic influence is partial and emerges gradually in the course of L2 development (Wakabayashi 2002) and that it persists when L2 argument structure constitutes a subset of its counterpart in L1 (Inagaki 2001) (see § 4.1.4 on the superset-subset relation).

### 4.1.2 Interlanguage

In L1 acquisition, learners can eventually arrive at a steady-state grammar of the native language. L2 learners arrive at a steady-state grammar as well. However, L2 grammar may not be the target grammar but an interlanguage (IL), which is incomplete, intermediate and optional but systematic through its development (Lakshmanan and Selinker 2001; Selinker 1972; Towell et al 1993; Zobl 1992).

Adjemian (1976) lists a number of characteristics of interlanguages such as systematicity, permeability and fossilization; interlanguages are treated as natural languages which are systematic from the start with an internally coherent structure (systematicity); they are susceptible to infiltration by L1 and L2 rules or forms and are subject to a number of impinging forces (permeability); non-target-like competence persists in interlanguages, resulting in fossilization, i. e. "the permanent cessation of IL learning before the learners have attained target language norms at all levels of linguistic structure and in all discourse domains in spite of the learner's positive ability, opportunity or motivation to learn or acculturate into target society" (Selinker and Lamendella 1978: 187). Interlanguage, therefore, is a partial outcome in that L2 learners fail to attain the ultimate full target competence (Davies 1984).

Proposals of the non-native nature of interlanguages are supported by empirical research findings ( e. g. Corver 2003; Hawkins and Liszka 2003; Tsimpli and Rousou 1991; Zhang 1995; Zobl 1989). In a study of L2 acquisition of the syntactic and semantic properties related to unaccusativity in Italian, Sorace (1993) finds that her English subjects exhibit incompleteness while the French subjects exhibit divergence: the former have indeterminate judgments about all restructured constructions, regardless of whether they are grammatical or ungrammatical, optional or obligatory; the latter seem to have acquired a divergent representation of restructuring and are radically different concerning optional changes of auxiliary. It is concluded that L2 learners are seemingly capable of native-like performance, but their knowledge representations, particularly in the case of restructured constructions, are substantially different from the native knowledge representations.

Even though interlanguage grammars may be non-native, claims that they are permanently fossilized seem to be too strong. L2 acquisition is a complex process, in which both grammatical factors and non-grammatical factors operate (Schachter and Yip 1990). The Fossilization Hypothesis (Selinker 1972) does not explain in what way or for what reason an interlanguage is fossilized. Research findings suggest that L2 learners perform like native speakers in tests relating to principles of UG (Birdsong 1992) and that native-like competence in L2 is achievable (White and Genesee 1996). As L2 proficiency increases, L2 learners are able to represent and process the language in the same way as native speakers do (Green 2003).

### 4.1.3 Functional categories

In generative grammar, lexical categories are the conceptual aspect of linguistic structure, bearing semantic features, in particular features having to do with θ-roles. In contrast, functional categories are the computational aspect: some of them bear agreement features; others play a role in triggering movement (Fukui 2001). These functional categories "erect a syntactic skeleton above lexical categories which serves to hold together the various syntactic relations that take place in the phrase" (Adger 2003: 165).

Given the nature and the role of functional categories, it is argued that "lexical categories are essentially invariant across languages" and that "only functional categories are subject to crosslinguistic variation" (Fukui 1988: 267). An implication is that L2 acquisition can be reduced to the acquisition of functional categories.

Proposals on L1 transfer and UG access discussed in § 4.1.1 are mostly related to functional categories. Proponents for full-transfer or full-access hypotheses argue that L1 functional categories transfer into L2 and that L2 functional categories can be projected because UG is fully operative in L2 acquisition. In contrast, proponents for partial-transfer or partial-access proposals argue that functional categories do not transfer or that they cannot be fully projected or fully specified in the L2 grammar.

There is no consensus as to whether functional categories can be fully projected in the L2 grammar. Some researchers claim that they can ( e. g. Grondin and White 1996; Lakshmanan 1993/1994; Lakshmanan and Selinker 1994; White 1996, 2003b), while others claim that they are impaired in interlanguage representations ( e. g. Beck 1997, 1998; Eubank and Grace 1998; Hawkins and Chan 1997; Hawkins and Liszka 2003 ). According to Meisel ( 1997 ), L1 acquisition and L2 acquisition differ in terms of the relationship between inflectional morphology and syntax. L1 acquirers have UG-constrained grammars so that there is some necessary connection between overt morphology and verb raising in L1 acquisition. Such connection, however, does not exist in the L2 grammar due to the unavailability of UG. As a result, L2 learners make no finite/nonfinite distinctions in L2 acquisition and L2 grammars suffer from global impairment in terms of functional categories. On similar grounds, Beck ( 1997, 1998 ) takes a "local impairment" view, arguing that the morphosyntactic features that require or prohibit thematic verb raising become impaired during the course of maturation so that L2 grammars allow optional verb raising when functional projections are present.

Some researchers argue that parameter-resetting is not always possible even if UG is available in L2 acquisition. Hawkins and Chan ( 1997) posit the Failed Functional Features Hypothesis, arguing that adult L2 learners are unable to acquire functional features that are different from those in the L1. In other words, they only have access to those functional features instantiated in the L1 ( also see Franceschina 2001; Hawkins and Liszka 2003). Tsimpli and Roussou ( 1991 ) take a similar view, arguing that L2 learners cannot reset parameters associated with functional categories whose values differ between L1 and L2. According to Smith and Tsimpli ( 1995 ), parametric variation between languages is associated exclusively with functional categories, which are a finite set of abstract categories that collectively constitute a component of UG referred to as the UG lexicon. It is these functional categories, i. e. the UG lexicon, rather than the UG principles, that are assumed to be subject to maturational development.[2] UG principles may still be available to L2 learners, but parameter setting, which only concerns functional categories or the UG lexicon, is not. If L1 and L2 differ parametrically, L2 learners cannot develop the same underlying grammatical representations as native speakers do despite their accessibility to UG principles.

A question that needs clarification is: what counts as the benchmark of the acquisition of functional categories? Should "absence of evidence" be treated as "evidence of absence" (White 2000: 139)? Do underspecified functional categories indicate lack of functional categories or otherwise? According to the Missing Surface Inflection Hypothesis (Haznedar 2003; Herschensohn 2001; Ionin and Wexler 2002; Lardiere 1998a, 1998b, 2000; Prévost and White 2000; Robertson 2000), underspecification may be related to a mapping problem: L2 learners have acquired the syntactic features but cannot map morphology onto the syntax. In this case, underspecification is evidence of presence rather than evidence of absence of functional projections.

### 4.1.4 Learnability problems

Learnability theory is "concerned explicitly with the conditions under which successful learning of a system of rules can take place within a finite amount of time" (Goodluck 1991: 145). It specifies "how a learner develops from an initial state to the target grammar with the available input and the given device" (Pienemann and Håkansson 1999: 385).

Learnability addresses two issues in language acquisition, the logical problem and the developmental problem (Gregg 1996): the former concerns how language learners are successful, while the latter concerns how learners enter and leave a developmental state. In accordance with the two problems are two types of principles available to L2 learners, language principles and learning principles (Wolfe-Quintero 1992). In generative grammar, language principles refer to principles of UG such as the Empty Category Principle, the Subjacency Principle and the Binding Principles. These principles constrain natural language grammars. Learning principles include the mechanisms required to process language input and the mechanisms required to represent language input.

One of the learning principles is the Subset Principle (Berwick 1985; Wexler and Manzini 1987; see Fodor and Crain 1987 for criticisms). A premise for the operation of this principle is the Subset Condition, illustrated in Figure 4.1 (from White 1989a: 145): Y is a subset and permits a smaller range of structures, whereas X is the superset of Y and allows a larger range of structures; X and Y form a superset-subset relation.

*Figure 4.1 The subset condition for two grammars*

Based on the "no negative evidence hypothesis", the Subset Principle posits that learners start with the narrowest possible hypothesis compatible with the available data. They will first construct a conservative grammar, i.e. Y, and subsequently expand the grammar to the more permissive grammar, i.e. X, on the basis of positive evidence.

The Subset Principle may be a learning principle in L1

acquisition, but it may not be applicable to L2 acquisition (Yip 1995). However, the subset-superset relation between L1 and L2 grammars does have some effect on the acquisition of L2 properties (White 1989a, 1989b). If L1 is a subset but L2 a superset, positive evidence in the L2 input will trigger parameter resetting appropriate to L2. However, if L1 is a superset but L2 a subset, L2 learners may initially adopt a wider grammar of the L1 before proceeding to a narrow grammar of the L2 (Thomas 1989; White 1991; Zobl 1988). In this case, the Subset Principle is overridden by transfer and becomes inoperative (Rutherford 1989). Due to lack of positive evidence in the L2 input to trigger parameter resetting, negative evidence via grammar teaching or error correction may be required to lead to the resetting from the superset to the subset value. However, the instruction or correction may improve L2 learners' performance, but may not necessarily change their underlying linguistic competence or help with parameter-resetting (Bialystok 1994; Ellis 1985; Jordens 1996; Trahey 1996; see Carroll and Swain 1993, Toth 2000, for different views). It is argued, therefore, that parameter is more difficult to reset by using negative evidence than using positive evidence[3] and that L2 learners have more difficulty acquiring a subset target representation than a superset target representation (Trahey and White 1993).

To trigger parameter-resetting, positive evidence is not only to be available, but also to be frequent and clear (Inagaki 2002), ready for processing[4] (VanPatten 1990). Positive evidence cannot play a role unless it is perceived and processed. Processing principles are independently needed for general human cognitive functions and cannot be reduced to language or learning principles.[5] Therefore, it may be a processing problem rather than a competence deficit that underlies learners' non-target representations (Juffs and Harrington 1995, 1996;

Schachter and Yip 1990).

## 4.2　SLA studies of causativity

The present research addresses the acquisition of causativity in Chinese. It includes two aspects, which are the acquisition of the non-causativeness of Chinese unaccusative verbs and psych verbs and the acquisition of Chinese causative representations such as resultative, compound causative and analytical causative constructions. As far as I am aware, no such research has been conducted. However, a few researches have been carried out on L2 acquisition of argument structure in relation to causativity. I will review some of the studies in the following sections.

### 4.2.1　Previous studies

The study of causativity in SLA concerns the acquisition of argument structure. To be more exact, it concerns acquisition of the links between thematic relations and syntax or the interface between morphology and syntax. In this section I will introduce some studies, in chronological order, on the acquisition of alternating unaccusative verbs and OE psych verbs to see whether L2 learners are able to acquire the inks or the interfaces.

#### 4.2.1.1　Juffs (1996b)

Juffs (1996b) investigated knowledge of semantics-syntax correspondences in SLA within the Principles and Parameters framework, with particular focus on the acquisition of change-of-state locatives and psych verbs in English by native Chinese speakers. I will only introduce the part concerning psych verbs, as it is also a part of my research reported in this thesis.

It was pointed out in Chapter 2 that English allows OE verbs but

Chinese does not due to different conflation parameters in the two languages (Juffs 1996a, 1996b, 2000): while a morphologically simple verb in English can incorporate the meaning components CAUSE and BECOME into a root morpheme, its Chinese counterpart cannot. As a result, OE verbs are allowed in English but disallowed in Chinese; analytical causative constructions must be used to express causativity in Chinese (see § 2.2).

Juffs carried out an experiment with adult Chinese-speaking learners of English to see whether L2 learners could acquire the conflation pattern in the L2. The experiment included 120 Chinese subjects, who were divided into four L2 proficiency groups, namely the low-level group, the intermediate group, the high-level group and the advanced group. A production task and a grammatical judgment (GJ) task were designed to determine L2 subjects' knowledge of the syntax and semantics of the verbs in English.

The result of the production task indicated that the low-level and intermediate learners, who produced significantly fewer sentences with OE verbs, differed significantly from the native speakers, whereas the advanced learners and the native speakers patterned together. The result of the GJ task showed a similar pattern: the low-level learners tended to reject OE verbs, but positive evidence in the L2 input seemed to enable the more proficient learners to reset the parameter to the L2 value. It was concluded from the experiment that the parameter concerning conflation pattern could be reset and learners were able to acquire knowledge of L2 syntax-semantics correspondences with the help of positive evidence.

As outlined in Chapter 2, Chinese and English form a subset-superset relation in terms of psych verbs. Positive evidence available in English can trigger parameter resetting concerning conflation pattern in the L2 grammar so that the CAUSE component of OE verbs is recognized and projected onto the syntax, as found in Juffs' study. However, it is unknown from the experiment whether L2 properties can be acquired when L2 is a subset like Chinese while L1 is a superset like English. In this case, can the CAUSE component of OE verbs in the L1 be pre-empted so that it is not projected onto the L2 syntax?

### 4.2.1.2　White et al (1999)

White et al (1999) studied how the argument structure of English psych verbs is realized in L2 English grammars.

English has both SE verbs and OE verbs. If linking from semantic structure to syntactic structure is arbitrary and must be learned on a case-by-case basis, L2 learners of English will be expected to perform randomly with both types of verbs, making such errors as *John frightens exams* and *Exams fear John*. In the study of White et al, it was hypothesized that SE verbs would present few problems since Experiencer links to a higher position than Theme in both the underlying structure and the surface structure, consistent with UTAH (Baker 1988). It was also hypothesized that errors if any would involve OE verbs only.

To test these hypotheses, three experiments were conducted, the first involving 35 Malagasy speakers and 18 Japanese speakers, the second involving 15 francophone and 12 Japanese-speaking learners of English, the third involving 27 Malagasy speakers and 29 Spanish speakers. The first experiment used a written elicited production task and a translation task (into L1); the other two experiments used picture identification tasks.

The result of the experiments indicated that all L2 groups showed greater accuracy on SE verbs than on OE verbs, which confirmed the hypotheses (also see White et al 1998). The problem that L2 learners had with the OE verbs is that they incorrectly took Experiencer as subject in their L2 grammars. The result indicated that L2 learners did not link thematic roles to syntactic positions in an arbitrary fashion. When in doubt, they linked Theme to the object position and Experiencer to a higher position, which was consistent with UTAH. L1 effect was also apparent, in particular with the Malagasy speakers, who had difficulties with SE verbs. They mistakenly promoted Theme to the subject position in the L2 with SE verbs ( e. g. *Exams fear John) because Theme is favoured in the subject position in their L1.

White et al concluded that the linking of Experiencer and Theme arguments to syntactic positions was not arbitrary in interlanguage grammars and that L2 learners were still guided by UTAH and the thematic hierarchy rather than by properties of the L1 grammar or the L2 input alone.

### 4. 2. 1. 3  Montrul (1999)

Montrul ( 1999 ) investigated the acquisition of causative/ inchoative alternation in Spanish by native speakers of English and Turkish in order to find out whether L2 learners could distinguish between unaccusative and unergative verbs on the one hand, and different subclasses of unaccusative verbs on the other hand. Due to morphological differences between English and Turkish in terms of alternating unaccusative verbs, L1 influence was also a target of investigation.

Crosslinguistically, causative/inchoative alternation is morphologically marked with covert or overt morphemes ( Haspelmath 1993, see § 2. 1. 3. 1). In English, covert morpheme is used so that alternating unaccusative verbs ( e. g. 'sink' ) are morphologically the same in the causative form ( e. g. *The enemy sank the ship*) and the inchoative form ( e. g. *The ship sank*). In Spanish, some change-of-state unaccusative verbs like *derretir* 'melt' (past tense *derritió*) use the root form to express causativity as shown in (2a) but an obligatory reflexive morpheme *se* to express inchoativity as shown in (2b), whereas others like *morir* 'die' (past tense *murió*) have a lexically suppletive causative counterpart like *matar* 'kill' (past tense *mató*) as in (2c). In Turkish, anticausative suffix -$ıl$ is used on some alternating unaccusative verbs like *kırmak* 'break' (past tense *kır-dı*) as in (3b), while causative suffix -$dır$ is used on other verbs like *batmak* 'sink' (past tense *bat-mış*) as in (3d) (the causative morpheme -$dır$ is subject to the vowel and consonant harmony rules of the language and occurs as -$ır$ in (3d)). In both Spanish and Turkish, the anticausative morphemes, i.e. *se* and *-il* respectively, are homophonous with the passive morpheme and also appear in middle constructions, but cannot be used with unergative verbs (examples in (2) and (3) quoted from Montrul 1999: 194-95).

(2) Spanish
    a. El cocinero derritió    la manteca.
       the cook    melt-PAST the butter
       'The cook melted the butter.'
    b. La manteca *se*    derritió.
       the butter REFL melt-PAST
       'The butter melted.'
    c. El delincuente *murió/mató*    al hombre.
       the vandal    die-PAST/kill-PAST ANIM-the man
       'The vandal died/killed the man.'

(3) Turkish
    *Anticausative suffix-ıl*
    a. H$ısız$ pencere-yi    k$ır$-d$ı$.
       thief window-ACC break-PAST
       'The thief broke the window.'

b. Pencere kır-*ıl*-dı.
   window break-ANTICAUS-PAST
   'The window broke. '

*Causative suffix -dır*

c. Gemi bat-mış.
   ship sink-PAST
   'The ship sank. '

d. Düşman gemi-yi bat-*ır*-mış.
   enemy ship-ACC sink-CAUS-PAST
   'The enemy sank the ship. '

Montrul's experiment involved 19 Turkish speakers and 15 English speakers, all of whom were intermediate learners of Spanish. The participants took a picture judgment task, which consisted of pairs of sentences presented in the context of a picture. Half of the pictures described an action involving an Agent and a Patient, while the other half described the same action but involved only one participant. Transitive pictures were accompanied by transitive sentences and intransitive pictures by intransitive sentences. The reflexive clitic *se* appeared with all the intransitive sentences, while the periphrastic causative verb *hacer* ' make ' appeared with the verb in all the transitive sentences. Each sentence in the pair was followed by a 7-point scale ranging from 3 ( very natural ) to -3 ( very unnatural ). Participants were asked to judge the sentences in the context provided by the picture both for their grammaticality and meaning.

Results indicated that L2 learners were very accurate at accepting alternating unaccusative verbs used in transitive configurations but very inaccurate at rejecting intransitive verbs used in transitive sentences with causative meaning, resulting in causative errors, i. e. errors made when an intransitive verb is used in a transitive configuration with causative meaning. With regard to the inchoative forms, the Turkish-speaking learners and the control group patterned together on both types of verb form: they correctly accepted the forms with reflexive morphology and correctly rejected the forms without the morphology. The English group showed the opposite pattern: they incorrectly rejected verb forms with reflexive morphology and incorrectly accepted the same verb forms without reflexive morphology. Given morphological differences between English and Turkish in terms of alternating unaccusative verbs, Montrul argued that L1 transfer played a role in L2 representations. The contrast indicated that English-speaking learners of Spanish had problems with the morphological representation of alternating unaccusative verbs rather than with the syntactic representation.

### 4. 2. 1. 4  Montrul (2000)

Montrul (2000) expanded her study on causative/transitive alternation from L2 Spanish to L2 English and Turkish. Four types of verbs were chosen in her study, which were alternating unaccusative verbs (e.g. *break*), non-alternating verbs (e.g. *paint*), non-alternating unaccusative verbs (e.g. *disappear*) and unergative verbs (e.g. *cry*). Research questions underlying the studies were as follows (Montrul 2000: 246): a) How do L2 learners learn transitivity alternations? Do they make errors similar to those reported in L1 acquisition?[6] b) How do UG and L1 constrain acquisition of the lexicon in interlanguage grammars? c) If L2 learners make errors, do similar developmental paths emerge in the three languages? Answers to these questions will lend support either to the Full Access Model (Epstein et al 1996) or to the Full Transfer/Full Access Hypothesis (Schwartz and Sprouse 1994, 1996): for the former, only UG is involved in the initial state of interlanguage development, while for the latter, the initial state is the L1 although UG plays a role as well.

The experiment involved subjects who studied English, Spanish and Turkish as second languages. The English study involved 29 Spanish speakers and 28 Turkish speakers; the Spanish study involved 31 English speakers and 19 Turkish speakers; the Turkish study involved 18 English speakers and 24 Spanish speakers. As in Montrul (1999), all participants took a picture judgment task. They were asked to judge a sentence for both its grammaticality and meaning in the context provided by the picture.

The results on non-alternating unaccusative verbs and unergative verbs in the three studies suggested that causative/transitive errors seemed to be related to learners' L2 proficiency rather than L1 influence. Such causative errors were better characterized as developmental in nature because they disappeared gradually over time and with learners' increasing proficiency. In terms of alternating verbs, learners in the three studies knew the transitivity possibilities of the four types of verb, but failed to reject some causative and anticausative errors: on the one hand, they were less accurate than native speakers at rejecting causative errors with the non-alternating classes, in particular with non-alternating unaccusative (e. g. *The magician disappeared the rabbit) and unergative (e. g. *The dentist cried the child) verbs; on the other hand, they failed to reject anticausative errors with transitive verbs (e. g. *The picture painted). Between transitive and intransitive verbs, they were more accurate with the transitive variant than with the intransitive one. With respect to the morphology of alternating verbs, the results in the three studies suggested apparent L1 effects: errors were systematic and could be traced back to the learners' respective L1s to a large extent. More detailed analysis of the results can be found in Montrul (2001b, 2001c).

Based on the experimental results, Montrul concluded that UG and L1 knowledge could not affect all linguistic domains in the same way at a given stage of development, but interacted in discrete ways in constraining interlanguage grammars by operating at different levels of linguistic structure and by reconfiguring at different times. It was proposed that L1 transfer was subject to modularity in interlanguage grammars. The conclusion was claimed to support the Full Transfer/ Full Access Hypothesis of Schwartz and Sprouse (1994, 1996).

### 4.2.1.5 Montrul (2001a)

In Montrul (2001a), experiments were conducted on the acquisition of causative or anticausative morphology with change-of-state verbs and psych verbs in L2 English, L2 Spanish and L2 Turkish by learners whose native languages were English, Japanese, Spanish and Turkish. Since the part on change-of-state verbs is included in Montrul (1999, 2000), which were introduced in § 4.2.1.3 and § 4.2.1.4, I will focus on the part concerning psych verbs here.

According to Montrul (2001a), psych verbs in English, Japanese, Spanish and Turkish are morphologically different in terms of causative/inchoative alternation. In English, only a few psych verbs (e.g. *worry*) participate in the alternation and can be used either causatively (as OE verbs) or inchoatively (as SE verbs). With most OE verbs (e.g. *frighten* in (4a)), causativity can also be expressed with the analytical causative verb make, as in (4c); the inchoative form is expressed periphrastically with the verb *get*, as shown in (4b). In Spanish, the root form of psych verbs expresses causativity as in (5a), while a reflexive clitic *se* is used obligatorily to express inchoativity, as shown in (5b). Transitive psych verbs in Spanish can be paraphrased with the analytical causative verb *hacer* 'make' (past tense *hizo*) as in (5c). In Japanese and Turkish, the inchoative form is morphologically simple, while the causative form has an overt causative suffix (-(s)ase in Japanese and -ut in

Turkish), as shown in (6) and (7) (examples (4), (5), (6) and (7) quoted from Montrul 2001a: 151-2, 175).

(4) English
    a. *Causative*  The lion frightened the hunter.
    b. *Inchoative*  The hunter got frightened.
    c. *Analytical*  The lion made the hunter frightened.

(5) Spanish
    a. *Causative*  El león asustó      al cazador.
                     the lion frighten-PAST ANIM-hunter
                     'The lion frightened the hunter.'
    b. *Inchoative*  El cazador se     asustó.
                     the hunter REFL frighten-PAST
                     'The hunter got frightened.'
    c. *Analytical*  El león *hizo*   asustar (se)   al cazador.
                     the lion made frighten (REFL) ANIM-hunter
                     'The hunter made the hunter frightened.'

(6) Japanese
    a. *Causative*  Lion-ga   ryooshi-no   kowagar-ase-ta.
                     lion-NOM hunter-ACC fear-CAUS-PAST
                     'The lion frightened the hunter.'
    b. *Inchoative*  Ryooshi-ga kowagatta.
                     hunter-NOM frightened
                     'The hunter got frightened.'

(7) Turkish
    a. *Causative*  Arshan auci-yi     kork-ut-muş.
                     lion  hunter-ACC fear-CAUS-PAST
                     'The lion frightened the hunter.'
    b. *Inchoative*  Auci  kork-muş.
                     hunter frighten-PAST
                     'The hunter got frightened.'

Montrul's hypotheses are based on the Full Transfer/Full Access Hypothesis proposed by Schwartz and Sprouse (1994, 1996): if the formal features of a given morpheme are expressed overtly in L1 but non-overtly in L2, L2 learners will have difficulty with zero-morphemes and will try to find a surrogate L2 specific phonological form on which to map the formal features of such a lexical item; if a morpheme is not phonetically realized in L1 but realized in L2, L2 learners are likely to assume that such a morpheme does not have an overt form in L2 either, at least initially.

Experiments were conducted to test these hypotheses. The English study involved 29 Spanish speakers and 18 Turkish speakers; the Spanish study involved 30 English speakers and 19 Turkish speakers; the Turkish study involved 18 English speakers, 9 Japanese speakers and 24 Spanish speakers. The principal test instrument was picture judgment (see § 4. 2. 1. 3 and § 4. 2. 1. 4).

In the English study, Spanish speakers patterned together with the native English control group as both English and Spanish use zero morphology on the causative form (i. e. OE verbs) and explicit morphology on the inchoative form (i. e. *get* in English and *se* in Spanish). In contrast, Turkish speakers rejected sentences with causative psych verbs (e. g. *The lion frightened the hunter*). They accepted ungrammatical sentences with zero-derived inchoative psych verbs (e. g. *\*The hunter frightened*) but took their grammatical counterparts (e. g. *The hunter got frightened*) as ungrammatical.

In the Spanish study, responses to intransitive sentences with *se* (e. g. *El cazador se asustó* 'The hunter got frightened' in (5b)) were significantly different between the native Spanish control group and L2 groups; while Turkish speakers accepted the anticausative pattern with these verbs, English speakers were inaccurate at rejecting the zero-derived forms with these verbs (e. g. *\* El cazador asustó*

'The hunter frightened').

In the Turkish study, the Spanish and English intermediate learners failed to reject the incorrect zero-derived transitive forms (e. g. *Arshan auci-yi korkmuş 'The lion frightened the hunter'), which, according to Montrul, could be explained by transfer of their L1 morphological patterns. However, they were more accurate at accepting the grammatical forms (i. e. sentences with the causative morpheme-*ut* as in (7a)) than rejecting the ungrammatical forms (i. e. sentences in which the psych verb is used as a zero-derived causative verb, e. g. *Arshan auci-yi korkmuş 'The lion frightened the hunter'). As for intransitive psych verbs as shown in (7b), L2 groups accepted these sentences as the control group did.

Montrul's conclusion is that errors with argument structure alternations are related to the way alternations are morphologically expressed in L1 and L2. Morphological errors in L2 are constrained by morphological properties of L1s so that L2 learners have problems merging features and forms. The findings are claimed to be consistent with the predictions of the Full Access/Full Transfer Hypothesis of Schwartz and Sprouse (1994, 1996).

4. 2. 1. 6  Cabrera and Zubizarreta (2003)

Cabrera and Zubizarreta's study was a replication and extension of Montrul's work on causative alternation. The purpose was to test whether L2 learners could distinguish between different classes of intransitives (i. e. unaccusatives and unergatives) when they made overgeneralizations. Their hypothesis was that if L2 learners overgeneralized the causative construction selectively, it should be the case that they would favour non-alternating unaccusatives and disfavour unergatives because such unaccusative verbs had properties of alternating unaccusative verbs.

Ninety-seven subjects were involved in the study: 47 took an acceptability judgment (AJ) test and 50 took a vocabulary translation task (VTT). In each test, subjects were divided into three groups, i. e. the beginner group, the intermediate group and the advanced group, according to their L2 Spanish proficiency. Four types of verb were tested in the experiment, which include non-alternating unaccusative verbs (e. g. *aparecer* 'appear'), alternating unaccusative verbs (e. g. *romper* 'break'), non-alternating transitive verbs (e. g. *pintar* 'paint') and unergative verbs (e. g. *llorar* 'cry').

The result of the AJ test indicated that L2 learners tended to accept overgeneralized causatives of non-alternating unaccusatives. However, only beginners tended to accept overgeneralized causatives with unergatives. There was no significant difference across L2 groups on alternating unaccusative verbs or non-alternating transitive verbs. Analysis of individual subjects indicated that among those who made overgeneralizations, some only overgeneralized non-alternating unaccusatives while others overgeneralized both non-alternating unaccusative verbs and unergative verbs. This phenomenon was considered to be related to the strategy that L2 learners employed in putting to use their grammatical knowledge. Two types of strategies were proposed, as shown in (8) (adapted from Cabrera and Zubizarreta 2003: 33):

(8) *Syntactic strategy*:
   The lexical information of particular verb classes is ignored. The following general form-meaning correspondence generalization is used:
   NP1 V NP2 ←→ [NP1 CAUSE [NP2 BECOME PREDICATIVE]]

*Lexico-syntactic strategy*:
   The correspondence between surface syntactic template and meaning is restricted to a lexico-syntactic class, namely unaccusatives.

Cabrera and Zubizarreta concluded that L2 learners start from the syntactic strategy and move toward the lexico-syntactic strategy and that more causative errors are made when L2 learners employ the syntactic strategy.

### 4.2.2  Summary of the findings

The studies on alternating unaccusative verbs and OE psych verbs are summarized in Table 4.1.

Studies reported in § 4.2.1 seem to support the Full Transfer/ Full Access Hypothesis (Schwartz and Sprouse 1994, 1996) that L2 learners start from L1 but have access to UG. The thematic hierarchy (Grimshaw 1990; Jackendoff 1990; Larson 1988) and UTAH (Baker 1988) seem to have effects on the acquisition of L2 argument structure. Results of these studies indicate that L2 learners make causative errors as in L1 acquisition and that L1 morphological properties play a role in the acquisition of L2 lexicon.

The studies on alternating unaccusative verbs and psych verbs discussed in this chapter all take Indo-European languages as L2s. It is unknown, therefore, whether findings of these studies apply to L2 acquisition of causativity in non-Indo-European languages like Chinese. The present study will tackle this problem and investigate the acquisition of L2 Chinese representations of causativity by native speakers of Indo-European languages like English and non-Indo-European languages like Japanese and Korean. Apart from typological differences, the four languages, i.e. Chinese, English, Japanese and Korean, also differ in the representation of grammatical functions: while Chinese does not have causative affixes or case markers, Japanese and Korean have both; both alternating unaccusative and OE psych verbs are allowed in English, but neither is allowed in Chinese, Japanese or Korean. Comparison between L2 Chinese grammars of different L1s is a good test of existing theories and findings.

Table 4.1 Previous studies on the acquisition of L2 alternating unaccusative verbs and psych verbs

| Studies | Focus | L1 | L2 | Subjects | Tasks | Main findings |
|---|---|---|---|---|---|---|
| Juffs (1996b) | change-of-state locatives and psych verbs | Chinese | English | 120 Chinese divided into 4 L2 proficiency groups | production GJ | Lexical parameter can be reset; learners can achieve knowledge of L2 syntax-semantics correspondences. |
| White et al (1999) | psych verbs | Malagasy Japanese French Spanish | English | 1. 35 Malagasy, 18 Japanese 2. 15 French, 12 Japanese 3. 27 Malagasy, 29 Spanish | written production translation picture identification | L2 learners have problem with OE verbs; L2 learners are guid ed by U-TAH and thematic hierarchy. |
| Montrul (1999) | causative/inchoative alternation | English Turkish | Spanish | 19 Turkish (intermediate) 15 English (intermediate) | picture judgment | L2 learners make causative errors; L1 plays a role in L2 representations. |
| Montrul (2000) | causative/transitive alternation | English Spanish Turkish | English as L2; 29 Spanish, 28 Turkish Spanish as L2; 31 English, 19 Turkish Turkish as L2; 18 English, 24 Spanish | picture judgment | UG and L1 knowledge interact in discreteways in constraining L2 grammars; L1 transfer is subject to modularity in L2 representations. |
| Montrul (2001a) | alternating unaccusative verbs and psych verbs | English Japanese Spanish Turkish | English as L2; 29 Spanish, 18 Turkish Spanish as L2; 30 English, 19 Turkish Turkish as L2; 18 English, 24 Spanish and 9 Japanese | picture judgment | Causative errors are related to the way alternations are morphologically expressed and are constrained by the morphological properties of L1s. |
| Cabrera and Zubizarreta (2003) | overgeneralization of causative constructions | not specified | Spanish | beginners intermediate learners advanced learners | AJ VTT | Learners accep t / produce causatives with unaccusatives more than with u-nergatives. |

## 4.3 Summary

In this chapter, I first gave a brief review of SLA studies in general with particular reference to such issues as L1 transfer, interlanguage, functional categories and learnability. Then I discussed some studies of the acquisition of causativity, in particular the acquisition of alternating unaccusative verbs and psych verbs in L2s. The purpose of this chapter is to provide a background for the present empirical study, which will be presented in the following chapters.

## Notes

[1] Kellerman (1995) further develops the "Transfer to Nowhere" Principle, arguing that it is not the syntactic features of L1 but its conceptual organization that transfers into L2. If language determines how speakers conceptualize experience, then a shift to a new language implies a change in the conceptual framework through which the speaker views the world. This will be a more challenging task than syntactic restructuring.

[2] Herschensohn (2000) makes a similar distinction between two aspects of UG, which are the form of grammar (product) and the strategy of language acquisition (process): the former includes universal components and principles such as "move" or "economy of derivation", which are available to L2 learners; the latter is the acquisition of L2 lexicon, which is not UG driven. Since UG as the form of the grammar is identical crosslinguistically and parametric variation is restricted to lexicon, the main task of L2 acquisition is the acquisition of L2 morpholexicon.

[3] In terms of positive/negative evidence, Schwartz (1993) argues that the type of knowledge resulting from negative evidence is not to be equated with linguistic competence and that only positive evidence can affect the construction of an interlanguage grammar. That is to say, positive and negative evidence play different roles in building an L2 grammar.

[4] Corder (1967) makes a distinction between "input" and "intake", the former referring to "what is available" and the latter to "what goes in". Intake is defined as "a subset of the

input that the learner actually perceives and processes" ( VanPatten 1990: 287 ). See Boulouffe ( 1986 ), Chaudron ( 1985 ), Leow ( 1993 ), Sharwood Smith ( 1993 ) and VanPatten and Cadierno ( 1993 ) for related discussion.

[5] Klein and Martohardjono ( 1999 ) make a distinction between properties and mechanism: language knowledge and its representation constitute the properties of the grammars which are constructed in acquisition; input, learnability, processing and triggering pertain to the mechanism or the process which drives the acquisition from one intermediate grammar representation to the next. In this proposal, property issues concern WHAT of the developing learner systems, while process issues address HOW a learner gets from one state of knowledge to another.

[6] Montrul ( 1999 ) reports that causative errors ( i. e. the use of an intransitive verb in a transitive frame to express a causative situation, e. g. *The magician disappeared the rabbit*) are well documented in L1 acquisition studies ( e. g. Allen 1996; Hochberg 1986; Morikawa 1991).

# 5 Research methodology of the present study

**导言**

　　本章重点介绍作者所做的实证研究的研究方法,是承前启后的一章,它把前几章中的问题融入试验设计中,为以后章节的实证结果分析做了铺垫。

　　作者首先对第二章和第三章中讨论过的汉、英、日、韩这四种语言中有关使动的语义和句法表征做了概括总结,随后联系第四章介绍过的第二语言习得理论,提出了实证研究将要探讨的问题:1)使动在以汉语为目标语的中介语中有怎样的表征? 2)在这些表征中,是否有第一语言迁移现象发生? 3)汉语结果补语和复合使动结构中包含的功能范畴(即体短语)能否在中介语中有适当表征?

　　接下来,作者对实证研究的试验设计做了介绍,试验对象包括 55 名母语为英语的汉语学习者、56 名母语为日语的汉语学习者和 73 名母语为韩语的汉语学习者,控制组由 28 名汉语本族语者构成。通过完形填空,作者对被试的汉语水平进行测试,并根据测试成绩分别把母语为英语、日语、韩语的学习者分为中低、中级和中高三组。具体试验中作者采用了三种试验工具,分别为产出测试、可接受性判断测试和理解测试。产出测试要求被试用所给的含有非宾格动词和心理动词的词语组句。可接受性判断测试要求被试对含有非宾格动词、心理动词、分析型使动结构、结果补语结构和复合使动结构的单句的可接受性做出判断。理解测试考察被试对汉语结果补语和复合使动结构的理解,这些结构分别以无语境单句和有图画语境单句两种形式给出。

# Research methodology of the present study

As mentioned at the beginning of the thesis, Chinese does not have lexical causatives, and, as a result, Chinese unaccusative verbs and psych verbs are non-causative in nature. Causativity in Chinese is represented by analytical causative, compound causative and resultative constructions. In the present research, I will examine representations of causativity in English, Japanese and Korean speakers' L2 Chinese grammars.

This chapter gives a description of the research methodology employed in the present study. Section 5.1 is a summary of representations of causativity in Chinese, English, Japanese and Korean; Section 5.2 proposes research questions and hypotheses; Section 5.3 provides information about participants in the experiment; Section 5.4 describes instruments of the experiment and data-collecting procedures.

## 5.1 Causativity in Chinese, English, Japanese and Korean

We studied properties of unaccusative and psych verbs in Chapter 2 and properties of compound causative and resultative constructions in Chapter 3. In this section, I will summarize representations of causativity in Chinese, English, Japanese and Korean, which I hope will enable the reader to understand my research methodology better.

As stated in Chapter 2, OE verbs and alternating unaccusative verbs are allowed in English but not allowed in Chinese, Japanese or Korean. Causative affixes are used to causativize psych verbs and unaccusative verbs in Japanese and Korean. Since Chinese does not have causative affixes, it employs free causative morphemes to causativize psych verbs and uses compound causatives to represent the cause-effect relation.

Alternating unaccusative verbs and OE psych verbs have a lexical semantic representation that involves semantic primitives CAUSE and BECOME (Levin and Rappaport Hovav 1995). In English, the two semantic components can be conflated together so that it is possible for one verb to express both meanings. When the lexical semantic representation is projected onto syntax, there will be a VP shell with the upper $v$P denoting CAUSE and the lower VP denoting BECOME. Since alternating unaccusatives and OE verbs in English are semantically causative (Levin and Rappaport Hovav 1995; Pesetsky 1995), they are attracted by the abstract light verb to the head position of the upper $v$P to have their causative features checked. In Chinese, the conflation of CAUSE and BECOME into one word is impossible (see §2.1.4.2 and §2.2.3). Thus, single verbs, whether they are unaccusative or psych verbs, are non-causatives and can only express BECOME. When the lexical semantic features are projected onto syntax, there will be a single VP headed by the non-causative unaccusative verb or psych verb. Japanese and Korean behave similarly in this respect. The lexical semantic representations and syntactic structures of unaccusative and psych verbs in the four languages are illustrated in (1):

(1) Unaccusative verbs and psych verbs
    a. Syntactic structures

(i) English

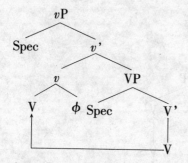

(ii) Chinese, Japanese and Korean

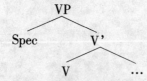

b. Semantic structures
English: [ [ x DO SOMETHING ] CAUSE [ y BECOME STATE ]]
Chinese, Japanese and Korean: [ y BECOME STATE ]

Analytical causatives in the four languages have the same syntactic structure, which involves a VP shell with the upper vP headed by an explicit causative morpheme. However, due to the SVO order in Chinese and English but the SOV order in Japanese and Korean, there is a parametric difference in surface representations. The semantic and syntactic structures of analytical causatives in the four languages are summarized in (2):

(2) Analytical causative constructions
  a. Semantic structure
      [[ x CAUSE [ y DO SOMETHING/BECOME STATE ]]
  b. Syntactic structures

(i) Chinese and English

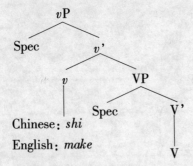

(ii) Japanese and Korean

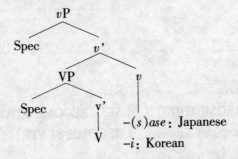

With regard to resultatives and compound causatives, Chinese involves an AspP between VP (headed by the activity predicate $V_1$) and XP (headed by the result predicate $V_2$) to delimit an activity which would be unbounded otherwise. The AspP is headed by an explicit morpheme *de* in the case of resultatives but a phonetically unrealised morpheme in the case of compound causatives. The two constructions have a syntactic structure as illustrated in (3b) (see §3.2.2.1 and §3.2.2.2). Since the result $V_2$ can be predicated either to $NP_1$ (i.e. *Zhangsan* in the examples) or $NP_2$ (i.e. *Lisi* in the examples), resultatives and compound causatives have a semantic structure as shown in (3a).

(3) Resultative and compound causative constructions in Chinese

a. Semantic structure

   $[[x\text{ CAUSE}[x/y\text{BECOME }z]\text{BY}[x\text{DO SOMETHING}(\text{TO }y)]]$

b. Syntactic structure

   $[_{vP}\text{Spec}[_{v'}[_{VP}\text{Spec}[_{V'}V_1[_{AspP}\text{Spec}[_{Asp'}(de)[_{XP}V_2]]]]]]]$

c. Examples (from (41) and (48) of Chapter 3)

   (a) Resultative with a single $V_1$

   Zhangsan <u>zhui</u> de  Lisi dou *lei* le.

   Zhangsan chase *de* Lisi even tire ASP

   'Zhangsan chased Lisi and Lisi got tired as a result.'

   (b) Resultative with a reduplicated $V_1$

   Zhangsan <u>zhui</u>  Lisi <u>zhui</u> de dou   *lei* le.

   Zhangsan chase Lisi chase *de* even tire ASP

   'Zhangsan chased Lisi and got tired as a result.'

   (c) Compound causative

   Zhangsan <u>zhui</u>-*lei*  le  Lisi.

   Zhangsan chase-tire ASP Lisi

   (i) 'Zhangsan chased Lisi and Lisi got tired as a result.'

   (ii) 'Zhangsan chased Lisi and got tired as a result.'

English has resultatives but does not have compound causatives. Unlike Chinese, English resultatives do not contain any functional category between the activity predicate and the result predicate (see § 3.1.2.3). Their semantic and syntactic structures are summarized in (4):

(4) Resultative constructions in English

   a. Semantic structure

   $[[x\text{CAUSE}[y\text{BECOME }z]\text{BY }[x\text{DO SOMETHING}(\text{TO }y)]]$

   b. Syntactic structure

   $[[_{vP}\text{Spec}[_{v'}[_{VP}\text{Spec}[_{V'}V_{activity}[_{XP}\text{Spec}[_{X'}X_{result}]]]]]]]$

   c. Examples (from (10) and (11) of Chapter 3)

      (a) Tom pounded the metal flat.

(b) The joggers ran their Nikes threadbare.
(c) They drank the pub dry.

Japanese has resultative (A-V) and compound causative ($V_1$-$V_2$) constructions, but neither involves any functional category. In resultatives, the two predicates, i. e. the adjective and the verb, denote a result-activity relation, while in a compound causative, the two predicates, i. e. $V_1$ and $V_2$, denote an activity-result relation. In the resultative construction, the result-denoting adjective forms a predication relation with the object. In the compound causative construction, both verbs (i. e. $V_1$ and $V_2$) are predicated of the subject. As Japanese has an SOV order, $V_2$ is the main predicate heading the result VP, while $V_1$ is the secondary predicate heading the XP of activity. The semantic and syntactic structures of Japanese resultatives and compound causatives are summarized in (5):

(5) Resultative and compound causative constructions in Japanese
 a. Semantic structure
  [[$x$ CAUSE[$y$ BECOME $z$]BY[$x$ DO SOMETHING TO $y$]]
 b. Syntactic structures
  Resultative: [$_{VP}$ Spec [$_{XP}$ Spec [$A_{result\ X'}$ ]$V_{activity\ V'}$ ]]
  Compound causative: [$_{VP}$ Spec [$_{XP}$ Spec [$V_{1\ X'}$ ] $V_{2\ V'}$ ]]
 c. Examples (from (52) of Chapter 3)
  (a) John-ga kabe-o aoku  nut-ta. (resultative)
   John-NOM wall-ACC blue paint-PAST
   'John painted the wall blue.'
  (b) John-ga Mary-o uti-korosi-ta.(compound causative)
   John-NOM Mary-ACC shoot-kill-PAST
   'John shot and killed Mary.'

As in Japanese, Korean resultatives have an A-V structure denoting a result-activity relation. Korean compound causatives have a $V_1$-$V_2$

structure denoting an activity-result relation. In contrast to Japanese, which does not employ any causative or resultative marker in the resultative and compound causative constructions, the Korean resultative construction is headed by an explicit marker -*key* and its compound causative is headed by an explicit causative morpheme -*i*. Korean is an SOV language, so $V_2$ is the main predicate of the $V_1$-$V_2$ compound while $V_1$ is the secondary predicate heading the XP of activity. The semantic and syntactic structures of Korean resultatives and compound causatives are summarized in (6):

(6) Resultative and compound causative constructions in Korean
   a. Semantic structure
      $[[x \text{ CAUSE}[y \text{ BECOME } z] \text{ BY}[x \text{ DO SOMETHING}(\text{TO } y)]]]$
   b. Syntactic structures
      Resultative: $[_{\text{VP}}\text{Spec}[_{\text{AspP}}\text{Spec}[_{\text{XP}}[A_{\text{result X'}}] \text{ -}key_{\text{Asp'}}]V_{\text{activity V'}}]]$
      Compound causative: $[_{\text{vP}} \text{ Spec}[_{\text{VP}} \text{ Spec}[_{\text{XP}}[V_{1 \text{ X'}}]V_{2 \text{ V'}}] \text{ -}i_{\text{v'}}]]$
   c. Examples (from (59b) and (60a) of Chapter 3)
     (a) resultative
        Mary-nun kumsok-ul napcakha-key twutulki-ess-ta.
        Mary-TOP metal-ACC flat-COMP hammer-PAST-DEC
        'Mary hammered the metal flat.'
     (b) compound causative
        John-i    Bill-ul    sswa-a-cwuk-i-ess-ta.
        John-NOM Bill-ACC shoot-die-CAUS-PAST-DEC
        'John shot Bill dead.'

Compared with unaccusative verbs and psych verbs, resultatives and compound causatives form a more complicated picture in the four languages, as we can see from the above summary.

    In this section, I summarized properties of unaccusative verbs, psych verbs, resultative constructions, compound causative constructions and analytical causative constructions in Chinese, English, Japanese and

Korean in relation to causativity. In the following empirical study, I will examine acquisition of these verbs and constructions in Chinese by native speakers of English, Japanese and Korean.

## 5.2 Research questions and hypotheses

As we know from the previous chapters and the last section, Chinese does not allow lexical causatives. As a result, unaccusative and psych verbs are non-causative in Chinese, and causativity is expressed with resultative, compound causative and analytical causative constructions. In terms of L2 Chinese acquisition, this implies that L2 learners have two tasks: on the one hand, they need to acquire representations of causativity in Chinese, including analytical causatives, compound causatives and resultatives; on the other hand, they need to acquire the non-causativeness of unaccusative verbs and psych verbs. The present research explores both aspects.

Given properties of the verbs and constructions in the four languages under study summarized in the last section and taking into account previous studies on the acquisition of argument structure which were introduced in §4.2.1, I will look into three issues in the present study: 1) How is causativity represented in L2 Chinese grammars? 2) Is there L1 effect in L2 Chinese representations of causativity? 3) Can functional categories involved in compound causatives and resultatives be projected in L2 Chinese grammars? The following questions and hypotheses are proposed on these issues in relation to the verbs and constructions under study.

### 5.2.1 Unaccusative verbs and psych verbs

The following questions are raised on the acquisition of Chinese unaccusative verbs and psych verbs.

1) In English change-of-state unaccusative verbs and OE psych

verbs project a VP shell, while in Chinese unaccusative verbs and psych verbs project a single VP, as shown in (1) of this Chapter. Regarding unaccusative verbs and psych verbs, English is a superset but Chinese a subset. Can English-speaking learners project a single VP rather than a VP shell in their L2 Chinese grammar without the availability of positive evidence?

2) Unaccusative verbs and psych verbs project a single VP in Chinese, Japanese and Korean. Can causative errors be avoided in Japanese- and Korean-speaking learners' L2 Chinese grammars?

3) Chinese unaccusative verbs and psych verbs have the same semantic structure and syntactic structure. Are these two types of verb represented in the same way in L2 Chinese grammars?

Hypotheses about the above questions are as follows:

1) If L1 transfer happens, as found in previous studies on psych verbs (Juffs 1996b; White et al 1998; White et al 1999; Yip 1995) and alternating unaccusative verbs (Montrul 1999, 2000, 2001a, 2001b, 2001c), English-speaking learners of Chinese will make causative errors at least initially. However, under the guidance of UG and with the increase in their L2 proficiency, they can acquire the semantic structure of Chinese unaccusative verbs and psych verbs which only contain the BECOME component as in (1) and consequently project a single VP in their L2 Chinese syntax, despite the unavailability of positive evidence.

2) If Japanese- and Korean-speaking learners of Chinese transfer the VP structure in their L1s into L2 Chinese grammar, causative errors will be avoided. However, this might not be the case because the way alternations are morphologically expressed in the three languages is different. Japanese and Korean employ causative affixes to causativize unaccusative verbs and psych verbs. Chinese, however, does not have causative affixes. The unavailability of causative affixes in Chinese may mislead Japanese- and Korean-speaking learners into

believing that Chinese allows covert causative morphemes. Consequently, they may accept the incorrect alternating unaccusative structure (e. g. *Zhangsan sui le na ge huaping 'Zhangsan broke the vase') and the incorrect OE-verb structure (e. g. *Zhe ge xiaoxi xingfen le Zhangsan 'This news excited Zhangsan') in Chinese.

It is also hypothesized that unaccusative verbs and psych verbs may be represented differently in L2 Chinese grammars. If UTAH (Baker 1988) and thematic hierarchy (Grimshaw 1990) play a role in L2 acquisition, as found in previous studies (White et al 1998; White et al 1999), the incorrect alternating unaccusative structure (e. g. *Zhangsan sui le na ge huaping 'Zhangsan broke that vase') will be more difficult to reject than the incorrect OE-verb structure (e. g. *Zhe ge xiaoxi xingfen le Zhangsan 'This news excited Zhangsan') because the former conforms to UTAH and thematic hierarchy in both the underlying structure and the surface structure with Agent (i. e. Zhangsan) occurring at a higher position than Theme (i. e. na ge huaping 'that vase'), while the latter, with Theme (i. e. zhe ge xiaoxi 'this news') occurring at a higher position than Agent (i. e. Zhangsan), violates thematic hierarchy in the surface structure. As pointed out in § 2.1.4.2.2, Chinese unaccusative verbs can assign partitive case (e. g. Zhangsan duan le yi tiao tui 'Zhangsan broke a leg', see (31) of Chapter 2). Due to lack of explicit case markers in Chinese, the partitive-case-marked NP (i. e. yi tiao tui 'one leg') may be mistaken as an accusative-case-marked NP. This kind of evidence may also mislead L2 learners into accepting the incorrect alternating unaccusative structure.

### 5.2.2 Resultative and compound causative constructions

The following questions are asked on the acquisition of Chinese resultative and compound causative constructions.

1) Chinese resultatives and compound causatives involve a functional category AspP as shown in (3), while English resultatives do not, as shown in (4). Can this functional category be projected in English-speaking learners' L2 Chinese?

2) Both Japanese and Korean allow compound causatives. Will this facilitate Japanese- and Korean-speaking learners in their acquisition of compound causatives in Chinese? Will the functional category AspP be projected in L2 Chinese grammars by Japanese-speaking learners, whose L1 does not involve any functional category in resultatives and compound causatives, as shown in (5b), and by Korean-speaking learners, whose L1 involves functional categories in resultatives and compound causatives, as shown in (6b)?

3) In Chinese, there are different types of compound causative constructions, which have the same syntactic structure but different semantic structures, as shown in (3). Will some compound causative constructions be acquired earlier than others because of different semantic structures that they have?

4) In Chinese, the functional category AspP has an overt head *de* in resultatives but a covert head in compound causatives. Will resultatives be easier to acquire than compound causatives because of the overt head they have?

The following are hypotheses about these questions.

1) Whether English-speaking learners can acquire the functional category AspP which is available in Chinese resultatives and compound causatives but unavailable in English resultatives will lend support either to proposals that functional categories can be projected in L2 grammar (e.g. Lakshmanan 1993/1994; Schwartz and Sprouse 1994, 1996; White 1996) or to proposals that they cannot (e.g. Franceschina 2001; Hawkins and Liszka 2003; Meisel 1991, 1997; Tsimpli and Roussou 1991). My hypothesis is that English-speaking

learners may transfer the syntactic structure of English resultatives into L2 Chinese at least initially, accepting resultatives like (7b) which do not involve the functional category AspP. However, with the increase in their L2 proficiency and with the help of positive evidence, the AspP can be projected for resultatives and compound causatives in their L2 Chinese grammar.

(7) a. Zhangsan ku de shoujuan    dou *shi* le.
       Zhangsan cry *de* handkerchief even wet ASP
    b. *Zhangsan ku shoujuan    dou *shi* le.
       Zhangsan cry handkerchief even wet ASP
       'Zhangsan cried the handkerchief soggy.'

2) Although Japanese and Korean have both resultatives and compound causatives, L2 Chinese learners of the two L1s may not find it easier to acquire the two constructions, in particular the compound causative construction, than English-speaking learners. One reason is that the AspP involved in Chinese compound causatives has a phonetically unrealised head, which has strong feature and triggers movement (see §3.2.2.2), different from functional categories in Japanese and Korean, which have weak features and do not trigger movement (see §3.3 and §3.4). If they fail to acquire the feature strength of Asp in Chinese compound causatives, errors as in (7b) will also arise. Another reason is that the semantic structures of resultatives and compound causatives in L1 Japanese and Korean are different from those of Chinese resultatives and compound causatives, as shown in (3b), (5b) and (6b). As a result, Japanese- and Korean-speaking learners may have problems with the interpretation of Chinese resultatives and compound causatives even if they have acquired the syntactic structure of these constructions.

3) Compound causatives in Chinese have the same syntactic structure but different semantic structures. As a result, some types of

compound causative may be acquired earlier than others if they can be acquired at all. Since all the compound causatives have the same syntactic structure, my hypothesis is that construction with a semantic structure as shown in (8a) and exemplified in (8b) is easier to acquire than other types of compound causative.

(8) a. [[x DO SOMETHING TO y] CAUSE [y BECOME STATE]]
b. Zhangsan da-*sui* le Lisi de huaping.
Zhangsan hit-break ASP Lisi's vase
'Zhangsan broke Lisi's vase'

(9)

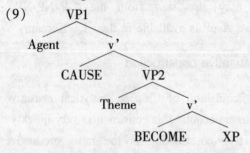

A reason why such a construction is easier to acquire is that it contains both a CAUSE component and a BECOME component and thus satisfies the causative template (ignoring the AspP in the compound causative construction) as in (9) (see §2.1.3.2). In (8b), for example, $NP_1$ (i. e. *Zhangsan*) is the Agent, while $NP_2$ (i. e. *Lisi de huaping* 'Lisi's vase') is the Theme; in the compound, $V_1$ (i. e. *da* 'hit') is the predicate of activity/cause, while $V_2$ (i. e. *sui* 'break') is the predicate of result/state; the Theme (i. e. *Lisi de huaping* 'Lisi's vase') and $V_2$ (i. e. *sui* 'break') form a predication relation.

4) Concerning acquisition pace, my hypothesis is that resultatives will be acquired earlier than compound causatives because the functional category AspP has a phonetically realized head *de* in resultatives but a phonetically null head in compound causatives. *De* has weak feature and does not trigger movement. In contrast, the phonetically unrealized

head in compound causatives has strong feature and attracts the result predicate to raise. The operation deriving compound causatives is thus more costly and will be acquired later. If L2 learners are constrained by the economy principle (Chomsky 1995), they will acquire Chinese resultatives earlier than compound causatives.

It is also hypothesized that if L1 transfer happens English- and Japanese-speaking learners will start from the "V-NP-XP" structure, which is allowed in their L1s (e.g. *Tom pounded the metal flat*) but not allowed in Chinese. If functional categories do not transfer, Korean-speaking learners may also start from the "V-NP-XP" structure although resultative AspP is available in their L1 Korean.

### 5.2.3 The analytical causative construction

The question on the acquisition of Chinese analytical causative construction is: Can L2 learners acquire this construction very quickly? Since the analytical causative construction is the most productive (Comrie 1985; Shibatani 1976a; Song 1996) and exists in the four languages under study with the same semantic and syntactic structures as shown in (2), it is hypothesized that L2 learners will acquire the analytical causative construction in Chinese without much difficulty.

An empirical research is conducted to test the above hypotheses on representations of causativity in L2 Chinese. The following sections provide an introduction to the experiment.

### 5.3 Participants

Participants in the empirical research include 55 English speakers (ES), 56 Japanese speakers (JS), 73 Korean speakers (KS) and 28 native Chinese speakers (NS) as controls. At the time of the experiment, the L2 subjects were studying Chinese at Peking University, Beijing Foreign Studies University, Capital Normal

University (Beijing), University of Foreign Economics and Trade (Beijing) and University of Cambridge. Subjects in the native control group were students of the Yutian Normal College. A minimum time of studying Chinese and living in a Chinese-speaking environment[1] was set for L2 subjects to ensure that they had already had necessary knowledge of the structures under study.

In the experiment, all the subjects did a cloze test first. In the SLA literature, cloze test is argued to be a reliable measure of learner' L2 proficiency (e. g. Fotos 1991; Laesch and van Kleeck 1987). Thus results of the cloze test are taken as representing subjects' L2 Chinese proficiency.

The cloze test consists of two passages,[2] which are given in both Chinese characters and in *pinyin*, the Romanization system of Chinese. The two passages contain forty blanks in total, with twenty in each. Subjects may choose either the character version or the *pinyin* version and fill in each blank with one character or with the *pinyin* standing for that character.

The body of the cloze test, i. e. the two passages (in character and in *pinyin*) with forty blanks, is the same for all participants, but explanations for possible new words are given in L2 subjects' native languages, i. e. English, Japanese and Korean. So is the instruction for the whole experiment. The purpose is to minimize potential problems caused by new words or by unclear instructions. Two examples are given in the instructions to illustrate what subjects are expected to do.

On the basis of the scores in the cloze test, each of the English, Japanese and Korean groups is classified into low-intermediate (LI), intermediate (IN) and high-intermediate (HI) subgroups. Information of each subject group is presented in Table 5.1 and results of the cloze test are given in Table 5.2. The present research includes comparisons between groups from the same L1 but at different Chinese proficiency levels and comparisons between groups from different L1s but at the same Chinese proficiency levels. The purpose of the former is to explore longitudinal development within subjects of the same L1, while the purpose of the latter is to find out possible variations between subject groups of different L1s.

Table 5.1 Information of the subjects in the study

| First language | Total N | Chinese proficiency level | N | Age Range | Age Mean | Time of learning[a] | Time of living[b] |
|---|---|---|---|---|---|---|---|
| English | 55 | low-intermediate | 26 | 19-23 | 20.4 | 24.1 | 4.4 |
| | | intermediate | 13 | 20-31 | 21.4 | 42.2 | 6.9 |
| | | high-intermediate | 16 | 19-36 | 22.9 | 45.6 | 18.6 |
| Japanese | 56 | low-intermediate | 15 | 20-27 | 22.7 | 25.9 | 19.3 |
| | | intermediate | 18 | 20-33 | 23.8 | 36.2 | 19.7 |
| | | high-intermediate | 23 | 19-36 | 22.3 | 47.6 | 26.4 |
| Korean | 73 | low-intermediate | 27 | 20-28 | 22.3 | 29.2 | 7.5 |
| | | intermediate | 25 | 20-25 | 22.0 | 32.7 | 11.3 |
| | | high-intermediate | 21 | 21-27 | 22.4 | 33.2 | 13.6 |
| Chinese | 28 | N/A | 28 | 19-22 | 20.8 | N/A | N/A |

a. Number of months for which a subject has learned Chinese;
b. Number of months for which a subject has lived in a Chinese-speaking environment.

Table 5.2 The mean score and standard deviation (SD) of each subject group in the cloze test (total score = 40)

| First language | Low-intermediate (range 15 – 29) | | Intermediate (range 30-33) | | High-intermediate (range 34-40) | | Chinese native | |
|---|---|---|---|---|---|---|---|---|
| | Mean | SD | Mean | SD | Mean | SD | Mean | SD |
| English | 23.23 | 3.35 | 31.62 | 1.04 | 36.31 | 1.92 | 38.61 | 1.29 |
| Japanese | 24.93 | 5.40 | 31.83 | 1.15 | 36.04 | 1.72 | | |
| Korean | 25.89 | 3.48 | 31.64 | 1.04 | 35.24 | 1.22 | | |

To make comparisons between proficiency groups possible, we need to know whether subgroups at the four proficiency levels (i. e. low-intermediate, intermediate, high-intermediate, and native Chinese) differ significantly in each of the L1 groups. One-way ANOVA tests were conducted on the cloze test scores between the four proficiency levels (i. e. low-intermediate, intermediate, high-intermediate and native Chinese) in the L1 English group, the L1 Japanese group and the L1 Korean group respectively. The results reveal significant differences between the four proficiency levels in the English group ($F(3,79) = 235.101$, $p < .001$), the Japanese group ($F(3,80) = 98.961$, $p < .001$) and the Korean group ($F(3,97) = 186.426$, $p < .001$). Post hoc Scheffé tests[3] indicate that in each L1 group, the three subgroups at different L2 proficiency levels (i. e. low-intermediate, intermediate and high-intermediate) differ significantly from each other ($p < .001$) and from the native Chinese control group ($p < .001$). This makes comparisons between proficiency groups possible.

To compare between different L1 groups, we need to know whether significant differences exist between groups from different L1s but at the same Chinese proficiency levels. One-way ANOVA tests were conducted on the cloze test scores between the low-intermediate groups, the intermediate groups, and the high-intermediate groups respectively. The results reveal no significant difference between the three low-intermediate groups ($F(2,65) = 3.075$, $p = .053$), between the three intermediate groups ($F(2,53) = 0.217$, $p = .806$) or between the three high-intermediate groups ($F(2,57) = 2.302$, $p = .109$). This means that groups from different L1s but at the same L2 Chinese proficiency levels are homogeneous, thus making comparisons between different L1 groups possible.

## 5.4 Procedures and Instruments

### 5.4.1 Data-collecting procedures

A pilot study was conducted four months before the main study. It involved 16 English speakers, 13 Japanese speakers and 17 Korean speakers. All the L2 subjects were language students at the University of Foreign Economics and Trade (Beijing). The control group consisted of 12 native speakers. After the pilot study, the testing materials were reviewed and revised for the main study.

The main study was carried out in the following procedures. In the first place, subjects were asked to read general introductions at the front page of the test booklet and provide personal information (see Appendix 1). Following was the cloze test (see Appendix 2). The experiment employed three instruments, i.e. a production test, an acceptability judgment (AJ) test and a comprehension test (see Appendixes 3, 4 and 5). Of the three instruments, the production test was conducted first, followed by the AJ test and the comprehension test respectively. Such an arrangement was to minimize subjects' awareness of what was tested so that their performance could reflect their L2 knowledge without being affected by extralinguistic factors. Each structure in the three tests had three tokens (i.e. testing items, see Appendix 6 for all the testing items used in the empirical study). Distracters were provided in the production test and the AJ test.

In the experiment, instructions were given in the subject's native language to ensure that they would not misunderstand any task. Only words with a high frequency of occurrence based on a frequency table were used in the tests. The frequency table was made by the State Language Work Committee of China on the frequency of occurrence of 3500 modern Chinese characters and was published by Yuwen Press

(Beijing) in 1989. In the tests, content words such as nouns, verbs and adjectives were provided with explanations in the subject's native language so that the effect of new words could be minimized. The explanation was given in a bracket following EACH sentence. At the beginning of each instrument, two examples were provided to illustrate what subjects were expected to do. The testing items and distracters were randomized and presented in two versions in reverse order to control the ordering effect and the fatigue effect.

The experiment was administered and conducted in the classroom. No time limit was set, but most subjects completed the tasks within one hour.

### 5.4.2 Instruments

In SLA studies, different instruments are used for different purposes (see Ellis 1991, Flynn 1986, Hedgcock 1993, Mandell 1999, Nagata 1988, Schachter and Yip 1990, White 1989a, for discussion of the advantages and disadvantages of each instrument). Some researchers (e.g. Crookes 1991; Hulstijn 1997) argue for more than one task in a study so that results attributable to the task itself can be avoided.

To ensure reliability of the experiment, three instruments were used in the present study: a production test, an AJ test and a comprehension test. The AJ test is the main body of the test. It examines L2 Chinese learners' judgments on unaccusative verbs, psych verbs, resultative constructions and compound causative constructions. The production test studies how unaccusative verbs and psych verbs are used in L2 Chinese. The comprehension test looks into L2 learners' interpretation of Chinese resultative and compound causative constructions.

## 5. 4. 2. 1　The production test

The aim of the production test is to find out how non-alternating unaccusative verbs, non-causative psych verbs and analytical causatives are represented in L2 Chinese. Accordingly the three types of structure are tested ( see Appendix 3 for this part in the test paper and Appendix 6 for the testing items).

The task of the production test is sentence making. A set of four words as exemplified in (10) is provided for each possible sentence and subjects are required to form grammatical sentences if possible with the words given. The words provided for a possible psych-verb structure include a human NP ( e. g. *Zhangsan*), an inanimate NP ( e. g. *na ge xiaoxi* 'that news'), a psych verb ( e. g. *xingfen* 'excite') and an aspectual marker *le*. Since Chinese does not allow OE verbs, a sentence like (10a) is ungrammatical. The psych verb provided for each testing item is an intransitive SE verb, so a sentence like (10b) is also ungrammatical. In fact, no grammatical sentence can be formed from the given words. In this case, subjects are required to mark " × " after the given words to indicate the impossibility explicitly, as shown in (10c). Psych verbs used in the three tokens are *xingfen* 'excite', *shengqi* 'anger' and *shiwang* 'disappoint'.

(10) Words: Zhangsan, na ge xiaoxi, le, xingfen
　　　　　　Zhangsan, that CL news, ASP, excite
　　⟹　a. *na ge xiaoxi xingfen le Zhangsan.
　　　　　　that CL news excite ASP Zhangsan
　　　　　　'That news excited Zhangsan. '
　　　　b. *Zhangsan xingfen le na ge xiaoxi.
　　　　　　Zhangsan excite ASP that CL news
　　　　　　*'Zhangsan excited the news. '
　　　　c. ×

For a potential analytical causative, the given words include a human NP (e. g. *Zhangsan*), an inanimate NP (e. g. *na ge xiaoxi* 'that news'), a psych verb (e. g. *xingfen* 'excite') with a modifier *hen* 'very', and the analytical causative marker *shi* 'make', from which a grammatical analytical causative sentence can be formed, as shown in (11). Psych verbs used in the three tokens for potential analytical causatives are *xingfen* 'excite', *shengqi* 'anger' and *shiwang* 'disappoint', which are the same as those used for potential psych-verb sentences. A minor difference is that the psych verb used for a potential analytical causative has a modifier *hen* 'very' to make the formed sentence more natural.

(11) Words: Zhangsan, na ge xiaoxi, hen xingfen, shi
⟹ Zhangsan, that CL news, very excite, *shi*
na ge xiaoxi shi Zhangsan hen xingfen.
that CL news make Zhangsan very excite
'That news made Zhangsan very excited.'

For a potential sentence with an unaccusative verb, the given words include a human NP (e. g. *Zhangsan*), an inanimate NP (e. g. *Lisi de huaping* 'Lisi's vase'), the word *ba* and an unaccusative verb with aspectual marker *le* (e. g. *sui le* 'broke'), as shown in (12). As pointed out in § 2.1.4.2, Chinese unaccusative verbs like *sui* 'break' do not have the CAUSE element. As a result they cannot project a causative VP shell and assign accusative case. Consequently, the potential Theme NP *Lisi de huaping* 'Lisi's vase' in (12) cannot be preposed by *ba*[4] and thus no grammatical sentences can be formed from the given words.[5] Unaccusative verbs used in the three tokens for potential sentences are *sui*, *duan* and *po*, which all mean 'break' roughly.

(12) Words: Lisi de huaping, Zhangsan, sui    le,  ba
           Lisi's vase,    Zhangsan, break ASP, ba
   ⇒    *Zhangsan *ba* Lisi de huaping sui   le.
           Zhangsan  ba Lisi's   vase    break ASP

In the production test, sets of words for the three types of potential sentence are presented in different orders to minimize subjects' awareness of the structures tested. The words in the three tokens for a potential structure are presented in different orders to reduce the effect of word order.

### 5.4.2.2 The acceptability judgment test

The AJ test is widely used in second language acquisition research within the generative framework. It is argued to be a reliable instrument in the test of L2 knowledge (e.g. Mandell 1999) despite being criticized for its decontextualized approach (Selinker 1996) and other potential shortcomings (Birdsong 1989).

The AJ test constitutes the main body of the experiment. It covers the two main areas of the study: the acquisition of Chinese unaccusative verbs and psych verbs, both of which project a single VP rather than a VP shell, and the acquisition of Chinese resultative constructions and compound causative constructions, both of which project a functional category AspP. The aim of the test is to find out how causativity is represented in L2 Chinese, whether L1 transfer happens and persists and whether functional categories can be projected in L2 Chinese grammars.

The AJ test contains 54 testing items and 30 distractors (see Appendix 4 for this part in the test paper and Appendix 6 for the testing items). Each of them is presented as an independent sentence in Chinese characters. For some testing items that contain no more than five characters, a brief context is provided in a bracket to make the sentence sound more natural. At the end of each sentence, there is a continuum scale from "-2" to "+2", standing for "completely unacceptable" and "completely acceptable" respectively. In between are "-1" for "probably unacceptable", "+1" for "probably acceptable" and "0" for "I don't know". The scale is presented in (13):

(13) Continuum scale in the acceptability judgment test

```
-2 ─────── -1 ─────── 0 ─────── +1 ─────── +2
completely   probably                probably      completely
                          I don't know
unacceptable unacceptable             acceptable    acceptable
```

Subjects are asked to judge the acceptability of each sentence and mark their choice on the scale.

In the following subsections, I will present categories used in the AJ test.

### 5.4.2.2.1 Psych verbs and unaccusative verbs in the AJ test

As outlined in Chapter 2, Chinese does not allow OE verbs or alternating unaccusative verbs. The purpose of including these categories in the AJ test is to see whether the non-causativeness of these verbs can be acquired by L2 Chinese learners and whether a single VP can be projected in L2 Chinese grammars.

Three structures as illustrated in (14) are included to test psych verbs in L2 Chinese: A) psych verbs used as SE verbs; B) psych verbs used in analytical causatives; and C) psych verbs misused as OE verbs. Of the three structures, Structures A and B are allowed in Chinese and therefore grammatical, while Structure C is disallowed and ungrammatical. There are three tokens for each structure and psych verbs used in the three tokens of each structure are *gaoxing* 'please', *shengqi* 'anger' and *jingya* 'surprise'.

(14) Psych-verb structures used in the AJ test

    A. Psych verbs used as SE verbs

(Tingdao zhe ge xiaoxi) Zhangsan hen gaoxing.
(hear    this CL news) Zhangsan very please
'(Hearing this news,) Zhangsan was very pleased.'

B. Psych verbs used in analytical causatives
Zhe ge xiaoxi shi Zhangsan hen gaoxing.
this CL news shi Zhangsan very please
'This news made Zhangsan very pleased.'

C. Pysch verbs misused as OE verbs
*Zhe ge xiaoxi gaoxing le    Zhangsan.
this CL news please    ASP Zhangsan
'This news pleased Zhangsan.'

Structure A tests whether subjects have knowledge of the psych verbs under study. For each token of the structure, a context is provided to make the short sentence sound more natural, as exemplified in (14A). Structure B looks into subjects' acquisition of analytical causatives with these psych verbs. Structure C examines whether these psych verbs are treated as causative verbs, i. e. OE verbs.

Three structures of unaccusative verbs are included in the AJ test: A) unaccusative verbs used in a one-argument structure, with the Theme argument occurring at the sentence-initial position as in (15A); B) unaccusative verbs misused as alternating verbs in the active form as in (15Ba); and C) unaccusative verbs misused as alternating verbs in the passive form headed by *bei*[6] as in (15Ca) (see Chu 1973, Ren 1991, Shi 1997, Tang 2001, Ting 1998, for discussion of Chinese passives). Structures B and C contain a human NP as Agent/Causer (e. g. *Zhangsan*), an inanimate definite NP as Theme (e. g. *Lisi de huaping* 'Lisi's vase') and an unaccusative verb (e. g. *sui* 'break'). Such a structure is ungrammatical because unaccusative verbs in Chinese lack the CAUSE component and consequently project a single VP rather than a VP shell. Structures B and C have corresponding control structures which contain a human NP as Agent (e. g. *Zhangsan*), an inanimate NP as Theme (e. g. *Lisi de huaping* 'Lisi's vase') and a transitive verb (e. g. *mai* 'sell'), as in (15Bb) and (15Cb).

(15) Unaccusative structures used in the AJ test
    A. One-argument structure
        Lisi de huaping sui   le.
        Lisi's vase     break ASP
        'Lisi's vase broke. '
    B. Two-argument structure in the active form
        a. Unaccusative verbs misused as alternating verbs (experimental)
        *Zhangsan sui    le   Lisi de huaping.
        Zhangsan break ASP Lisi's vase
        'Zhangsan broke Lisi's vase. '
        b. Transitive structure (control)
        Zhangsan mai le    Lisi de huaping.
        Zhangsan sell ASP Lisi's   vase
        'Zhangsan sold Lisi's vase'.
    C. Two-argument structure in the passive form
        a. Unaccusative verbs misused as alternating verbs (experimental)
        *Lisi de huaping bei    Zhangsan sui le.
        Lisi's vase        PASS Zhangsan break ASP
        'Lisi's vase was broken by Zhangsan. '
        b. Transitive structure (control)
        Lisi de huaping bei    Zhangsan mai le.
        Lisi's vase        PASS Zhangsan sell ASP
        'Lisi's vase was sold by Zhangsan. '

As we can see from the examples, the experimental unaccusative structures and the corresponding transitive control structures differ only in the verb. If any difference is found in a subject's judgment of the two structures, it can be reduced to the use of different types of verb. The active structures (both experimental and control) and their corresponding passive structures form pairs, which differ only in voice.

Why are control structures used in the test? As found in previous studies (e.g. Cabrera and Zubizarreta 2003; Montrul 1999), L2 subjects make causative errors with non-alternating unaccusative verbs. If L2 Chinese learners make causative errors with unaccusative verbs, the experimental alternating unaccusative verbs as in (15Ba) and (15Ca) will have the same representation in L2 grammars as transitive verbs in (15Bb) and (15Cb), at least at earlier developmental stages. Since L2 subjects in the present study are intermediate learners of Chinese, we cannot tell what their initial-state L2 Chinese grammars are like. However, by comparing subjects' judgments on the experimental structures with their judgments on the control structures, we may find out whether L2 learners are able to distinguish syntactically between the two types of verb without the help of causative affixes or case markers that are absent in Chinese. Since Japanese and Korean have both causative affixes and case markers, another purpose of comparison between judgments on the two types of verb is to find out the effect of L1 morphological properties on the acquisition of certain L2 structures.

5.4.2.2.2 Resultative and compound causative constructions in the AJ test

Purposes of including resultative and compound causative constructions in the AJ test are: 1) to see whether English speakers can acquire Chinese resultatives, which are different from English resultatives in syntactic structure, and compound causatives, which do not exist in English; 2) to find out whether L1 transfer occurs in Japanese and Korean speakers' L2 Chinese grammars and in what way if it does; 3) to see whether the acquisition of different types of compound causative occurs at the same time or exhibits a hierarchy in terms of acquisition order; and 4) to find out whether resultatives are easier to acquire due to the existence of the explicit resultative marker *de*.

Three types of resultative constructions are included in the AJ test, which are illustrated in (16):

(16) Resultative constructions used in the AJ test
    A. Unergative $V_1$
        Zhangsan <u>ku</u> de shoujuan     dou *shi*   le.
        Zhangsan cry *de* handkerchief even soggy ASP
        'Zhangsan cried the handkerchief soggy.'
    B. Psych verb $V_1$
        Zhangsan <u>gaoxing</u> de *you  chang you tiao.*
        Zhangsan please  *de* both sing   and dance
        'Zhangsan was so pleased that he both sang and danced.'
    C. Type B used in analytical causative headed by *shi*
        Zhe ge xiaoxi shi Zhangsan <u>gaoxing</u> de *you chang you tiao.*
        this CL news *shi* Zhangsan please *de* both sing and dance
        'This news made Zhangsan so pleased that he both sang and danced.'

In Structure A, the main predicate $V_1$ (e.g. *ku* 'cry') is an unergative verb while the result predicate $V_2$ is an adjective (e.g. *shi* 'wet') and the resultative marker *de* is followed by a clause (e.g. *shoujuan dou shi le* 'handkerchief got wet') in the surface structure. In Structure B, the main predicate $V_1$ is a psych verb (e.g. *gaoxing* 'please') and *de* is followed by a result VP (e.g. *you chang you tiao* 'both sing and dance'). Structure C is an extension of Structure

B with a projection of the analytical causative construction.

Type A ( e. g. *ku de...shi* ' cry *de...* wet ' ) has a compound causative counterpart ( e. g. *ku-shi* ' cry-wet ' ) ( see ( 18C ) ). Comparison between results on the resultative and results on the corresponding compound causative may tell us whether learners acquire the two structures at the same time or whether the acquisition of one is easier than that of the other. Comparison will also be made between results on Structure A of the resultative construction and results on the incorrect resultative structure without *de* ( i. e. the V-NP-XP structure as found in English resultatives) as shown in (17). If the two structures are treated differently, the difference can only be reduced to the presence of *de* in one structure but absence of *de* in the other.

(17) Resultative construction without *de* (i. e. the V-NP-XP structure)
  *Zhangsan ku shoujuan    dou  shi le.
  Zhangsan cry handkerchief even wet ASP
  ' Zhangsan cried the handkerchief soggy. '

Six types of compound causatives as exemplified in (18) are included in the AJ test. They are classified into three groups in terms of the nature of $V_1$ or $V_2$.

(18) Compound causative constructions used in the AJ test
  *Group* 1. *Transitive* $V_1$ :
    A. Unaccusative $V_2$
      Zhangsan da-*sui*    le   Lisi de huaping.
      Zhangsan hit-break ASP Lisi's vase
      ' Zhangsan broke Lisi's vase. '
      ( $V_1 = da$ ' hit ' , $V_2 = sui$ ' break ' )
    B. Unergative $V_2$
      Zhangsan ma-*ku*    le   Lisi.

Zhangsan scold-cry ASP Lisi
'Zhangsan scolded Lisi and Lisi cried.'
($V_1 = ma$ 'scold', $V_2 = ku$ 'cry')

**Group 2. Unergative $V_1$**

C. Adjective $V_2$

Zhangsan ku-*shi*　le　shoujuan.
Zhangsan cry-wet ASP handkerchief
'Zhangsan cried the handkerchief soggy.'
($V_1 = ku$ 'cry', $V_2 = shi$ 'wet')

D. Psych verb $V_2$

Zhangsan ku-*fan*　le　Lisi.
Zhangsan cry-bore ASP Lisi
'Zhangsan cried and Lisi got bored as a result.'
($V_1 = ku$ 'cry', $V_2 = fan$ 'bore')

**Group 3. Transitive $V_1$ + Psych verb $V_2$**

E. Inanimate $NP_2$

Zhangsan ting-*fan*　le　na shou ge.
Zhangsan listen-bore ASP that CL song
'Zhangsan listened to that song (time and again) and got bored.'
($V_1 = ting$ 'listen', $V_2 = fan$ 'bore', $NP_2 = na\ shou\ ge$ 'that song')

F. Animate/human $NP_2$

Zhangsan zhui-*lei*　le　Lisi.
Zhangsan chase-tire ASP Lisi
(i) 'Zhangsan chased Lisi and Lisi got tired as a result.'
(ii) 'Zhangsan chased Lisi and got tired.'
($V_1 = zhui$ 'chase', $V_2 = lei$ 'tire', $NP_2 = Lisi$)

Group 1 contains two structures of compound causative constructions, A and B. In both structures the activity predicate $V_1$ is transitive (e. g. *da* 'hit' in (18A) and *ma* 'scold' in (18B)), but the result predicate is unaccusative (e. g. *sui* 'break' in (18A)) or unergative

(e. g. *ku* 'cry' in (18B)). $V_1$ is predicated of $NP_1$, i.e. the sentence subject like *Zhangsan*, while $V_2$ is predicated of $NP_2$ like *Lisi de huaping* 'Lisi's vase' in (18A) and *Lisi* in (18B). The two structures have semantic representations as shown in (19), in which $x$ and $y$ represent $NP_1$ and $NP_2$ respectively:

(19) Type A:
 [[$x$ DO SOMETHING TO $y$] CAUSE [$y$ BECOME STATE]]
Type B:
 [[$x$ DO SOMETHING TO $y$] CAUSE [$y$ DO SOMEHTING]]

Group 2 contains two structures, C and D. In both structures the activity predicate $V_1$ is unergative (e. g. *ku* 'cry'), while the result predicate $V_2$ is an adjective (e. g. *shi* 'wet' in (18C)) or psych verb (e. g. *fan* 'bore' in (18D)). The two structures have the same semantic representation as shown in (20), in which $x$ and $y$ represent $NP_1$ and $NP_2$:

(20) Type C and D:
 [[$x$ DO SOMETHING] CAUSE [$y$ BECOME STATE]]

Group 3 contains Type E and Type F. In the two structures the activity predicate is transitive (e. g. *ting* 'listen to' in (18E) and *zhui* 'chase' in (18F)), while the result predicate is a psych verb (e. g. *fan* 'bore' in (18E) and *lei* 'tire' in (18F)). In terms of $NP_2$, it is inanimate in Type E (e. g. *na shou ge* 'that song') but animate or human in Type F (e. g. *Lisi*). The difference in the animacy of $NP_2$ results in the interpretational difference between the two structures: in Type E, the psych verb (e. g. *fan* 'bore') cannot be predicated of the inanimate $NP_2$ (e. g. *na shou ge* 'that song') and can only form a predication relation with $NP_1$ (e. g. *Zhangsan*); in Type F, however, the psych verb (e. g. *lei* 'tire') can be predicated of both $NP_1$ (e. g. *Zhangsan*) and $NP_2$ (e. g. *Lisi*), thus generating ambiguous readings.

The two structures have semantic representations as illustrated in (21):

(21) Type E:
   [[xDO SOMETHING TO y]CAUSE[x/*y BECOME STATE]]
   Type F:
   [[xDO SOMETHING TO y]CAUSE[x/y BECOME STATE]]

Through the AJ test I intend to find out whether the functional category AspP can be projected in L2 Chinese grammars and whether different types of compound causative constructions can be acquired at the same time and, if they are not, which type is acquired earlier than others.

### 5.4.2.3 The comprehension test

The purpose of the comprehension test is to find out the semantic representations of resultatives and compound causatives in L2 Chinese grammars. Two resultative constructions and one compound causative construction are used in the test, as illustrated in (22) and (23). In each of the three structures, $NP_1$ and $NP_2$ are both animate/human NPs like *Zhangsan* and *Lisi* in the examples. $V_1$ is a transitive verb like *zhui* 'chase', while $V_2$ is a psych verb like *lei* 'tire'.

(22) Resultative constructions used in the comprehension test
   A. Resultative with single $V_1$
      Zhangsan zhui de Lisi dou lei le.
      Zhangsan chase *de* Lisi even tire ASP
      'Zhangsan chased Lisi and Lisi got tired as a result.'
      ($V_1$ = *zhui* 'chase', $V_2$ = *lei* 'tire')
   B. Resultative with reduplicated $V_1$
      Zhangsan zhui Lisi zhui de dou lei le.
      Zhangsan chase Lisi chase *de* even tire ASP

'Zhangsan chased Lisi and got tired as a result. '
($V_1 = zhui$ 'chase', $V_2 = lei$ 'tire')
(23) Compound causative construction used in the comprehension test
(Type F in the AJ test)
Zhangsan zhui-*lei*　le　Lisi.
Zhangsan chase-tire ASP Lisi
(i) 'Zhangsan chased Lisi and got tired as a result. '
(ii) 'Zhangsan chased Lisi and Lisi got tired as a result. '
($V_1 = zhui$ 'chase', $V_2 = lei$ 'tire')

The two resultative constructions in the comprehension test differ in that one structure contains a single $V_1$ as in (22A) but the other a reduplicated $V_1$ as in (22B). Each token in one construction has a corresponding token in the other construction and the only difference between the two tokens lies in whether $V_1$ is reduplicated or not, as shown in (22A) and (22B). Since all the lexical items in a token of one construction are the same as those in the corresponding token of the other construction, any difference in subjects' interpretation of the two constructions can be attributed to the (un)reduplication of $V_1$. The two constructions have different meanings as indicated in the translation because they involve different syntactic operations (see § 3.2.2.1).

The compound causative construction used in the comprehension test is Type F of the compound causative used in the AJ test (see (18F)). This construction allows ambiguous readings because the result element can be predicated of either $NP_1$ or $NP_2$ (i.e. *Zhangsan* and *Lisi* respectively in the exemplar token) (see § 3.2.2.2, in particular (50) in Chapter 3, for the syntactic derivation).

The comprehension task is a multiple-choice test. Each sentence is followed by a question and five options, A, B, C, D and E. Of the five options, A stands for "the sentence is ungrammatical" and E for "I don't know". Options B, C and D concern which argument the result predicate assigns a θ-role to. Let us take the compound causative in (23) as an example. Option B stands for a situation in which the result predicate (i.e. *lei* 'tire') assigns a θ-role to NP$_1$ (i.e. *Zhangsan*); Option C stands for a situation in which the result predicate (i.e. *lei* 'tire') assigns a θ-role to NP$_2$ (i.e. *Lisi*); Option D stands for ambiguous readings in which the result predicate (i.e. *lei* 'tire') assigns a θ-role either to NP$_1$ (i.e. *Zhangsan*) or NP$_2$ (i.e. *Lisi*). The question and five options are illustrated in (24):

(24) Zhangsan zhui-*lei*　le　Lisi.
　　Zhangsan chase-tire ASP Lisi

　　*Question*: *Shui lei le* (*who got tired*)?
　　A) The sentence is ungrammatical.
　　B) 'Zhangsan got tired'.
　　C) 'Lisi got tired'.
　　D) 'Either Zhangsan or Lisi got tired'.
　　E) I don't know.

Each token of the resultative constructions and the compound causative construction in the comprehension test is presented in three ways. Take the token of the compound causative construction in (23) again as an example. First, it is presented as an independent sentence without contextual clues, as shown in (25). Second, it is presented in a pictorial context that is biased toward Option B (i.e. "Zhangsan got tired"), as shown in (26). Third, it is presented in a pictorial context that is biased toward Option C (i.e. "Lisi got tired"), as shown in (27) (see Appendix 5 for the pictures used in the comprehension test and Appendix 6 for the testing items).

(25) Tokens presented as independent sentences without contextual clues
　　Zhangsan zhui-*lei*　le　Lisi.

Zhangsan chase-tire ASP Lisi
Question: *Shui lei le* (*who got tired*)?
A) The sentence is ungrammatical.
B) 'Zhangsan got tired'.
C) 'Lisi got tired'.
D) 'Either Zhangsan or Lisi got tired'.
E) I don't know.

(26) Tokens presented in a pictorial context biased toward Option B
Zhangsan zhui-*lei* le Lisi.
Zhangsan chase-tire ASP Lisi

Question: *Shui lei le* (*who got tired*)?
A) The sentence is ungrammatical.
B) 'Zhangsan got tired'.
C) 'Lisi got tired'.
D) 'Either Zhangsan or Lisi got tired'.
E) I don't know.

(27) Tokens presented in a pictorial context biased toward Option C
Zhangsan zhui-*lei* le Lisi,
Zhangsan chase-tire ASP Lisi

# 5 Research methodology of the present study

Question: *Shui lei le (who got tired)*?
A) The sentence is ungrammatical.
B) 'Zhangsan got tired'.
C) 'Lisi got tired'.
D) 'Either Zhangsan or Lisi got tired'.
E) I don't know.

As we can see in (25), (26) and (27), each token appears in three different ways. Of the three structures in the comprehension test, the two resultative constructions exemplified in (22) are unambiguous irrespective of the contexts in which they occur. In contrast, the compound causative construction illustrated in (23) has ambiguous readings, which may be influenced by the context.

The two resultative constructions and the compound causative construction in the comprehension test have altogether nine tokens (3 tokens × 3 structures). The testing items are arranged as follows. First, the nine tokens are randomised and presented as independent sentences without contextual clues. Then, they are presented in the two pictorial contexts.

The picture judgment test is a commonly used instrument in SLA studies (e.g. Juffs 1996b; Hirakawa 1995; Montrul 1999, 2000, 2001a, 2001b, 2001c; White et al 1998; White et al 1999) and is believed to be a reliable way of tapping L2 learners' knowledge. The purpose of presenting the two resultative and one compound causative in different ways is to find out how L2 Chinese learners interpret these constructions and whether pictorial contexts have an impact on their interpretation.

## 5.5 Summary

In this chapter, I first summarized representations of causativity in Chinese, English, Japanese and Korean. On the basis of different causative representations in the four languages, I proposed research questions and hypotheses in the present study. Then I presented a description of the empirical study, including participants, procedures and instruments. In the following chapters, results of the empirical study will be presented and discussed.

## Notes

[1] The minimum time for studying Chinese and living in a Chinese-speaking environment (i.e. staying in Mainland China or Taiwan) set for L2 subjects in the present study is eight months and three months respectively. The criterion is arbitrary, but it is believed that L2 subjects who meet the two conditions have had contact with the structures tested in the experiment.

[2] The two passages used in the cloze test are both established ones: the first was used by Yuan in his research on L2 Chinese acquisition (e.g. Yuan 1999, 2001), while the second is adapted from an IGCSE Chinese paper (Edexcel 2000).

[3] In the present study, the Scheffé test is used in one-way ANOVA post hoc multiple comparisons. The reason for using this test is that it is the most conservative in the sense that it is least likely to find significant differences between groups and that it is exact for unequal numbers of subjects in the groups (Bryman and Cramer 1999).

[4] According to Y.-H. Li (1990) and Chao (1968), *ba* is a preposition, which can prepose an accusative-case assigned NP, as in (i):

(i) a. Zhangsan mai le zixingche.
   Zhangsan sell ASP bicycle
   'Zhangsan sold his bicycle.'
   b. Zhangsan *ba* zixingche mai le.
   Zhangsan *ba* bicycle sell ASP
   'Zhangsan sold his bicycle.'

In (ia), the NP *zixingche* 'bicycle' is the Theme and is assigned accusative case, therefore it can be preposed by *ba*.

[5] It is believed that L2 subjects who meet the two conditions of selection (i.e. studying Chinese for eight months and living in Chinese-speaking environment for three months) have studied the *ba*-structure. Thus, their responses can be attributed to the unaccusative verbs rather than to the *ba*-structure.

[6] It is believed that L2 subjects in the present study have learned Chinese passive structures.

# 6 Results and discussion: psych verbs and unaccusative verbs

**导言**

　　本章和第七章是对试验结果的描述、分析和讨论,本章主要针对试验中有关非宾格动词和心理动词的习得情况。汉语中,这两类动词都没有使动用法,这部分试验的目的在于考察汉语学习者能否掌握它们的非使动特征、它们在中介语中是否具有同样表征。从可接受性判断测试和产出测试结果来看,不同母语背景的汉语学习者能够掌握由"使"引导的分析型使动结构,能够掌握心理动词的非使动特征。不过,在汉语非宾格动词的习得上,使动错误经常出现,而且这类动词在中介语中的表征也没有随着学习者汉语水平的提高而有所发展,这种僵化现象在母语为日语和韩语的学习者身上表现尤为明显。

　　心理动词和非宾格动词的习得为什么呈现这么大的差异? 作者认为,非宾格动词被误用作使动动词后,其语义结构与使动模块相一致,因此学习者很难将这类动词与使动动词区分开,容易产生使动错误。而心理动词被误用作使动动词后,其语义结构与使动模块不一致,因此学习者容易辨别这一类使动错误。为什么母语为日语和韩语的汉语学习者在非宾格动词习得上会出现僵化现象呢? 作者认为,这很可能与日语、韩语多形态变化而汉语缺乏形态变化有关。在没有形态标记的情况下,汉语学习者不能从语法关系上对句子做出正确判断。这表明,第一语言迁移受制于两种语言的形态变化。第一语言有丰富的形态变化而第二语言没有,会增加习得难度,甚至会导致僵化现象的产生。

# Results and discussion: psych verbs and unaccusative verbs

In this chapter, I will present results of the experiment on Chinese unaccusative verbs and psych verbs to see whether L2 Chinese learners can acquire the non-causative nature of these verbs and project a single VP in their L2 Chinese grammars. Results of psych verbs and unaccusative verbs in the AJ test and the production test will be presented in § 6.1 and § 6.2 respectively, followed by comparisons between results on the two types of verbs in § 6.3 and discussion in § 6.4.

## 6.1 Psych verbs

As outlined in Chapter 2, Chinese allows SE psych verbs but disallows OE psych verbs. Syntactically, Chinese psych verbs project a single VP rather than a VP shell. When causation is expressed with psych verbs, the analytical causative structure headed by *shi* 'make' is used. As in Chinese, OE verbs are disallowed in Japanese and Korean. When causation is to be expressed, causative affixes must be used in the two languages. Unlike Chinese, Japanese and Korean, English allows both SE verbs and OE verbs. OE verbs in English project a VP shell where the psych verb undergoes head movement from the lower VP to the upper $v$P.

In this section, results of the AJ test and the production test on psych verbs will be reported. As pointed out in § 5.2, purposes of these tests are to find out whether L1 transfer happens and whether learners can project a single VP rather than a VP shell in their L2 Chinese grammars concerning psych verbs. Given that OE verbs are allowed in English but disallowed in Chinese, Japanese and Korean, it is hypothesized that English-speaking learners of Chinese may make more causative errors with psych verbs and have more difficulty projecting a single VP than Japanese- and Korean-speaking learners in their L2 Chinese grammars if L1 transfer happens and L1 effect lasts. Due to existence of causative morphemes in the four languages, it is also hypothesized that L2 learners will not have much difficulty with the analytical causative construction in Chinese. We will see whether these hypotheses are borne out by the results.

### 6.1.1 Results of the AJ test

As stated in § 5.4.2.2.1, three types of structures involving psych verbs were tested in the AJ test: a) intransitive SE verbs that only select Experiencer as sentence subject; b) psych verbs used in analytical causatives; and c) psych verbs incorrectly used as OE verbs. Examples of the three types of structures are given in (1), repeated from (14) of Chapter 5.

(1) The three types of psych-verb structures used in the AJ test
    a. Intransitive SE verbs used in a one-argument structure
      (Tingdao zhe ge xiaoxi) Zhangsan hen gaoxing.
      (hear    this CL news) Zhangsan very please
      '(Hearing this news,) Zhangsan was very pleased.'
    b. Psych verbs used in analytical causatives
      Zhe ge xiaoxi shi Zhangsan hen gaoxing.
      this CL news *shi* Zhangsan veryplease
      'This news made Zhangsan very pleased.'
    c. Psych verbs misused as OE verbs
      *Zhe ge xiaoxi gaoxing le   Zhangsan.
      this CL news please   ASP Zhangsan
      'This news pleased Zhangsan.'

# 6 Results and discussion: psych verbs and unaccusative verbs

The mean scores of each group in judging the three structures are illustrated in Figure 6.1[1] (see Tables 1, 2 and 3 in Appendix 7 for descriptive statistics):

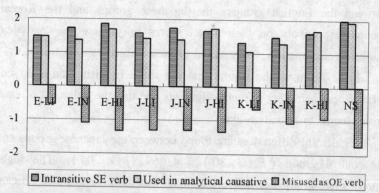

Figure 6.1 Psych-verb structures: mean scores in the AJ test

Recall that a 5-point scale from "-2" to "+2" is used in the AJ test. If we take "+1" and above as a sign of acceptance while "-1" and below as a sign of rejection, we will find that all the groups accept psych verbs when they are used in one-argument sentences as SE verbs as in (1a) or when they are used in analytical causatives as in (1b), indicating that learners do not have problems with these verbs or with the analytical causative construction. All the learner groups show degrees of rejection to the incorrect OE-verb structure: the intermediate and high-intermediate English groups, the three Japanese groups and the intermediate Korean group reject it (mean score $\leqslant -1$), while the low-intermediate English group, the low-intermediate and high-intermediate Korean groups tend to reject it (mean score ranging between -1 and 0).

Next, I will compare results on the analytical causative structure and the OE-verb structure between learner groups to see whether the hypotheses are confirmed.

### 6.1.1.1 Psych verbs used in the analytical causative construction

One-way ANOVA and following Scheffé tests were conducted between the English groups, the Japanese groups and the Korean groups respectively on their mean scores in judging the analytical causative construction, with native Chinese subjects as controls.

It is shown in the results that the three English groups do not differ from each other in their judgments and that the judgment of each group seems to be native-like.[2]

Significant differences are found between the Japanese groups and the control group ($F(3, 80) = 4.669$, $p < .05$). The high-intermediate group has native-like judgment as there is no significant difference between this group and the control group. However, both the low-intermediate group and the intermediate group differ significantly from the control group ($p = .049$ and $p = .019$ respectively). No significant difference is found between the three Japanese groups.

Significant differences are also found between the Korean groups and the control group ($F(3,97) = 7.020$, $p < .001$). While the three Korean groups do not differ from each other, the low-intermediate group and the intermediate group differ significantly from the control group ($p = .001$ and $p = .033$ respectively). The judgment of the high-intermediate Korean group seems to be native-like.

Comparisons are also made between groups from different L1s but at the same Chinese proficiency levels. One-way ANOVA tests reveal no significant difference between the low-intermediate groups ($F(2,65) = 2.155$, $p = .124$), between the intermediate groups ($F(2,53) = 0.056$, $p = .946$) or between the high-intermediate groups ($F(2,57) = 0.047$, $p = .955$), which seems to suggest that learners' L1s are irrelevant to the development of the L2 Chinese analytical causative construction.

Results of the AJ test indicate that L2 Chinese learners can acquire the analytical causative construction at least at the high-intermediate stage and that L2 Chinese groups of different L1s follow a similar pace in their acquisition of this construction.

### 6.1.1.2 Psych verbs misused as OE verbs

One-way ANOVA and pair-wise Scheffé tests were conducted on the mean scores of the incorrectly used OE verb as in (1c) between the English, Japanese and Korean groups respectively, each with the native Chinese group as a control.

Significant differences are found between the English groups ($F(3,79) = 11.831$, $p < .001$). The judgment of the low-intermediate group differs significantly from that of the high-intermediate group ($p = .015$). No significant difference is found between the low-intermediate and intermediate groups ($p = .195$) or between the intermediate and high-intermediate groups ($p = .874$). Both the intermediate and the high-intermediate English groups seem to have native-like judgment ($p = .097$ and $p = .392$ respectively), but the low-intermediate group does not ($p < .001$).

No significant difference is found between the Japanese groups and the control group ($F(3,80) = 2.411$, $p = .073$). The three Japanese groups all have native-like judgments on these Chinese verbs. They reject sentences where Chinese psych verbs are incorrectly used as OE verbs at the three developmental stages under examination.

The three Korean groups do not differ from each other in their judgments of the incorrect OE-verb structure, but significant difference is found between Korean groups and the control group ($F(3,97) = 7.142$, $p < .001$): the low-intermediate group and the high-intermediate group differ significantly from the control group

($p < .001$ and $p < .05$ respectively), but the intermediate Korean group has native-like judgment.

Now let us find out whether there are variations between groups from different L1s but at the same Chinese proficiency levels in judging the incorrect OE-verb structure. One-way ANOVA tests reveal no significant difference between the intermediate groups ($F(2,53) = 0.395$, $p = .676$) or the high-intermediate groups ($F(2,57) = 1.305$, $p = .279$), but the three low-intermediate groups differ significantly ($F(2,65) = 3.742$, $p < .05$). Pair-wise Scheffé tests reveal significant difference between the English group and the Japanese group ($p = .037$) at the low-intermediate stage.

As pointed out in Chapter 2, English allows OE verbs while Chinese does not. If the Full Transfer/Full Access Hypothesis (Schwartz 1998; Schwartz and Sprouse 1994, 1996) is on the right track, English-speaking learners will transfer the causative structure of OE verbs into Chinese and project a VP shell in the initial-state L2 Chinese grammar. Since our subjects are intermediate (including low-intermediate, intermediate and high-intermediate) learners of Chinese, we cannot determine whether L1 transfer happens at the initial stage of L2 Chinese acquisition. What we do find in the test results is that the incorrect OE-verb structure is more acceptable to English-speaking learners than to Japanese-speaking learners at the low-intermediate stage. From the results, we may postulate that L1 transfer happens in English-speaking learners' initial-state L2 Chinese grammars and that the difference between English and Japanese speakers at the low-intermediate stage is a sign of L1 effect.

### 6.1.2 Results of the production test

Two types of structures involving psych verbs were tested in the production test: psych verbs used in the analytical causative construction and psych verbs incorrectly used as OE verbs.

### 6.1.2.1 Psych verbs used in the analytical causative construction

Recall that a set of four words was given for each potential sentence in the production test and that subjects were required to use all the given words to form a grammatical sentence. A set of four words provided for a potential analytical causative structure includes a psych verb[3] (e. g. *hen xingfen* 'very excited'), a human NP (e. g. *Zhangsan*), an inanimate NP (e. g. *na ge xiaoxi* 'that news') and the analytical causative marker *shi* 'make', from which a grammatical analytical causative sentence can be formed (e. g. *na ge xiaoxi shi Zhangsan hen xingfen* 'That news made Zhangsan very excited') (see Example (11) of Chapter 5). The number of grammatical analytical causatives formed and its percentage out of the total number of sentences formed are given in Table 6.1. The number of consistent subjects who formed such sentences and its percentage out of the total number of subjects in each group are also given in Table 6.1. Here, a consistent subject refers to one who formed three grammatical analytical causative sentences out of the three sets of words provided.

As shown in Table 6.1, more than 60 percent of the sentences formed are grammatical analytical causative sentences in all the learner groups and more than half of the learners consistently formed grammatical analytical causative sentences. It is also shown that the percentage of grammatical sentences and that of consistent subjects rise with the increase in subjects' L2 Chinese proficiency. More than 80 percent of the sentences formed by high-intermediate learners are grammatical analytical causatives and more than 70 percent of these learners are consistent subjects.

Table 6.1 The number and percentage of grammatical analytical causative sentences formed and consistent subjects who formed such sentences in the production test

| Subject groups | Grammatical analytic causatives | | Consistent subjects | |
| --- | --- | --- | --- | --- |
| | N | % | N | % |
| English LI (26) | 53 | 68 | 14 | 54 |
| English IN (13) | 29 | 74 | 8 | 62 |
| English HI (16) | 41 | 85 | 13 | 81 |
| Japanese LI (23) | 34 | 76 | 9 | 60 |
| Japanese IN (18) | 46 | 85 | 12 | 67 |
| Japanese HI (15) | 68 | 99 | 22 | 96 |
| Korean LI (27) | 57 | 70 | 15 | 56 |
| Korean IN (25) | 55 | 73 | 14 | 56 |
| Korean HI (21) | 53 | 84 | 16 | 76 |
| Native control (28) | 84 | 100 | 28 | 100 |

Note: The total number of sentences formed in each group = number of subjects × 3

The result of the production test was transformed into numerical data with " +1" for each grammatical analytical causative formed and "0" for other cases. The mean scores of each subject group from the transformed data are presented in Figure 6.2.

One-way ANOVA and pair-wise Scheffé tests were conducted on the mean scores of the transformed data between the English groups, the Japanese groups and the Korean groups respectively, with the native group as a control. Significant differences are found between the English groups and the control group ($F(3, 79) = 4.413$, $p < .05$): the three English groups do not differ from each other, but the low-intermediate English group differs significantly from the control group ($p = .006$); the results of the intermediate and high-intermediate English groups are native-like.

# 6 Results and discussion: psych verbs and unaccusative verbs

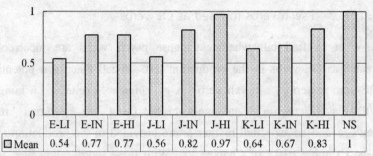

Figure 6. 2 *Analytical causative construction: mean scores of the transformed data in the production test*

Significant differences are found between the Japanese groups and the control group ($F(3,80) = 6.294, p < .05$): the low-intermediate group differs significantly from the high-intermediate group ($p = .006$) and the control group ($p = .002$), but no significant difference is found between other groups.

Significant differences are also found between the Korean groups and the control group ($F(3,97) = 4.802, p < .05$): the low-intermediate group and the intermediate group differ significantly from the control group ($p = .013$ and $p = .028$ respectively), but the result of the high-intermediate group is native-like; the three Korean groups do not differ significantly from each other.

One-way ANOVA tests were also conducted on the transformed data to see whether there were any variations between L2 groups from different L1s but at the same Chinese proficiency levels. The results reveal no significant difference between the low-intermediate groups ($F(2,65) = 0.196, p = .822$), between the intermediate groups ($F(2,53) = 0.790, p = .459$), or between the high-intermediate groups ($F(2,57) = 1.718, p = .189$).

The results of the production test concerning the analytical causative construction roughly match the results of the AJ test. Both suggest that L2 Chinese learners can acquire the analytical causative construction.

## 6.1.2.2 Psych verbs misused as OE verbs

Let us find out whether Chinese psych verbs are incorrectly treated as OE verbs in the production test. Recall that for a potential OE-verb sentence, a psych verb (e. g. *xingfen* 'excite'), a human NP (e. g. *Zhangsan*), an inanimate NP (e. g. *na ge xiaoxi* 'that news') and an aspectual marker *le* are provided in the production test (see Example (10) of Chapter 5). With these words, however, no grammatical sentence can be formed because Chinese does not allow OE verbs (*\* Na ge xiaoxi xingfen le Zhangsan* 'That news excited Zhangsan') and because the given psych verb is intransitive (*\* Zhangsan xingfen le na ge xiaoxi* '(literally) Zhangsan excited that news').

Three types of structures in the production test were counted: a) formation rejected (FR), where subjects indicate explicitly by drawing "×" that no grammatical sentence can be formed; b) the given psych verb (e. g. *xingfen* 'excite') incorrectly used as an OE verb (*\* Na ge xiaoxi xingfen le Zhangsan* 'That news excited Zhangsan'); c) the given psych verb (e. g. *xingfen* 'excite') incorrectly used as a transitive SE verb (*\* Zhangsan xingfen le na ge xiaoxi* '(literally) Zhangsan excited that news'). Table 6.2 presents the number and percentage of the three structures counted. Other structures formed are irrelevant to the study and are therefore ignored.

Table 6.2 *Psych verbs: the number and percentage of three types of structure formed and subjects who consistently formed such structures in the production test*

| Subject groups | Structures formed | | | Consistent subjects | | |
|---|---|---|---|---|---|---|
| | FR | * As OE | * As trans | FR | * As OE | * As trans |
| LI(26) | 51(65%) | 14(18%) | 9(12%) | 11(42%) | 1(3%) | 1(3%) |
| English IN (13) | 29(74%) | 6(15%) | 1(3%) | 9(69%) | 1(8%) | 0 |
| HI (1) | 39(81%) | 8(17%) | 1(2%) | 12(75%) | 0 | 0 |

# 6 Results and discussion: psych verbs and unaccusative verbs

| Subject groups | | Structures formed | | | Consistent subjects | | |
|---|---|---|---|---|---|---|---|
| | | FR | *As OE | *As trans | FR | *As OE | *As trans |
| | LI (15) | 18 (40%) | 0 | 25(56%) | 4(27%) | 0 | 5(33%) |
| Japanese | IN (18) | 24(44%) | 8(15%) | 22(41%) | 5(28%) | 1(6%) | 2(11%) |
| | HI (23) | 43 (62%) | 8(12%) | 16(23%) | 11(48%) | 0 | 2(9%) |
| | LI (27) | 49 (60%) | 5 (6%) | 15 (19%) | 12 (44%) | 1(4%) | 2(8%) |
| Korean | IN (25) | 44 (59%) | 7 (9%) | 22 (29%) | 11(44%) | 1(4%) | 4(16%) |
| | HI (21) | 53 (84%) | 3 (5%) | 6 (10%) | 14 (67%) | 0 | 0 |
| Native control(28) | | 83(99%) | 1 1 | 0 | 27(96%) | 0 | 0 |

Note: The total number of tokens in each group = number of subjects × 3.

As seen from Table 6.2, more than 40 percent of possible formations are rejected and less than 20 percent of incorrect OE-verb sentences are formed in all the learner groups. The English groups make more incorrect OE-verb sentences than the corresponding Japanese and Korean groups. In terms of consistent subjects, the percentage of Japanese groups indicating explicitly the impossibility of making grammatical sentences from the given words is lower than that of the corresponding English and Korean groups. At the same time, Japanese- and Korean-speaking learners make more ungrammatical sentences with psych verbs as transitive SE verbs. At the high-intermediate stage, none of the L2 Chinese learners from any of the three L1s forms OE-verb sentences consistently.

Why are Japanese- and Korean-speaking learners more likely to use intransitive psych verbs as transitive ones? Both Japanese and Korean allow dative-subject constructions (e.g. Sugioka 1985). In the case of psych verbs, a dative-case-marked Experiencer argument can occur at the sentence-initial position,[4] as shown in (2a) (from Sugioka 1985: 156). According to Ura (1999: 234), psych verbs that can be used in dative-subject constructions project a VP shell, as illustrated in (2b). In this structure, the light verb $v$ has a static meaning and does not trigger syntactic movement.

(2) a. Taroo-ni    hebi-ga    kowa-i. (Japanese)
   Taroo-DAT snake-NOM fearful-PRES
   'Taroo is fearful of snakes.'
   b. ($_{vP}$ Experiencer-DAT ($_{VP}$ Theme ($V_{V'}$)$_{v'}$))

If Ura's proposal is correct, then Japanese- and Korean-speaking learners may project a VP shell for Chinese psych verbs. As Chinese does not have case markers, the Experiencer argument that occurs at the sentence-initial position may be taken as being marked with abstract dative case. An ungrammatical sentence like *Zhangsan xingfen le na ge xiaoxi* '(literally) Zhangsan excited that news' is thus derived provided the headedness direction of VP is reset from the L1 value (i.e. OV) to the Chinese value (i.e. VO).

The information provided in Table 6.2 is descriptive, which does not tell us whether significant differences exist between groups at different Chinese proficiency levels or between groups from different L1s. In order to discover possible significant differences between learner groups, I transformed the results of the production test into numerical data, with " + 1 " for each token where any possible formation is rejected, "-1" for each token where an ungrammatical OE-verb structure is formed and "0" for other cases. The mean scores of the transformed data in each group are presented in Figure 6.3.

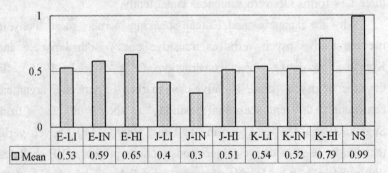

*Figure* 6.3 *Psych verbs*: *mean scores of the transformed data in the production test*

## 6 Results and discussion: psych verbs and unaccusative verbs

One-way ANOVA and pair-wise Scheffé tests were conducted on the mean scores of the transformed data between the English groups, the Japanese groups and the Korean groups respectively, with the native group as a control. Significant differences are found between the English groups and the control group ($F(3,79) = 4.534, p < .05$): the three English groups do not differ from each other, but the low-intermediate group differs significantly from the control group ($p = .011$); the results of the intermediate and high-intermediate English groups do not show any significant difference from the result of the control group. The result of the production test on OE verbs roughly matches that of the AJ test.

Significant differences are found between the Japanese groups and the control group ($F(3, 80) = 15.006, p < .001$). Pair-wise comparisons indicate that the three Japanese groups do not differ significantly from each other, but they all differ from the control group significantly (J-LI vs. NS, $p < .001$; J-IN vs. NS, $p < .001$; J-HI vs. NS, $p < .05$). Recall that no significant difference was found in the AJ test either between the three Japanese groups or between the Japanese groups and the control group (see § 6.1.1). The discrepancy between the AJ test results and the production test results seems to suggest that instruments of the experiment play a role in L2 learners' performance. In fact, however, results of the two tests are not contradictory. In the AJ test, learners were asked to judge the OE-verb structure only, while in the production test they had freedom to form sentences in their own way. Since rejection of the OE-verb structure and acceptance of the dative-subject construction are both possible in Japanese, optionality thus arises in L2 Chinese concerning psych verbs if L1 transfer happens.

Significant differences are also found between the Korean groups and the control group ($F(3,97) = 7.664, p < .001$): the three

Korean groups do not differ from each other, but the low-intermediate group and the intermediate group differ significantly from the control group ($p = .002$ and $p = .001$ respectively); no significant difference is found between the high-intermediate group and the control group ($p = .458$). The result of the Korean groups in the production test roughly matches that in the AJ test.

One-way ANOVA tests were conducted between groups from different L1s but at the same Chinese proficiency levels on the mean scores of the transformed data, but no significant difference is found between the low-intermediate groups ($F(2,65) = 0.346$, $p = .709$), between the intermediate groups ($F(2,53) = 1.258$, $p = .293$) or between the high-intermediate groups ($F(2,57) = 2.531$, $p = .088$). The significant difference between the low-intermediate English and Japanese groups found in the AJ test is not found in the production test.

To sum up, the results of the production test concerning psych verbs roughly match those of the AJ test except for the Japanese groups whose performances are native-like in the AJ test but non-native-like in the production test. Performance of L2 Chinese learners from different L1s but at the same L2 Chinese proficiency levels seem to be alike in the production test concerning psych verbs. Effect of L1 transfer is not seen in the production test except for the scrambling in Japanese-speaking learners' data.

### 6.1.3 Summary

Results of the tests on Chinese psych verbs are summarized in Table 6.3.

# 6 Results and discussion: psych verbs and unaccusative verbs

Table 6.3 Summary of results on the analytical causative construction and the incorrect OE-verb structure in the AJ test and the production test: pair-wise comparisons

| Groups | | Analytical causative construction | | | | | | *Psych verbs as OE verbs | | | | | |
|---|---|---|---|---|---|---|---|---|---|---|---|---|---|
| | | AJ test | | | Production test | | | AJ test | | | Production test | | |
| | | IN | HI | NS | IN | HI | NS | IN | HI | NS | IN | HI | NS |
| English | LI | | | | | √ | | √ | √ | | | | √ |
| | IN | | | | | | | | | | | | |
| | HI | | | | | | | | | | | | |
| Japanese | LI | √ | | | √ | √ | | | | | √ | | |
| | IN | √ | | | | | | | | | √ | | |
| | HI | | | | | | | | | | √ | | |
| Korean | LI | √ | | | | √ | | √ | | | √ | | |
| | IN | √ | | | | √ | | √ | | | √ | | |
| | HI | | | | | | | | | √ | | | |

"√" stands for significant difference found in pair-wise Scheffé tests

Results reported in this part indicate that L2 Chinese learners from different L1s do not seem to have much difficulty in acquiring the analytical causative construction and that their performances are native-like at least at the high-intermediate stage. Results of the production test on the analytical causative construction do not vary much from results of the AJ test except for the Japanese groups.

It is shown in the results that L2 Chinese learners seem to have knowledge of the behaviour of Chinese psych verbs and that they correctly produce and accept sentences where psych verbs are used as intransitive SE verbs. When these verbs are incorrectly used as OE verbs in the AJ test, all L2 groups show degrees of rejection and most of them have native-like judgments. The Japanese subjects perform differently in the two tests: their judgments are native-like in the AJ test but non-native-like in the production test.

Performances of subjects who are from different L1s but at the same L2 Chinese proficiency levels are mostly alike on both the analytical causative construction and the incorrect OE-verb structure.

Significant differences are only found between the low-intermediate Japanese and English groups in judging incorrectly used OE verbs: the former rejects these verbs significantly more than the latter. If such difference is attributed to the persistence of L1 effect in the English group, then such effect is not seen in comparisons between English and Korean subjects at all developmental stages: they seem to have similar mental representations of psych verbs in their L2 Chinese grammars.

A hypothesis concerning psych verbs is that English speakers will make more causative errors than Japanese and Korean speakers because OE verbs are allowed in English but disallowed in Japanese and Korean. This hypothesis is confirmed by comparisons between the low-intermediate English group and the low-intermediate Japanese group, but it is not borne out by comparisons between the English and Korean groups. The hypothesis that L2 Chinese learners will not have much difficulty in acquiring the analytical causative construction is confirmed by the results.

Results of the tests on Chinese psych verbs seem to suggest that L1 transfer may occur and remain available at later stages in L2 Chinese grammars, but it does not occur or last in all cases.

## 6.2 Unaccusative verbs

In this section I will present results of the AJ test and the production test concerning Chinese unaccusative verbs.

### 6.2.1 Results of the AJ test

As outlined in §5.4.2.2.1, three types of unaccusative structures were used in the AJ test: a) unaccusative verbs used in a one-argument structure with Theme occurring at the sentence-initial position; b) unaccusative verbs incorrectly used as alternating verbs in the active form; and c) unaccusative verbs incorrectly used as alternating verbs in the passive form. For b) and c), transitive control structures are used. The purpose is to find out whether unaccusative verbs and transitive verbs are treated differently in L2 learners' Chinese grammars.

First, let us look into L2 learners' judgments of the unaccusative structure with the Theme argument occurring at the sentence-initial position. The structure is exemplified in (3) (repeated from (15A) of Chapter 5) and the mean scores on this structure are illustrated in Figure 6.4 (see Table 4 in Appendix 7 for descriptive statistics).

(3) Lisi de huaping sui le.
    Lisi's vase    break ASP
    'Lisi's vase broke.'

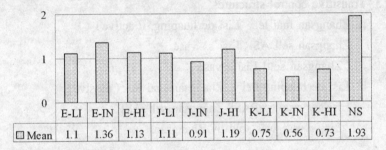

Figure 6.4 *The unaccusative structure with the Theme argument as sentence subject: mean scores in the AJ test*

As shown in Figure 6.4, none of the L2 Chinese groups shows any rejection to the unaccusative structure with Theme as sentence subject. All the English groups and the low- and high-intermediate Japanese groups accept this structure (mean score ≥ 1), while the intermediate Japanese group and the three Korean groups, whose mean scores vary between 0.5 and 1, tend to accept this structure.

Now let us find out how these verbs are treated when they are incorrectly used as alternating unaccusative verbs. Examples of the alternating unaccusative structures and their transitive control structures are given in (4) and (5) (repeated from (15) of Chapter 5). As stated in Chapter 2, Chinese does not allow alternating unaccusative verbs. The alternating unaccusative structures are therefore unacceptable whether they occur in the active form as in (4a) or in the passive form as in (4b).

(4) Alternating unaccusative structures
    a. *Zhangsan sui   le   Lisi de huaping. (active)
       Zhangsan   break ASP Lisi's  vase
       'Zhangsan broke Lisi's vase.'
    b. *Lisi de huaping bei    Zhangsan sui   le. (passive)
       Lisi's   vase     PASS Zhangsan break ASP
       'Lisi's vase was broken by Zhangsan.'

(5) Transitive control structures
    a. Zhangsan mai le   Lisi de huaping. (active)
       Zhangsan sell ASP Lisi's  vase
       'Zhangsan sold Lisi's vase.'
    b. Lisi de huaping bei    Zhangsan mai le. (passive)
       Lisi's   vase     PASS Zhangsan sell ASP
       'Lisi's vase was sold by Zhangsan.'

The mean scores on these structures are illustrated in Figure 6.5 (see Tables 5, 6, 7 and 8 in Appendix 7 for descriptive statistics). As shown in the Figure, the mean scores of the L2 groups are all positive except for the high-intermediate English group's judgment of the active form of alternating unaccusative verbs. In most groups, especially Japanese and Korean groups, the mean scores of the ungrammatical alternating unaccusative structures do not vary much from the mean scores of the grammatical transitive control structures, indicating that L2 learners make causative errors with unaccusative verbs, as found in previous studies (e.g. Cabrera and Zubizarreta 2003; Montrul 1999, 2000, 2001a; see § 4.2.1).

# 6 Results and discussion: psych verbs and unaccusative verbs

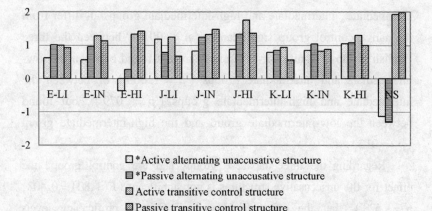

*Figure 6.5 The incorrect alternating unaccusative structures and the correct transitive control structures: mean scores in the AJ test*

### 6.2.1.1 L2 Chinese learners' judgments on the ungrammatical alternating unaccusative structures

Let us compare the mean scores on the incorrect alternating unaccusative structures (including both the active form as in (4a) and the passive form as in (4b)) between different learner groups.

General Linear Model (GLM) repeated measures were conducted between the English, Japanese, and Korean groups respectively, each with the native group as a control. The ungrammatical alternating unaccusative structures, both active and passive, constitute the within-subject factor and learners' Chinese proficiency levels the between-subject factor. Bonferroni test[5] were conducted for pair-wise comparisons.

Comparisons between the English groups reveal a significant effect for the unaccusative structures ($F(1,79) = 6.575$, $p < .05$) and for learners' Chinese proficiency levels ($F(3,79) = 30.092$, $p < .001$), but not for the interaction between the two factors

· 195 ·

($F(3,79) = 2.399$, $p = .074$). Bonferroni tests indicate that the low-intermediate, intermediate and high-intermediate groups all differ from the native control group significantly ($p < .001$); between the three English groups, significant differences are not found between the low-intermediate and intermediate groups ($p = 1.000$) or between the intermediate and high-intermediate groups ($p = .079$), but found between the low-intermediate group and the high-intermediate group ($p = .012$).

Regarding the three Japanese groups and the control group, the effect for the unaccusative structures is not significant ($F(1,80) = 0.402$, $p = .528$), but the effect for learners' Chinese proficiency levels ($F(3,80) = 39.546$, $p < .001$) and the effect for the interaction between the unaccusative structures and learners' Chinese proficiency levels ($F(3,80) = 3.232$, $p < .05$) are both significant. Pair-wise comparisons suggest that the three Japanese groups differ significantly from the control group ($p < .001$) but do not differ significantly from each other ($p = 1.000$).

Concerning the Korean groups and the control group, the effect for the unaccusative structures is not significant ($F(1,97) = 0.149$, $p = .700$) but the effect for learners' proficiency levels is ($F(3,97) = 44.528$, $p < .001$). Pair-wise comparisons show that the three Korean groups do not differ significantly from each other ($p = 1.000$), but they all differ significantly from the native control group ($p < .001$). The effect for the interaction between the unaccusative structures and learners' proficiency levels is not significant ($F = (3,97) = 0.865$, $p = .462$).

GLM repeated measures were also conducted between the low-intermediate groups, the intermediate groups, and the high-intermediate groups from different L1s respectively, with the two ungrammatical alternating unaccusative structures as the within-subject factor and learners' L1s as the between-subject factor. Between the three low-intermediate groups, there is no significant effect for the unaccusative structures ($F(1,65) = 0.030$, $p = .863$), for learners' L1s ($F(2,65) = 0.174$, $p = .841$) or for the interaction between the unaccusative structures and learners' L1s ($F(2,65) = 2.474$, $p = .092$).

The intermediate groups pattern together with the low-intermediate groups: no significant effect is found for the unaccusative structures ($F(1,53) = 3.681$, $p = .060$), for learners' L1s ($F(2,53) = 0.334$, $p = .717$) or for the interaction between the unaccusative structures and learners' L1s ($F(2,53) = 0.205$, $p = .815$).

Regarding the high-intermediate groups, significant effects are found for the unaccusative structures ($F(1,57) = 10.415$, $p < .05$) and for learners' L1s ($F(2,57) = 8.175$, $p < .05$), but not for the interaction between these two factors ($F(2,57) = 2.360$, $p = .104$). Bonferroni tests indicate that the English group differs significantly from the Japanese group ($p < .05$) and the Korean group ($p < .05$) at the high-intermediate stage: the English group shows more rejection to the ungrammatical alternating unaccusative structures than the corresponding Japanese and Korean groups.

Rejected and accepted tokens of each of the incorrect alternating unaccusative structures (active and passive) and subjects who consistently rejected or accepted the three tokens of each structure were counted. Their percentages are given in Table 6.4. The percentage of rejected tokens and that of subjects who showed consistent rejection are shaded.

On the active form of the structure, more than 40% of the tokens are accepted by all the L2 groups. The high-intermediate English group is the only group that rejects it more readily than accepts it. On the passive form, more than 60% of the tokens are accepted by the L2 groups and more than 40% of the subjects in each group consistently accept the structure.

Table 6.4 *Percentage of rejected and accepted tokens of each of the incorrect alternating unaccusative structures and percentage of subjects who consistently rejected or accepted the three tokens of each structure in the AJ test*

| Subject groups | | *Active form | | | | *Passive form | | | |
|---|---|---|---|---|---|---|---|---|---|
| | | Tokens | | Consistent subjects | | Tokens | | Consistent subjects | |
| | | Reject % | Accept % | Reject % | Accept % | Reject % | Accept % | Reject % | Accept % |
| English | LI | 27 | 65 | 12 | 27 | 15 | 76 | 8 | 62 |
| | IN | 28 | 62 | 0 | 46 | 18 | 74 | 8 | 62 |
| | HI | 56 | 42 | 38 | 6 | 35 | 60 | 19 | 44 |
| Japanese | LI | 13 | 84 | 0 | 67 | 29 | 69 | 13 | 53 |
| | IN | 22 | 76 | 11 | 61 | 13 | 87 | 11 | 83 |
| | HI | 22 | 78 | 4 | 61 | 12 | 86 | 4 | 74 |
| Korean | LI | 23 | 65 | 4 | 48 | 23 | 65 | 4 | 56 |
| | IN | 24 | 69 | 4 | 44 | 17 | 73 | 0 | 52 |
| | HI | 17 | 73 | 0 | 38 | 13 | 75 | 0 | 43 |
| Native control | | 80 | 20 | 71 | 0 | 88 | 12 | 75 | 0 |

To sum up, comparisons between proficiency groups within each L1 indicate that representations of Chinese unaccusative verbs in Japanese and Korean speakers' L2 grammars do not develop toward native norms with the increase of their Chinese proficiency. Among the English groups, however, development is seen from the low-intermediate stage to the high-intermediate stage. Comparisons also indicate that L2 learners from the three L1s seem to have similar mental representations of Chinese unaccusative verbs at the low-intermediate stage and the intermediate stage, but at the high-intermediate stage English-speaking learners show more rejection to the ungrammatical alternating unaccusative structures than Japanese- and Korean-speaking learners. However, none of the L2 Chinese groups has native-like judgment at any developmental stage. The overall picture seems to suggest that syntactically a VP shell rather than a single VP is projected in L2 Chinese grammars and that in

Japanese- and Korean-speaking learners' L2 Chinese grammars the mental representations of alternating unaccusative structures tend to be fossilized, a term first used by Selinker (1972) to mean that L2 learners stabilize at some point in their grammatical development short of native-like attainment (see §4.1.2).

6.2.1.2 Comparisons between judgments on unaccusative verbs and transitive verbs

As we know from Chapter 2, non-alternating unaccusative verbs project a single VP, while alternating unaccusative verbs project a VP shell. In terms of syntactic structures, alternating unaccusative verbs and transitive verbs behave similarly in that both project a VP shell. As shown in Figure 6.5, most L2 Chinese groups accept (mean score $\geqslant +1$) or tend to accept (mean score ranging between 0 and $+1$) both the incorrect alternating unaccusative structures and the correct transitive control structures. If unaccusative verbs are treated as alternating verbs, the two types of verbs will have similar representations in L2 Chinese grammars. Next, we will find out whether this is the case.

Comparisons are made between judgments on the incorrect alternating unaccusative structure and judgments on the corresponding transitive control structure. As shown in (4) and (5), tokens for the two structures differ only in the verb. If a learner's judgments on the two structures differ, the difference can only be attributed to the verb used. Paired-samples T tests between these two structures were conducted within each subject group. The results are presented in Table 6.5.

Table 6.5 Comparisons between judgments on the incorrect alternating unaccusative structures and the correct transitive control structures in paired-samples T tests

| Subject groups | | df | Active *Unaccusative vs. transitive | | Passive *Unaccusative vs. transitive | |
|---|---|---|---|---|---|---|
| | | | t | p (2-tailed) | t | p (2-tailed) |
| English | LI | 25 | -2.457* | .021 | 0.778 | .444 |
| | IN | 12 | -2.438* | .031 | -1.022 | .327 |
| | HI | 15 | -5.735** | .000 | -3.252* | .005 |
| Japanese | LI | 14 | -0.268 | .792 | 0.397 | .698 |
| | IN | 17 | -1.679 | .111 | -1.039 | .314 |
| | HI | 22 | -3.980* | .001 | 0.947 | .354 |
| Korean | LI | 26 | -0.841 | .408 | 1.526 | .139 |
| | IN | 24 | 0.116 | .908 | 0.839 | .410 |
| | HI | 20 | -1.117 | .277 | 0.459 | .651 |
| Native control | | 27 | -20.211** | .000 | -27.268** | .000 |

*$p < .05$; **$p < .001$

Regarding the active pair of the incorrect alternating unaccusative structure as in (4a) and the transitive control structure as in (5a), significant differences are found in the three English groups but not in any of the Korean groups; the high-intermediate Japanese group judges the two structures differently in a significant way, but the low-intermediate and intermediate groups treat them similarly. Regarding the passive pair as in (4b) and (5b), significant differences are only found in the judgments of the high-intermediate English group. The two structures seem to be indistinguishable to the other L2 groups.

The results of the paired-samples T tests seem to indicate that unaccusative verbs (e.g. *sui* 'break') are more likely to be treated causatively or transitively in the passive form like (4b) than in the active form like (4a). When they occur in the passive form, only the high-intermediate English group seems to be able to differentiate them from transitive verbs. However, when they occur in the active form, the three English groups and the high-intermediate Japanese groups are all able to differentiate them from transitive verbs. The discrepancy might be attributed to the passive marker *bei* in Chinese passive sentences. It seems to play a role of validating the status of unaccusatives as transitives or causatives in L2 Chinese grammars.

### 6.2.2 Results of the production test

Recall that a set of four words is provided in the production test for a potential sentence involving an unaccusative verb. In each set of words, there is a human NP (e.g. *Zhangsan*), an inanimate NP (e.g. *Lisi de huaping* 'Lisi's vase'), an unaccusative verb with aspectual marker *le* (*sui le* 'broke') and the word *ba*, which is an accusative case assigner (cf. Y.-H. Li 1990) or a causative marker (cf. Sybesma 1992) (see Example (12) of Chapter 5). With the four given words, however, no grammatical sentences can be formed because Chinese does not allow alternating unaccusative verbs. Errors will be made if learners make sentences with the structure "human NP + *ba* inanimate NP + unaccusative verb" like *\*Zhangsan ba Lisi de huaping sui le* '(literally) Zhangsan *ba* Lisi's vase broke', the intended meaning of which is 'Zhangsan broke Lisi's vase'.

Two types of structure in the production result were counted: a) formation rejected (FR), where subjects indicate explicitly by drawing a "×" that no grammatical sentences can be formed; and b) unaccusative verbs incorrectly treated as alternating verbs (i.e. *\*Zhangsan ba Lisi de huaping sui le* 'Zhangsan broke Lisi's vase'). The number and percentage of the two types of structure produced are given in Table 6.6. The number and percentage of consistent subjects (i.e. subjects who formed three sentences of the same structure from the three sets of given words) are also given in Table 6.6. Other types of structures formed are irrelevant to the present study and are therefore ignored and not included in this table.

Table 6.6 Unaccusative verbs: number and percentage of two types of structure formed and consistent subjects who formed such structures in the production test

| Subject groups | | Formation rejected | | *Unaccusative as causative | |
|---|---|---|---|---|---|
| | | Individual tokens | Consistent subjects | Individual tokens | Consistent subjects |
| English | LI (26) | 13 (17%) | 0 | 54 (69%) | 15 (58%) |
| | IN (13) | 9 (23%) | 0 | 30 (77%) | 8 (62%) |
| | HI (16) | 24 (50%) | 4 (25%) | 24 (50%) | 7 (44%) |
| Japanese | LI (15) | 8 (18%) | 1 (7%) | 29 (64%) | 8 (53%) |
| | IN (18) | 12 (22%) | 1 (6%) | 39 (72%) | 12 (67%) |
| | HI (23) | 22 (32%) | 2 (9%) | 47 (68%) | 12 (52%) |
| Korean | LI (27) | 17 (21%) | 0 | 48 (59%) | 15 (56%) |
| | IN (25) | 23 (31%) | 1 (4%) | 49 (65%) | 12 (48%) |
| | HI (21) | 18 (26%) | 2 (10%) | 44 (70%) | 14 (67%) |
| Native control (28) | | 82 (98%) | 26 (93%) | 0 | 0 |

Note: The total number of tokens in each group = number of subjects × 3

As shown in Table 6.6, at least 40% of L2 learners consistently made causative errors in all the L2 groups and every learner group formed a large proportion of sentences belonging to the incorrect alternating unaccusative structure. This seems to suggest that L2 Chinese learners project a causative VP shell rather than a single VP for unaccusative verbs and that L2 Chinese grammars concerning unaccusative verbs tend to be fossilized and do not seem to be able to converge on the target grammar.

The information in Table 6.6 does not tell us whether learner groups differ significantly from each other. To find out whether such differences exist, I transformed the result of the production test into numerical data with " +1 " for each token where formation is rejected, "-1" for each token where an ungrammatical alternating unaccusative sentence is formed and "0" for other cases. The mean scores of the transformed data in each group are given in Figure 6.6.

# 6 Results and discussion: psych verbs and unaccusative verbs

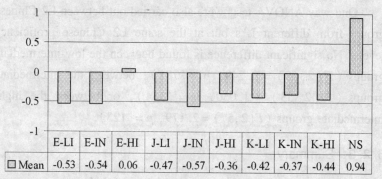

*Figure 6.6 Unaccusative verbs: mean scores of the transformed data in the production test*

One-way ANOVA and pair-wise Scheffé tests were conducted on the mean scores of the transformed data in the English, Japanese and Korean groups with the native group as a control. Significant differences are found between the English groups ($F(3,79) = 55.936$, $p < .001$): the production result of the high-intermediate group differs significantly from that of the low-intermediate group ($p = .007$) and that of the intermediate group ($p = .025$); no significant difference is found between the low-intermediate group and the intermediate group ($p = 1.000$). None of the three English groups' production results is native-like ($p < .001$).

Significant differences are found between the Japanese groups and the control group ($F(3,80) = 50.119$, $p < .001$): the three Japanese groups all differ significantly from the control group ($p < .001$), but they do not differ from each other.

Significant differences are also found between the Korean groups and the control group ($F(3,97) = 53.177$, $p < .001$). The three Korean groups do not differ from each other, but they all differ significantly from the control group ($p < .001$). The Korean groups and the Japanese groups show the same pattern in the production test on unaccusative verbs.

One-way ANOVA tests were also carried out between L2 Chinese groups from different L1s but at the same L2 Chinese proficiency levels. No significant difference is found between the low-intermediate groups ($F(2,65) = 0.249$, $p = .781$), between the intermediate groups ($F(2,53) = 1.030$, $p = .364$), or between the high-intermediate groups ($F(2,57) = 2.179$, $p = .123$).

### 6.2.3 Summary

In §6.2.1 and §6.2.2, results of the AJ test and the production test on the ungrammatical alternating unaccusative structures were reported. They are summarized in Table 6.7.

*Table 6.7 Summary of results on the ungrammatical alternating unaccusative verbs in the AJ test and the production test: pair-wise comparisons*

| Subject groups | | The AJ test | | | The production test | | |
|---|---|---|---|---|---|---|---|
| | | IN | HI | NS | IN | HI | NS |
| English | LI | √ | √ | | √ | √ | |
| | IN | | √ | | √ | √ | |
| | HI | | | √ | | | √ |
| Japanese | LI | | | √ | | | √ |
| | IN | | | √ | | | √ |
| | HI | | | √ | | | √ |
| Korean | LI | | | √ | | | √ |
| | IN | | | √ | | | √ |
| | HI | | | √ | | | √ |

"√" stands for significant difference found in pair-wise Scheffé or Bonferroni tests

It is shown in Table 6.7 that L2 Chinese grammars concerning unaccusative verbs do not develop in the Japanese and Korean groups with the increase of their L2 Chinese proficiency and that their mental representations of Chinese unaccusative verbs seem to remain non-native-like from the low-intermediate stage throughout to the high-intermediate stage. The English groups' L2 Chinese grammars concerning unaccusative verbs develop with the increase of their L2

# 6 Results and discussion: psych verbs and unaccusative verbs

Chinese proficiency, but they still differ significantly from the target grammar even at the high-intermediate stage. Most L2 Chinese groups treat unaccusative verbs causatively or transitively (see Table 6.5), which seems to suggest that Chinese unaccusative verbs are very difficult to acquire. As stated in Chapter 2, these verbs project a single VP syntactically and do not contain the CAUSE element semantically in the native Chinese grammar. The results suggest that L2 Chinese learners tend to project a VP shell with these verbs rather than a single VP and that the semantic structure for these verbs seems to contain a CAUSE element.

L2 groups from different L1s but at the same Chinese proficiency levels do not differ from each other in the production test. In the AJ test, only the judgment of the high-intermediate English group differs from that of the high-intermediate Japanese and Korean groups. This seems to suggest that L2 Chinese grammars concerning unaccusative verbs have little to do with learners' L1s at least at the low-intermediate and intermediate stages. Where there is significant difference between groups of different L1s as found between the high-intermediate groups in the AJ test, it is the English group who shows more rejection than the corresponding Japanese and Korean groups, contrary to my expectation.

## 6.3 Comparisons between psych verbs and unaccusative verbs in the group's judgments

One of my hypotheses is that L2 Chinese learners will make more errors with unaccusative verbs than with psych verbs as far as causativity is concerned (see § 5.2). To find out whether this is the case, comparisons are made between learners' judgments on the incorrect alternating unaccusative verbs and their judgments on the incorrect OE psych verbs. The mean scores on the OE-verb structure like (1c) (*Zhe ge xiaoxi gaoxing le Zhangsan 'This news pleased Zhangsan') and the active alternating unaccusative structure like (3a) (*Zhangsan sui le Lisi de huaping 'Zhangsan broke Lisi's vase') in the AJ test are illustrated in Figure 6.7.

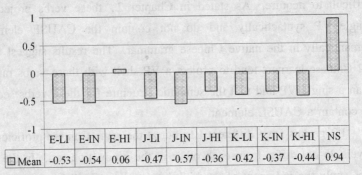

Figure 6.7 *The incorrect OE-verb structure and the incorrect alternating unaccusative structure: mean scores in the AJ test*

As shown in Figure 6.7, except for the high-intermediate English group whose mean scores on the two structures are both negative, the other learner groups reject (mean score ≤ -1) or tend to reject (means score ranging between -1 and 0) the incorrect OE-verb structure but accept (mean score ≥ +1) or tend to accept (mean score ranging between 0 and +1) the incorrect alternating unaccusative structure.

The percentage of rejected (mean score ≤ -1) and accepted (mean score ≥ +1) tokens of each of the two structures and the percentage of subjects who consistently rejected or accepted the three tokens of a structure in the AJ test are illustrated in Table 6.8. The percentage of rejected tokens and that of subjects who show consistent rejection are shaded. As shown in the Table, learners in all the groups reject the OE-verb structure more readily than they reject the alternating unaccusative structure. All the learner groups show more rejection of the incorrect OE-verb structure than acceptance of it, but most of them show more acceptance of the incorrect alternating unaccusative structure than rejection of it. On the alternating unaccusative structure, the high-intermediate English group is the only group in which rejected tokens outnumber accepted tokens and subjects showing consistent rejection outnumber those showing consistent acceptance.

Table 6.8 The OE-verb structure and the active unaccusative structure: percentage of accepted/rejected tokens and that of consistent subjects in the AJ test

| Subject groups | | *OE-verb structure | | | | *Unaccusative structure (active) | | | |
|---|---|---|---|---|---|---|---|---|---|
| | | Tokens | | Cons. subjects | | Tokens | | Cons. Subjects | |
| | | Reject % | Accept % | Reject % | Accept % | Reject % | Accept % | Reject % | Accept % |
| English | LI | 58 | 33 | 26 | 6 | 27 | 65 | 12 | 27 |
| | IN | 74 | 18 | 38 | 0 | 28 | 62 | 0 | 46 |
| | HI | 81 | 19 | 69 | 0 | 56 | 42 | 38 | 6 |
| Japanese | LI | 84 | 9 | 60 | 0 | 13 | 84 | 0 | 67 |
| | IN | 81 | 13 | 67 | 0 | 22 | 76 | 11 | 61 |
| | HI | 87 | 13 | 70 | 4 | 22 | 78 | 4 | 61 |
| Korean | LI | 59 | 25 | 33 | 7 | 23 | 65 | 4 | 48 |
| | IN | 72 | 20 | 52 | 0 | 24 | 69 | 4 | 44 |
| | HI | 67 | 16 | 48 | 5 | 17 | 73 | 0 | 38 |
| Native control | | 95 | 5 | 89 | 0 | 80 | 20 | 71 | 0 |

The difference between L2 learners' judgments on the two structures seems to suggest that L2 learners have more problems with the incorrect alternating unaccusative structure than with the incorrect OE-verb structure. The hypothesis is thus borne out.

## 6.4 Discussion

Results of the AJ test and the production test reported in this chapter confirm that a) L2 Chinese learners do not have much difficulty in acquiring the analytical causative construction; b) a single VP can be projected for psych verbs, but a VP shell is projected for unaccusative verbs in L2 Chinese grammars; and c) Japanese- and

Korean-speaking learners' L2 Chinese grammars concerning unaccusative verbs tend to be fossilized. I will now look into some factors which could account for these phenomena.

### 6.4.1 The acquisition of Chinese analytical causative construction

We have seen from §6.1.1.1 and §6.1.2.1 that L2 Chinese learners can acquire the analytical causative construction at least at the high-intermediate stage. This is not unexpected because the analytical causative construction is the most productive type of causative (Comrie 1985; Shibatani 1976a; Song 1996) and exists in the four languages under study with the same semantic and syntactic representations as shown in (2) of Chapter 5. In these languages, a VP shell is projected for analytical causatives with a causative marker heading the upper $v$P. When psych verbs are involved in these constructions, these verbs project structures as in (6):

(6) a. Chinese and English
　　($_{vP}$Causer/Agent($_{v'}$ shi/make ($_{VP}$ Experiencer ($_{v'}$ V))))
b. Japanese and Korean
　　($_{vP}$Causer/Agent ($_{VP}$Experiencer (V $_{v'}$) -(s)ase/-i $_{v'}$))

Causative markers *shi* in Chinese and *make* in English are both free morphemes, which have weak features and do not trigger movement. Although causative markers -(s)ase in Japanese and -i in Korean are affixes, they have weak features as well and do not induce syntactic operations (e.g. Harada 2002). Thus, derivations of analytical causatives in the four languages are costless and therefore easier to acquire. If L1 transfer happens, L2 Chinese learners can transfer the VP-shell structure from their L1s into the L2 and, if they are Japanese and Korean speakers, reset the headedness direction of VP to accommodate L2 Chinese input.

## 6.4.2 Causative errors with unaccusative verbs

L2 Chinese learners have more difficulty acquiring unaccusative verbs than psych verbs, as we have seen from § 6.3. They accept or tend to accept the incorrect alternating unaccusative structures but reject or tend to reject the incorrect OE-verb structures. The tendency is more clearly seen from the percentage of accepted and rejected tokens and from the percentage of subjects who consistently accepted or rejected the three tokens of each structure as shown in Table 6.8.

Given that both alternating unaccusative verbs and OE verbs have a causative VP-shell structure, the results seem to imply that L2 Chinese learners project a single VP for psych verbs but a VP shell for unaccusative verbs. Let us find out why unaccusative verbs are more difficult to acquire.

According to Grimshaw (1990: 8), argument structure is constructed in accordance with the thematic hierarchy as in (7). The structural organization of the argument array is determined by universal principles based on semantic properties of the arguments. Under UTAH (Baker 1988), an argument that fulfils the same thematic function with respect to a given verb occupies the same position in the underlying structure. The two approaches lead to Belletti and Rizzi's (1988) proposal that the subject of the OE-verb structure is the internal Theme argument in the underlying structure and that movement is involved in deriving OE-verb sentences (cf. Pesetsky 1995).

(7) (Agent (Experiencer (Goal/Source/Location (Theme))))

If UTAH and the thematic hierarchy play a role in L2 acquisition of argument structure as found in previous studies (White et al 1998;

White et al 1999), then it is predictable that L2 Chinese learners will have more difficulty rejecting the incorrect alternating unaccusative structure than the incorrect OE-verb structure. The reason is that the alternating unaccusative structure conforms to the thematic hierarchy and UTAH, while the OE-verb structure does not, as shown in (8) and (9):

(8) a. *Zhangsan sui    le    Lisi de huaping.
       Zhangsan break ASP Lisi's vase
       'Zhangsan broke Lisi's vase'
　　b. (Agent (Theme))
(9) a. *Zhe ge xiaoxi gaoxing le    Zhangsan
       this CL news   please ASP Zhangsan
       'This news excited Zhangsan.'
　　b. (Theme (Experiencer))

The alternating unaccusative structure as in (8a) contains two NPs, i.e. *Zhangsan* and *Lisi de huaping* 'Lisi's vase'. If the subject *Zhangsan* is treated as Agent while *Lisi's de huaping* 'Lisi's vase' is treated as Theme, the sentence has a thematic structure as in (8b), which conforms to the thematic hierarchy in (7). In the OE-verb structure as in (9a), *Zhangsan* is Experiencer and *zhe ge xiaoxi* 'this news' is Theme. It has a thematic structure as in (9b), which violates the thematic hierarchy in (7).

The thematic hierarchy and UTAH have two possible effects on L2 acquisition in relation to our study. One effect is that L2 learners will reject the OE-verb structure but accept the SE-verb structure because the former involves movement of the Theme argument to the subject position and does not conform to the thematic hierarchy in the surface structure while the latter conforms to the thematic hierarchy in both the underlying structure and the surface structure. This effect has been confirmed by previous studies such as Juffs (1996b), White et al (1998) and White et al (1999) (see § 4.2.1). The present study provides further evidence to such an effect: on the one hand, L2 Chinese learners accept the SE-verb structure (see § 6.1.1); on the other hand, they do not find it difficult to reject the incorrect OE-verb structure (see § 6.1.1.2 and § 6.1.2.2).

The other effect of the thematic hierarchy and UTAH is that L2 learners tend to make causative errors with non-alternating verbs and unergative verbs because such errors have an "Agent-V-Theme" order, which conforms to the thematic hierarchy in both the underlying structure and the surface structure (Cabrera and Zubizarreta 2003; Ju 2000; Juffs 1996b; Montrul 1999, 2000, 2001a; see § 4.2.1). In the present study, it is found that L2 Chinese learners make causative errors with non-alternating unaccusative verbs as shown in (8a) because such sentences do not violate the thematic hierarchy. Results reported in this chapter seem to indicate that both the thematic hierarchy and UTAH have effect on the acquisition of L2 Chinese argument structure.

### 6.4.3 Fossilized representations of unaccusative verbs

It is well documented in the linguistic literature that L2 learners make errors with non-causative verbs such as non-alternating unaccusative verbs and unergative verbs regardless of their L1s (e.g. Cabrera and Zubizarreta 2003; Ju 2000; Juffs 1996b; Helms-Park 2001; Montrul 1999, 2001a, 2001b), as exemplified in (10) (from Montrul 2001a). According to Montrul (1999), the reason for which L2 learners make overgeneralized causative errors is that they lack semantic knowledge of these verbs and therefore cannot distinguish between verbs that are involved in causative alternation and those that are not. When they are able to discriminate verb classes semantically with the increase in their L2 proficiency, causative errors will diminish.

(10) a. *The magician disappeared the rabbit.
   b. *The dentist cried the child.

The present study seems to provide further evidence for causative errors with non-alternating unaccusative verbs. It is shown in § 6.2.1.1 that L2 Chinese learners make a large portion of causative errors with unaccusative verbs and that Japanese and Korean speakers' representations of these verbs tend to be fossilized. It is shown in § 6.2.1.2 that unaccusative verbs and transitive verbs seem to have similar mental representations in Japanese- and Korean-speaking learners' L2 Chinese, which means that a VP shell rather than a single VP is projected in their L2 Chinese syntax.

Why do L2 learners persistently make causative errors with unaccusative verbs at the developmental stages under study? Why is no development observed in Japanese- and Korean-speaking learners' L2 Chinese representations of unaccusative verbs? These phenomena could be explained in terms of misleading evidence in Chinese and morphological properties in the L1s.

As mentioned in Chapter 2, unaccusative verbs in Chinese can assign partitive case as in (11a) despite their incapability of assigning accusative case as shown in (11b) (see § 2.1.4.2.2). It seems that some unaccusative verbs in modern Chinese have not lost the entire causative meaning that they had in ancient Chinese and are still used causatively in some Chinese idiomatic expressions like *duan houlu* '(literally) break the back route' in (11c).

(11) a. Zhangsan duan le yi tiao tui.
   Zhangsan break ASPone CL leg
   'Zhangsan broke a leg.'
   b. *Zhangsan duan le Lisi de tui.
   Zhangsan break ASP Lisi's leg
   'Zhangsan broke Lisi's leg(s).'

c. Youjidui duan le diren de houlu.
   guerrilla break ASP enemy's back route
   'The guerrilla cut off the enemy's retreat'

Due to the lack of case markers in Chinese, there is no morphological distinction between a partitive-case assigned NP and an accusative-case assigned NP. Evidence like (11a) and (11c) may mislead L2 Chinese learners into believing that Chinese unaccusative verbs are alternating verbs which are capable of assigning accusative case. As a result, ungrammatical sentences like (11b) are not rejected and a VP shell rather than a single VP is projected for these verbs in L2 Chinese grammars.

How do morphological properties in the L1s influence Japanese and Korean speakers' acquisition of L2 Chinese grammar concerning unaccusative verbs? As outlined in Chapter 2, unaccusative verbs in Chinese, Japanese and Korean behave similarly in terms of causativity and project a single VP. In Japanese and Korean, the Theme argument of an unaccusative verb undergoes vacuous movement to be assigned nominative case as in (12a) due to the SOV order in the two languages (e.g. Miyagawa 1989). Causative suffixes (i.e. $-(s)ase$ in Japanese and $-i$ in Korean) are used obligatorily if causation is expressed with these verbs, as shown in (12b).

(12) a. ($_{VP}$Theme ($_{V'}$ V))
   b. ($_{vP}$Agent ($_{VP}$Theme ($V_{V'}$)-(s)ase/-$i_{v'}$)))
   c. Taiyo-ga yuki-o tok-ase-ta. (Japanese)
      sun-NOM snow-ACC melt-CAUS-PAST
      'The sun melted the snow.'
   d. theyang-i elum-ul nok-i-ass-ta. (Korean)
      sun-NOM ice-ACC melt-CAUS-PAST-DEC
      'The sun melted the ice.'

In Japanese and Korean, grammatical relations are represented with verbal inflections and case markers. An unaccusative verb contains the BECOME element only and the CAUSE element is represented explicitly with causative suffixes. A causativized unaccusative verb selects an Agent argument and a Theme argument, with the former explicitly marked with nominative case and the latter with accusative case, as shown in (12c) and (12d) (repeated from Chapter 2). In terms of case markings, unaccusative verbs that are causativized through causative markers are similar to transitive verbs.

Chinese has neither verbal inflections nor explicit case markers. Therefore, Japanese- and Korean-speaking learners cannot rely on morphological properties to represent grammatical relations in L2 Chinese. Consequently, they may resort to the universal default causative template, as shown in (13) (see Baker 1988; Hale and Keyser 1993):

(13)

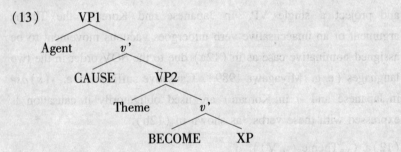

It is reported in the linguistic literature that children rely on this template in L1 acquisition and make causative errors with non-causative verbs (e.g. Bowerman 1990; Pinker 1989) and that L2 learners are also guided by the template (e.g. Juffs 1996b; Montrul 1999). If the template plays a role in Japanese- and Korean-speaking learners' acquisition of L2 Chinese, unaccusative verbs like *sui* 'break' will be used causatively and project a VP shell rather than a single VP, as we have seen from § 6.2.1.

## 6 Results and discussion: psych verbs and unaccusative verbs

In a study of L2 acquisition of English unaccusative verbs, Hirakawa (1995) found that Japanese-speaking learners were uncertain in their judgments about both alternating and non-alternating unaccusative verbs and that the uncertainty was attributed to the morphological markings that are present in Japanese but absent in English. The present study suggests that Japanese-speaking learners accept or tend to accept Chinese unaccusative verbs both in the non-alternating form (grammatical) and the alternating form (ungrammatical) (see Figures 6.4 and 6.5). Their acceptance of the ungrammatical alternating unaccusative structure (see Figure 6.5) may also be attributed to the morphological markings present in L1 Japanese but absent in L2 Chinese. Lack of morphological markings and the presence of misleading evidence in L2 Chinese result in Japanese- and Korean-speaking learners' non-native-like representations of Chinese unaccusative verbs.

As we have seen from the results reported in § 6.2.1, while Japanese- and Korean-speaking learners' non-native-like representations of Chinese unaccusative verbs (i.e. allowing alternating unaccusative verbs) are likely to be fossilized, English-speaking learners' L2 Chinese grammars concerning unaccusative verbs develop toward the native grammar with the increase in their L2 proficiency although representations of these verbs remain non-native-like at the three intermediate stages under study. One reason is that English speakers may transfer the causative VP shell in L1 English into L2 Chinese, which results in causative errors as can be seen from Figure 6.5. However, as their L2 Chinese develops, they can distinguish between unaccusative verbs and transitive verbs, as shown in Table 6.5 (the active pair). This implies that they have different mental representations of these two types of verbs in their L2 Chinese.

Like Chinese, English does not have phonetically realized case markers. Neither does it have phonetically realized causative markers used on alternating unaccusative verbs. As a result, English-speaking learners of Chinese are unable to depend on these markers to represent grammatical relations and may pay more attention to semantic structures to distinguish between different types of verb. Since unaccusative verbs and transitive verbs have different semantic structures in both English and Chinese, English-speaking learners of Chinese are able to distinguish between them (see Table 6.5) and project different syntactic structures for them.

To conclude, results of the tests on Chinese psych verbs and unaccusative verbs have shown that L2 Chinese learners are able to acquire the argument structure of psych verbs but have difficulty with unaccusative verbs. UTAH and the thematic hierarchy seem to play a role in L2 acquisition of Chinese so that learners reject the incorrect OE-verb structure but accept the correct SE-verb structure and the incorrect alternating unaccusative structure. We have argued that L2 Chinese learners' difficulty with unaccusative verbs results from misleading evidence in the L2 and different morphological properties between L1s and the L2. The results seem to suggest that English-speaking learners can acquire the properties of Chinese psych verbs although English is a superset while Chinese is a subset regarding psych verbs (see § 4.1.4 for discussion of superset-subset relation and § 2.2.1, § 2.2.2 and § 2.2.3 for discussion of properties of psych verbs in Chinese and English). It is also suggested that L1 transfer is constrained by L1 morphological properties and the thematic hierarchy.

## Notes

[1] In the figures and tables of the thesis, E-LI refers to the low-intermediate English group, which means that members of this group are English subjects whose L2 Chinese is of low-intermediate level as found in the cloze test reported in § 5.3. Likewise, E-IN refers to the intermediate English group, E-HI to the high-intermediate English group, J-LI to the low-intermediate Japanese group, J-IN to the intermediate Japanese group, J-HI to the high-intermediate Japanese group, K-LI to the low-intermediate Korean group, K-IN to the intermediate Korean group, and K-HI to the high-intermediate Korean group.

[2] A significant difference is found between the three English groups and the control group in a one-way ANOVA test ($F(3,79) = 3.699$, $p < .05$). However, the following pair-wise Scheffé test shows no significant difference between the three English groups or between the English groups and the control group. The discrepancy between the result of the one-way ANOVA test and that of the Scheffé test probably results from the conservativeness of the Scheffé test (see Bryman and Cramer 1999). Using the Tukey test, the high-intermediate group's judgment is found to be native-like, but the low-intermediate group and the intermediate group are found to be significantly different from the native control group ($p = .033$ and $p = .036$ respectively). Anyway, we may safely conclude that English-speaking learners can acquire the analytical causatives construction at least at the high-intermediate stage.

[3] As noted in Chapter 2 (see § 2.2.3.3), Chinese does not have a clear-cut distinction between verbs and adjectives. Psych verbs (e.g. *xingfen* 'excite') used in the production test for potential analytical causatives can be treated as adjectives because they have a modifier *hen* 'very', which is considered to be a modifier of adjectives (Zhu 1982).

[4] In the case of Japanese, this could also be a result of scrambling. Japanese allows scrambling and it is possible for arguments of a verb to occur in different positions in the surface structure (see Fukui 1993, Saito 1992, for detailed discussion).

[5] In the present study, the Bonferroni test is used for multiple comparisons in repeated measures. A reason for using this test is that it modifies the significance level to take account of the fact that more than one comparison is being made (see Bryman and Cramer 1999).

# 7 Results and discussion: resultative and compound causative constructions

**导言**

　　本章对实证研究中有关结果补语结构和复合使动结构这两部分的试验结果进行描述、分析和讨论。结果显示，英、日、韩这三种母语背景的汉语学习者能够习得以"得"为中心词的结果补语结构，而且母语为英语和日语的学习者，其结果补语结构的句法表征能够达到汉语本族语者的水平，对结果补语结构的理解也与汉语本族语者的语感接近。

　　与结果补语结构部分的试验结果形成对照的是，汉语复合使动结构在中介语中的句法表征与在本族语者中的句法表征有显著差异，而且在中介语语法中表现出僵化现象。为探究形成这一现象的原因，作者对试验中使用的六种复合使动结构的测试结果进行了具体分析，发现母语为英、日、韩的汉语学习者能够习得其中一种结构，但在习得其他五种结构上出现困难，对复合使动结构的理解也受到第一语言中相关语义结构的影响。作者认为，学习者能够习得一种复合使动结构，说明这种结构中包含的功能范畴（即体短语）在中介语中能够具有适当表征。在其他复合使动结构上出现的僵化现象，原因在于中介语语法不能为复合使动结构中的行为动词或结果成分指派适当的论元角色。作者认为，结果补语结构比复合使动结构容易习得，主要是因为功能范畴的中心词在前者中具有词汇形式，而在后者中没有。作者还指出，尽管复合使动结构在中介语中能够具有适当的句法表征，但其语义结构会受到第一语言的影响，这是从理解测试中得出的结论。

# Results and discussion: resultative and compound causative constructions

As stated in previous chapters, causativity in Chinese is expressed with analytical causative, compound causative and resultative constructions. In Chapter 6, we learned that L2 Chinese learners do not have much difficulty acquiring the analytical causative construction. In this chapter, we will examine through the AJ test and the comprehension test whether they can acquire resultative and compound causative constructions. Results of the tests on resultatives and compound causatives will be presented in § 7.1 and § 7.2 respectively, followed by comparisons between results on the two constructions in § 7.3 and summary and discussion of the results in § 7.4.

## 7.1 Resultative constructions

Two instruments, i.e. an AJ test and a comprehension test, were employed to examine the acquisition of resultative constructions by L2 Chinese learners.

### 7.1.1 Results of the AJ test

The resultative construction is one way of representing causativity in Chinese. As mentioned in Chapter 3, Chinese resultative constructions contain a functional category AspP headed by *de*. In this section, we will find out whether L2 Chinese learners can acquire this construction and project the functional AspP in their L2 grammars.

It was pointed out in Chapter 5 that three types of resultative constructions were examined in the AJ test: Type A contains an unergative $V_1$ like *ku* 'cry'; Type B contains a psych verb $V_1$ like *gaoxing* 'please'; Type C is used with the analytical causative construction headed by *shi*. Type C is an extension of Type B. That is, while only the result component is represented (by *de*) in Type B, both the cause and the result are morphologically represented (by *shi* and *de* respectively) in Type C. The three types of structures are exemplified in (1), repeated from (16) of Chapter 5. Unergative verbs in Type A and psych verbs in Type B are non-causatives and do not denote cause-effect relation. Used in the resultative construction, however, they can express causativity through the resultative marker *de*.

(1) Resultative constructions used in the AJ test
    A. Unergative $V_1$
        Zhangsan <u>ku</u> de shoujuan    dou *shi* le.
        Zhangsan cry *de* handkerchief even wet ASP
        'Zhangsan cried the handkerchief soggy.'
    B. Psych verb $V_1$
        Zhangsan <u>gaoxing</u> de *you chang you tiao*.
        Zhangsan please  *de* both sing and dance
        'Zhangsan was so pleased that he both sang and danced.'
    C. Analytical causative and resultative
        Zhe ge xiaoxi shi Zhangsan <u>gaoxing</u> de *you chang you tiao*.
        this CL news  *shi* Zhangsan please  *de* both sing and dance
        'This news made Zhangsan so pleased that he both sang and danced.'

The three types of constructions are all grammatical in Chinese. The mean scores of each learner group in judging these constructions in the AJ test are illustrated in Figure 7.1 (see Tables 9, 10 and 11 in Appendix 7 for descriptive statistics). As shown in the figure, all the learner groups accept (mean score $\geq +1$) or tend to accept (mean score ranging between 0 and +1) the three types of resultative constructions. In most groups, L2 learners show more acceptance of these constructions with the increase in their L2 Chinese proficiency.

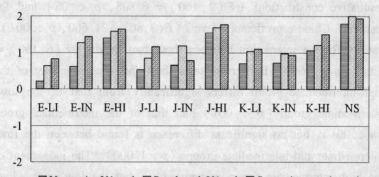

Figure 7.1 Resultative constructions: mean scores in the AJ test

GLM repeated measures and pair-wise Bonferroni tests were conducted between the English groups, the Japanese groups and the Korean groups respectively, with the native Chinese group as a control. The mean scores of the three types of resultative constructions constitute the within-subject factor and learners' Chinese proficiency levels constitute the between-subject factor.

Between the English groups, the effects for both the resultative constructions ($F(2,158) = 12.128$, $p < .001$) and learners' Chinese proficiency levels ($F(3,79) = 32.630$, $p < .001$) are significant, but the effect for the interaction between these two factors is not ($F(6,158) = 1.374$, $p = .228$). Pair-wise comparisons suggest that the judgement of the low-intermediate group differs significantly from that of the intermediate group ($p < .05$) and that of the high-intermediate group ($p < .001$), but no significant difference is found between the intermediate and high-intermediate groups ($p = .165$); the low-intermediate and intermediate groups differ significantly from the control group in their judgments ($p < .001$), but the high-intermediate group seems to have native-like judgement on these constructions.

Between the Japanese groups, there is a significant effect for the resultative constructions ($F(2,160) = 6.808$, $p < .05$) and for learners' Chinese proficiency levels ($F(3,80) = 21.660$, $p < .001$), but not for the interaction between these two factors ($F(6,160) = 1.547$, $p = .166$). Bonferroni tests show that the judgement of the high-intermediate group differs significantly from that of the low-intermediate group ($p < .001$) and that of the intermediate group ($p < .001$), but no significant difference is found between the low-intermediate and intermediate groups ($p = 1.000$). The judgement of the high-intermediate group is native-like, but the low-intermediate and intermediate Japanese groups differ significantly from the native control group ($p < .001$).

Regarding the Korean groups, there is a significant effect for the resultative constructions ($F(2,194) = 6.809$, $p < .05$) and for learners' Chinese proficiency levels ($F(3,97) = 13.551$, $p < .001$), but not for the interaction between these two factors ($F(6,194) = 0.650$, $p = .690$). Pair-wise comparisons indicate that the three Korean groups differ significantly from the control group ($p < .05$) but do not differ from each other.

The results of each proficiency group in relation to other proficiency groups and the control group are summarized in Table 7.1.

Table 7.1 Summary of the results on resultative constructions in the AJ test: pair-wise Bonferroni comparisons

|    | English groups | | | Japanese groups | | | Korean groups | | |
| --- | --- | --- | --- | --- | --- | --- | --- | --- | --- |
|    | LI | IN | HI | LI | IN | HI | LI | IN | HI |
| IN | √ |   |   |   |   |   |   |   |   |
| HI | √ |   |   | √ | √ |   |   |   |   |
| NS | √ | √ |   | √ | √ |   | √ | √ | √ |

"√" stands for a significant difference found in pair-wise Bonferroni tests

As seen in Table 7.1, comparisons between judgements of L2 proficiency groups seem to suggest that English- and Japanese-speaking learners' L2 Chinese grammars with regard to resultative constructions develop toward the target grammar with the increase in their L2 Chinese proficiency and that the high-intermediate English and Japanese groups have native-like mental representations of these constructions. No significant development is seen in the Korean groups and their judgments on Chinese resultative constructions remain non-native-like from the low-intermediate stage throughout to the high-intermediate stage.

Results of the AJ test seem to suggest that the functional AspP headed by the resultative marker *de* can be properly projected in English- and Japanese-speaking learners' L2 Chinese grammars although the functional category in question is unavailable in the resultative constructions of L1 English and Japanese. In contrast, Korean-speaking learners have more problems acquiring Chinese resultative constructions although the functional category AspP is present in the resultative construction of L1 Korean. The effect of L1 Korean on L2 Chinese seems to be negative rather than positive, as we will see in the discussion in § 7.4.1. The results seem to imply that the unavailability of certain functional categories (e.g. AspP) in the L1s does not put L2 Chinese learners from these L1s at a disadvantage with regard to the acquisition of these functional categories.

GLM repeated measures were also conducted between L2 groups from different L1s but at the same Chinese proficiency levels with the mean scores on the resultative constructions as the within-subject factor and learners' L1s as the between-subject factor. Between the three low-intermediate groups, there is a significant effect for the resultative constructions ($F(2,130) = 10.858, p < .001$) but not for learners' L1s ($F(2,65) = 2.035, p = .139$) or for the interaction ($F(4,130) = 0.260, p = .903$).

The intermediate groups pattern together with the low-intermediate groups: the effect for the resultative constructions is significant ($F(2,106) = 4.852$, $p < .05$), but the effect for learners' L1s ($F(2,53) = 0.400$, $p = .672$) and the effect for the interaction ($F(4,106) = 1.048$, $p = .386$) are not.

Between the high-intermediate groups, effects for the resultative constructions ($F(2,114) = 4.362$, $p < .05$) and for learners' L1s ($F(2,57) = 3.570$, $p < .05$) are significant, but the effect for the interaction between the two factors is not ($F(4,114) = 0.316$, $p = .867$). Pair-wise Bonferroni tests show that the Japanese group accepts Chinese resultative constructions more than the Korean group ($p < .05$) at the high-intermediate stage. Given that the functional category AspP is present in Korean resultative constructions as in Chinese, Korean speakers are expected to accept Chinese resultative constructions more than English and Japanese speakers. However, this prediction is not borne out by the comparisons between groups from different L1s. We will go to this problem in § 7.4.1.

### 7.1.2 Results of the comprehension test

The aim of the comprehension test is to examine semantic structures of Chinese resultative constructions in L2 Chinese grammars. Two types of resultative constructions as illustrated in (2) (repeated from (23) of Chapter 5) were used in the comprehension test. Following each token of these constructions, a question is asked about which of the two NPs (i.e. $NP_1$ like *Zhangsan* and $NP_2$ like *Lisi*) the result element (e.g. *lei* 'tire') is predicated of, as shown in the examples.

(2) Resultative constructions used in the comprehension test
    A. Resultative with single transitive $V_1$
        Zhangsan zhui de Lisi dou lei le.
        Zhangsan chase *de* Lisi even tire ASP

'Zhangsan chased Lisi and Lisi got tired as a result. '
( $V_1$ = *zhui* 'chase', $V_2$ = *lei* 'tire' )
*Question*: *Shui lei le* (*who got tired*)?

B. Resultative with reduplicated transitive $V_1$
Zhangsan <u>zhui</u> Lisi zhui *de* dou *lei* le.
Zhangsan chase Lisi chase *de* even tire ASP
'Zhangsan chased Lisi and got tired. '
( $V_1$ = *zhui* 'chase', $V_2$ = *lei* 'tire' )
*Question*: *Shui lei le* (*who got tired*)?

Recall that five options are provided for each question, of which "A" stands for "the sentence is ungrammatical" and "E" for "I don't know". The other three options suggest different ways of comprehension. Let us take tokens in (2) as examples to illustrate what they mean. Option B stands for a situation where the result predicate (i. e. *lei* 'tire') assigns a θ-role to $NP_1$ (i. e. *Zhangsan*), implying a reading that "Zhangsan got tired"; Option C stands for a situation where the result predicate (i. e. *lei* 'tire') assigns a θ-role to $NP_2$ (i. e. *Lisi*), implying a reading that "Lisi got tired"; Option D stands for a situation where the result predicate (i. e. *lei* 'tire') assigns a θ-role either to $NP_1$ (i. e. *Zhangsan*) or to $NP_2$ (i. e. *Lisi*), suggesting ambiguous readings that "either Zhangsan or Lisi got tired".

If a learner chooses A or E, he takes the construction as either ungrammatical or incomprehensible. If he chooses B, C or D, it indicates that he understands the construction in a certain way. Since the aim of the test is to look into the semantic structure of resultative constructions in L2 Chinese grammars, tokens where subjects choose A or E will be excluded when results are analysed.

The two resultative constructions (i. e. Type A and Type B as shown in (2)) used in the comprehension test were presented in three ways (see § 5.4.2.3 for illustrations): a) in sentences without a context; b) in a pictorial context biased toward Option B (i.e. 'Zhangsan got tired'); c) in a pictorial context biased toward Option C (i.e. 'Lisi got tired'). Since both the two resultative constructions used in the test are unambiguous, their interpretations are not determined by the contexts. Through pictorial contexts biased toward a certain interpretation, we hope to find out whether learners' L2 Chinese syntax allows ambiguous readings of the resultative constructions tested.

### 7.1.2.1 Resultative construction: Type A

Let us first look at the results on Type A, i.e. resultatives with a single transitive $V_1$. Three different meanings as shown in (3(i)), (3ii) and (3(iii)) can be generated from this construction exemplified in (2A) if the result predicate (i.e. *lei* 'tire') assigns a θ-role to different NPs, $NP_1$ (i.e. *Zhangsan*) and $NP_2$ (i.e. *Lisi*). Options B, C and D stand for the three possible readings as stated in (3(i)), (3ii) and (3(iii)) respectively. Of the three possible readings, only (3ii) (i.e. Option C) is allowed in the native Chinese grammar. The semantic structure of this type of resultative is illustrated in (4).

(3) Zhangsan zhui de Lisi dou lei le.
   ($V_1$ = *zhui* 'chase', $V_2$ = *lei* 'tire')
   Zhangsan chase de Lisi even tire ASP
   (i) *'Zhangsan chased Lisi and got tired as a result.' (Option B)
   (ii) 'Zhangsan chased Lisi and Lisi got tired as a result.'(Option C)
   (iii) *'Zhangsan chased Lisi and either Zhangsan or Lisi got tired as a result.' (Option D)
(4) [[xDO SOMETHINGTO y]CAUSE [yBECOME STATE]]

To find out how this construction is interpreted by L2 Chinese learners, I counted the occurrences of each of the three interpretations (B, C or D). The percentage of interpretations for each option out of the total number of interpreted tokens is given in Table 7.2.[1] I also counted subjects who consistently choose the same option (B, C or D) on the three tokens of the construction. The percentage of such consistent subjects out of those who show a certain way of understanding (i. e. choosing B, C or D on the three tokens) is given in Table 7.3. The percentage of the correct interpretation (i. e. Option C) is shaded in Table 7.2 and Table 7.3.

Table 7.2 *Type A of the resultative construction in the comprehension test: frequency (in percentage) of each of the interpretations*

| Subject groups | | In sentences without a context | | | In context biased toward Option B | | | In context biased toward Option C | | |
|---|---|---|---|---|---|---|---|---|---|---|
| | | B % | C % | D % | B % | C % | D % | B % | C % | D % |
| English | LI | 25 | 29 | 46 | 40 | 37 | 23 | 19 | 55 | 27 |
| | IN | 38 | 34 | 28 | 43 | 22 | 35 | 32 | 52 | 16 |
| | HI | 27 | 63 | 10 | 25 | 61 | 14 | 22 | 68 | 10 |
| Japanese | LI | 39 | 25 | 36 | 37 | 41 | 22 | 47 | 27 | 27 |
| | IN | 53 | 33 | 13 | 32 | 59 | 9 | 29 | 65 | 6 |
| | HI | 14 | 67 | 19 | 8 | 62 | 30 | 6 | 70 | 25 |
| Korean | LI | 34 | 26 | 40 | 40 | 28 | 32 | 32 | 41 | 26 |
| | IN | 22 | 47 | 31 | 37 | 46 | 17 | 26 | 48 | 26 |
| | HI | 28 | 44 | 28 | 44 | 37 | 20 | 33 | 46 | 22 |
| Native control | | 1 | 96 | 3 | 13 | 80 | 7 | 1 | 98 | 1 |

Table 7.3 Type A of the resultative construction in the comprehension test: percentage of subjects who consistently chose the same option (B, C or D) on the three tokens of the construction

| Subject groups | | In sentences without a context | | | In context biased toward Option B | | | In context biased toward Option C | | |
|---|---|---|---|---|---|---|---|---|---|---|
| | | B % | C % | D % | B % | C % | D % | B % | C % | D % |
| English | LI | 11 | 5 | 11 | 11 | 6 | 6 | 0 | 22 | 6 |
| | IN | 14 | 14 | 14 | 40 | 0 | 20 | 14 | 14 | 0 |
| | HI | 30 | 50 | 10 | 0 | 33 | 0 | 8 | 42 | 0 |
| Japanese | LI | 14 | 0 | 14 | 0 | 0 | 0 | 29 | 14 | 0 |
| | IN | 38 | 0 | 0 | 20 | 20 | 0 | 25 | 38 | 0 |
| | HI | 0 | 43 | 0 | 0 | 29 | 0 | 0 | 40 | 0 |
| Korean | LI | 6 | 0 | 18 | 21 | 0 | 7 | 6 | 12 | 6 |
| | IN | 0 | 25 | 38 | 8 | 23 | 0 | 0 | 27 | 0 |
| | HI | 11 | 0 | 22 | 10 | 0 | 0 | 17 | 25 | 8 |
| Native control | | 0 | 81 | 0 | 0 | 64 | 0 | 0 | 92 | 0 |

When the construction is presented without a context (see the column "in sentences without a context" in Table 7.2), the correct interpretation, i.e. Option C, is the dominant one of the three possible readings (i.e. options B, C and D) in the three high-intermediate L2 Chinese groups. In the high-intermediate English and Japanese groups, the correct interpretation (i.e. Option C) constitute more than 60 percent of the tokens treated as grammatical and comprehensible, and more than 40 percent of the subjects in the two groups consistently choose this option in sentences without a context, as shown in Table 7.3. In contrast, none of the high-intermediate Korean subjects consistently chooses the correct option (i.e. Option C) although a quarter of the Korean subjects choose this option at the intermediate stage, as seen in Table 7.3.

The results presented in Tables 7.2 and 7.3 seem to suggest that pictorial contexts play a role in learners' comprehension of the construction. However, the direction may not be necessarily such as the picture hints. When the picture is biased toward the correct interpretation, i. e. Option C, the percentage of selections for this option rises in all groups, as shown in Table 7.2, and the percentage of consistent subjects for this option rises in most groups, as shown in Table 7.3. When the picture is biased toward the non-target interpretation, i. e. Option B, the percentage of this option and the percentage of consistent subjects for this option only rise in some groups. Of groups at different L2 proficiency levels, the high-intermediate groups from the three L1s show the least variation in terms of the rate of correct interpretations when the structure is presented in different ways (see Table 7.2): it ranges from 61% to 68% in the high-intermediate English group, from 29% to 40% in the high-intermediate Japanese group, and from 37% to 46% in the high-intermediate Korean group. This seems to indicate that high-intermediate learners' interpretations are less liable to biased contexts.

### 7.1.2.2 Resultative construction: Type B

Type B of the resultative construction contains a reduplicated transitive $V_1$ like *zhui* 'chase' in (5). It may have three possible readings as illustrated in (5i), (5ii) and (5iii), which Options B, C and D in the test stand for respectively, depending on which of the NPs (i. e. $NP_1$ *Zhangsan* and $NP_2$ *Lisi*) is assigned a θ-role by the result predicate $V_2$ (i. e. *lei* 'tire'). Of the three possible readings, only (5i) (i. e. Option B) is allowed in the native Chinese grammar and the resultative construction has a semantic structure as illustrated in (6).

(5) Zhangsan zhui  Lisi zhui  de dou   lei le.
    Zhangsan chase Lisi chase *de* even tire ASP
    ($V_1 = zhui$ 'chase', $V_2 = lei$ 'tire')
    (i) 'Zhangsan chased Lisi and got tired as a result.'(Option B)
    (ii) * 'Zhangsan chased Lisi and Lisi got tired as a result.'(Option C)

(iii) * 'Zhangsan chased Lisi and either Zhangsan or Lisi got tired as a result. ' (Option D)

(6) [[x DO SOMETHING TOy] CAUSE [xBECOME STATE]]

Now let us find out how learners interpret this type of resultative construction. The percentage of interpretations for each option (B, C or D) out of the total number of interpreted tokens is given in Table 7.4. The percentage of consistent subjects (i. e. subjects who consistently choose the same option on the three tokens of the construction) out of those who show a certain way of understanding (i. e. choosing B, C or D on the three tokens) is given in Table 7.5. The percentage of the correct interpretation (i. e. Option B) is shaded.

Table 7.4 Type B of the resultative construction in the comprehension test: frequency (in percentage) of each of the interpretations

| Subject groups | | In sentences without a context | | | In context biased toward Option B | | | In context biased toward Option C | | |
|---|---|---|---|---|---|---|---|---|---|---|
| | | B % | C % | D % | B % | C % | D % | B % | C % | D % |
| English | LI | 45 | 13 | 42 | 40 | 19 | 40 | 27 | 32 | 41 |
| | IN | 54 | 17 | 29 | 67 | 9 | 24 | 43 | 22 | 35 |
| | HI | 72 | 12 | 16 | 69 | 5 | 26 | 67 | 0 | 33 |
| Japanese | LI | 70 | 15 | 15 | 59 | 8 | 32 | 66 | 9 | 26 |
| | IN | 92 | 2 | 6 | 83 | 6 | 11 | 70 | 2 | 27 |
| | HI | 85 | 9 | 6 | 83 | 2 | 15 | 78 | 6 | 16 |
| Korean | LI | 54 | 20 | 26 | 56 | 19 | 25 | 31 | 46 | 23 |
| | IN | 77 | 7 | 17 | 64 | 11 | 25 | 54 | 11 | 36 |
| | HI | 59 | 25 | 16 | 66 | 12 | 22 | 64 | 13 | 23 |
| Native control | | 90 | 1 | 8 | 93 | 1 | 6 | 81 | 10 | 8 |

*Table 7.5 Type B of the resultative construction in the comprehension test: percentage of subjects who consistently chose the same option (B, C or D) on the three tokens of the construction*

| Subject groups | | In sentences without a context | | | In context biased toward Option B | | | In context biased toward Option C | | |
|---|---|---|---|---|---|---|---|---|---|---|
| | | B % | C % | D % | B % | C % | D % | B % | C % | D % |
| English | LI | 15 | 0 | 10 | 9 | 0 | 18 | 5 | 5 | 24 |
| | IN | 40 | 0 | 20 | 25 | 0 | 13 | 36 | 9 | 18 |
| | HI | 46 | 0 | 7 | 55 | 0 | 9 | 60 | 0 | 30 |
| Japanese | LI | 33 | 0 | 0 | 27 | 0 | 9 | 63 | 0 | 0 |
| | IN | 80 | 0 | 0 | 62 | 0 | 0 | 62 | 0 | 15 |
| | HI | 68 | 0 | 0 | 67 | 0 | 5 | 62 | 0 | 10 |
| Korean | LI | 24 | 0 | 6 | 31 | 0 | 8 | 11 | 11 | 6 |
| | IN | 57 | 0 | 0 | 44 | 0 | 25 | 27 | 0 | 33 |
| | HI | 33 | 7 | 0 | 47 | 0 | 12 | 39 | 0 | 11 |
| Native control | | 81 | 0 | 0 | 82 | 0 | 0 | 75 | 0 | 0 |

As shown in Table 7.4, the construction is more likely to be interpreted as Option B (i.e. the target interpretation), which stands for the reading that 'Zhangsan chased Lisi and got tired as a result', than otherwise by most groups and in most situations. The tendency is more clearly seen from the percentage of consistent subjects shown in Table 7.5. When the construction occurs independently of contexts, few subjects interpret it as ambiguous (i.e. as Option D) and even fewer interpret it as Option C (i.e. the reading that 'Zhangsan chased Lisi and Lisi got tired as a result'). In fact, none of the subjects in the English and Japanese groups chooses Option C, an incorrect interpretation. When the construction occurs in a context biased toward the correct interpretation, i.e. Option B, none of the subjects chooses the incorrect Option C consistently in any of the learner groups. Even when the context is biased toward the incorrect interpretation (i.e. Option C), none of the high-intermediate subjects consistently interprets it as the context suggests. This seems to indicate that L2 Chinese learners do not have much difficulty in interpreting this type of resultatives.

The two types of resultative constructions used in the comprehension test as illustrated in (3) and (5) do not have ambiguous readings, but some tokens are interpreted as ambiguous (i. e. as Option D) as shown in Table 7.2 and Table 7.4, and a few subjects consistently treat the constructions as ambiguous as seen in Table 7.3 and Table 7.5. The misinterpretation most probably results from the word *dou* in the testing items. *Dou* has different meanings. It may function either as a universal quantifier meaning "all" or as an adverb of degree meaning "to the extent" (see Cheng 1995, J. Li 1995, among others, for detailed discussion). In the testing items, explanation of *dou* as an adverb of degree was provided, but L2 Chinese learners probably overlooked the explanation and still took it as a universal quantifier because the word is usually learned first as a quantifier. Since *dou* occurs before the result predicate like *lei* 'tire', it is possible for L2 Chinese learners to interpret sentences like (3) and (5) as 'both Zhangsan and Lisi got tired'. Because none of the options provided stands for such an interpretation, L2 Chinese learners may choose Option D, the option that allows the result element to be predicated of either $NP_1$ (i. e. *Zhangsan*) or $NP_2$ (i. e. *Lisi*).

### 7.1.3 Summary

In § 7.1.1 and § 7.1.2, results of the AJ test and the comprehension test on Chinese resultative constructions were reported. As seen in the AJ test results (see Figure 7.1 and Table 7.1), English- and Japanese-speaking learners of L2 Chinese have native-like judgments on the resultative constructions at least at the high-intermediate stage, while Korean-speaking learners' judgments are non-native-like. The results of the comprehension test indicate that the resultative constructions are more likely to be interpreted in the target way than otherwise. Although lexical items (e. g. *dou* 'to an extent') and biased contexts may play a role in learners' comprehension, their effects are not dominant.

Given that Korean resultatives involve an AspP while English and Japanese resultatives do not, the results seem to suggest that the AspP in L1 Korean is not transferred into Korean-speaking learners' L2 Chinese and that the absence of AspP in L1 resultatives does not put English- and Japanese-speaking learners at a disadvantage in their acquisition of Chinese resultatives.

## 7.2 Compound causative constructions

### 7.2.1 Results of the AJ test

Recall that six types of compound causative constructions were used in the AJ test. Examples of each type are given in (7), repeated from (18) of Chapter 5. Of the six types of compound causative, Type F has ambiguous readings. We will examine learners' interpretation of this type of construction by analysing the result of the comprehension test in § 7.2.2.

(7) Compound causative constructions used in the AJ test
    *Group* 1. *Transitive* $V_1$:
      A. Unaccusative $V_2$
        Zhangsan da-*sui* le Lisi de huaping.
        Zhangsan hit-break ASP Lisi's vase
        'Zhangsan broke Lisi's vase.'
        ($V_1 = da$ 'hit', $V_2 = sui$ 'break')
      B. Unergative $V_2$
        Zhangsan ma-*ku* le Lisi.
        Zhangsan scold-cry ASP Lisi

'Zhangsan scolded Lisi and Lisi cried.'
($V_1 = ma$ 'scold', $V_2 = ku$ 'cry')

Group 2. Unergative $V_1$

C. Adjective $V_2$

Zhangsan ku-shi le shoujuan.

Zhangsan cry-wet ASP handkerchief

'Zhangsan cried the handkerchief soggy.'
($V_1 = ku$ 'cry', $V_2 = shi$ 'wet')

D. Psych verb $V_2$

Zhangsan ku-fan le Lisi.

Zhangsan cry-bore ASP Lisi

'Zhangsan cried and Lisi got bored as a result.'
($V_1 = ku$ 'cry', $V_2 = fan$ 'bore')

Group 3. Transitive $V_1$ + Psych verb $V_2$

E. Inanimate $NP_2$

Zhangsan ting-fan le na shou ge.

Zhangsan listen-bore ASP that CL song

'Zhangsan listened to that song (time and again) and got bored.'
($V_1 = ting$ 'listen to', $V_2 = fan$ 'bore', $NP_2 = na\ shou\ ge$ 'that song')

F. Animate/human $NP_2$

Zhangsan zhui-lei le Lisi.

Zhangsan chase-tire ASP Lisi

(i) 'Zhangsan chased Lisi and got tired as a result.'

(ii) 'Zhangsan chased Lisi and Lisi got tired as a result.'

($V_1 = zhui$ 'chase', $V_2 = lei$ 'tire', $NP_2 = Lisi$)

The mean scores of each type of compound causative construction are illustrated in Figure 7.2 (see Tables 13 to 18 in Appendix 7 for descriptive statistics).

# Results and discussion: resultative and compound causative constructions

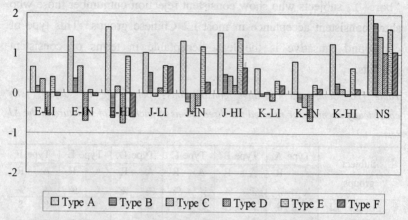

*Figure 7.2 Compound causative constructions: mean scores in the AJ test*

Of the six types of compound causatives in the test, Type A, which contains a transitive $V_1$ (e.g. *da* 'hit') and an unaccusative $V_2$ (e.g. *sui* 'break'), is most acceptable to all the L2 groups, although the mean scores in the low-intermediate English and Korean groups and the intermediate Korean group do not reach the benchmark of acceptance (mean score $\geq +1$). In terms of mean scores, the high-intermediate and intermediate Japanese groups accept Type E.

Individual subjects who consistently accept (choosing "+1" and "+2" on the three tokens of a construction) or reject a structure (choosing "-1" or "-2" on the three tokens of a construction) were counted, and the percentage of such subjects in each group is given in Table 7.6. The percentage of subjects who show consistent acceptance of a structure is shaded.

As illustrated in Table 7.6, more than half of the intermediate and high-intermediate subjects in each learner group consistently accept Type A. Both the mean scores and the percentage of consistent subjects seem to suggest that Type A is the most acceptable compound causative construction. In the case of Type D, which contains an unergative $V_1$ (e.g. *ku* 'cry') and a psych verb $V_2$ (e.g. *fan*

· 235 ·

'bore'), subjects who show consistent rejection outnumber those who show consistent acceptance in most L2 Chinese groups. This type of compound causative is the least acceptable in terms of consistent subjects.

*Table 7.6 Compound causative constructions: percentage of subjects who consistently accepted or rejected the three tokens of each type of structure in the AJ test*

| Subject groups | | Type A | | Type B | | Type C | | Type D | | Type E | | Type F | |
|---|---|---|---|---|---|---|---|---|---|---|---|---|---|
| | | A % | R % | A % | R % | A % | R % | A % | R % | A % | R % | A % | R % |
| English | LI | 42 | 8 | 27 | 12 | 23 | 8 | 8 | 27 | 23 | 8 | 8 | 8 |
| | IN | 79 | 0 | 15 | 0 | 31 | 8 | 0 | 38 | 8 | 8 | 8 | 8 |
| | HI | 100 | 0 | 7 | 31 | 31 | 19 | 7 | 44 | 50 | 7 | 7 | 31 |
| Japanese | LI | 40 | 0 | 33 | 13 | 0 | 7 | 20 | 7 | 33 | 0 | 33 | 7 |
| | IN | 78 | 0 | 0 | 11 | 0 | 7 | 11 | 22 | 77 | 7 | 22 | 0 |
| | HI | 83 | 0 | 35 | 9 | 30 | 0 | 22 | 4 | 70 | 0 | 43 | 4 |
| Korean | LI | 37 | 4 | 11 | 15 | 15 | 15 | 4 | 15 | 19 | 4 | 15 | 4 |
| | IN | 52 | 4 | 12 | 12 | 4 | 28 | 0 | 37 | 32 | 12 | 8 | 12 |
| | HI | 77 | 0 | 14 | 0 | 10 | 19 | 5 | 19 | 33 | 0 | 14 | 29 |
| Native control | | 100 | 0 | 93 | 0 | 75 | 0 | 75 | 0 | 89 | 0 | 82 | 4 |

A = accept; R = reject

## 7.2.1.1 Comparisons between L2 proficiency groups and comparisons between L2 groups from different L1s

Let us consider whether there are significant differences between groups at different Chinese proficiency levels and between L2 groups from different L1s. GLM repeated measures were conducted on the mean scores between the English groups, the Japanese groups and the Korean groups respectively, with the native group as a control. The six types of compound causatives form the within-subject factor and learners' Chinese proficiency levels form the between-subject factor. Bonferroni tests were used in pair-wise comparisons.

Between the English groups, there is a significant effect for the compound causatives ($F(5,395) = 52.555$, $p < .001$), for learners' Chinese proficiency levels ($F(3,79) = 40.345$, $p < .001$) and for the interaction between these two factors ($F(15, 395) = 5.711$, $p < .001$). Results of the three English groups do not differ from each other ($p = 1.000$), but they all differ significantly from the native control group ($p < .001$). This seems to suggest that English-speaking learners' L2 Chinese concerning compound causatives does not develop significantly from the low-intermediate stage to the high-intermediate stage and remains non-native-like throughout.

The Japanese groups pattern together with the English groups. The effect for the compound causatives ($F(5,400) = 37.616$, $p < .001$), for learners' Chinese proficiency levels ($F(3,80) = 26.760$, $p < .001$) and for the interaction ($F(15, 400) = 4.031$, $p < .001$) are all significant. A significant difference ($p < .05$) is found between the intermediate and high-intermediate groups in pair-wise comparisons, but the three Japanese groups all differ significantly from the native control group ($p < .001$).

Between the Korean groups, there is a significant effect for the compound causatives ($F(4, 485) = 22.642$, $p < .001$) and for learners' Chinese proficiency levels ($F(3,97) = 45.238$, $p < .001$) but not for the interaction ($F(15,485) = 1.584$, $p = .074$). While the three Korean groups do not differ from each other in their mean scores, all of them differ significantly from the control group ($p < .001$).

Comparisons between groups at different Chinese proficiency levels seem to suggest that Chinese compound causative constructions in L2 grammars are non-native-like at the three developmental stages under examination and that English- and Korean-speaking learners' L2 Chinese grammars concerning these constructions are likely to be fossilized.

To find out whether there is any variation between results of L2 groups from different L1s, GLM repeated measures were conducted between the low-intermediate groups, the intermediate groups and the high-intermediate groups, with the mean scores on the six types of compound causatives as the within-subject factor and learners' L1s as the between-subject factor.

Between the low-intermediate groups, there is a significant effect for the compound causatives ($F(5,325) = 10.031$, $p < .001$), but not for learners' L1s ($F(2,65) = 1.967$, $p = .148$) or for the interaction ($F(10,325) = 1.460$, $p = .153$).

Regarding the intermediate groups, the effect is non-significant for learners' L1s ($F(2,53) = 2.123$, $p = .130$), but significant for the compound causatives ($F(5,265) = 27.041$, $p < .001$) and for the interaction between the two factors ($F(10,265) = 3.957$, $p < .001$).

Between the high-intermediate groups, the effect for the compound causatives ($F(5,285) = 34.961$, $p < .001$), for learners' L1s ($F(2,57) = 4.967$, $p < .05$) and for the interaction ($F(10,285) = 2.780$, $p < .05$) are all significant. Bonferroni tests reveal a significant difference between the English group and the Japanese group ($p < .05$): the Japanese subjects show more acceptance to Chinese compound causatives than the English subjects at the high-intermediate stage.

Comparing the results of the six types of compound causative constructions as a whole between learner groups may give us an impression that L2 Chinese learners are unable to achieve native-like mental representations of Chinese compound causatives as none of the L2 Chinese groups in the study has native-like judgment. Given that the compound causative construction in Chinese involves a functional category AspP (see § 3.2.2), the results may imply that the AspP cannot be projected in L2 Chinese compound causatives. Such a conclusion, however, seems to be oversimplified because learners of the L2 groups show considerable variation in judging different types of compound causative construction. Thus we need to look at their judgments in more detail to find out what happens in their L2 Chinese grammars.

### 7.2.1.2 A closer examination of different types of compound causatives

In this section, we will examine test results of L2 Chinese learners on different types of compound causative to see which type can be acquired by L2 Chinese learners at the developmental stages under study.

First let us have a closer look at Type A (repeated in (8)), the most acceptable compound causative construction in terms of mean scores and number of consistent subjects (see Table 13 in Appendix 7 for descriptive statistics of this type of compound causative).

(8) Zhangsan da-sui    le   Lisi de huaping.
    Zhangsan hit-break ASP Lisi's vase
    'Zhangsan broke Lisi's vase.'
    (Transitive $V_1 = da$ 'hit', unaccusative $V_2 = sui$ 'break')

One-way ANOVA and following Scheffé tests were conducted between the English groups, the Japanese groups and the Korean groups independently on learners' mean scores in judging this type of compound causative with the native group as a control.

Significant differences are found between the English groups and the control group ($F(3, 79) = 23.187$, $p < .001$). The low-intermediate group differs significantly from the intermediate group ($p = .006$) and the high-intermediate group ($p < .001$), but no significant difference is found between the intermediate and high-intermediate groups ($p = .779$). The judgement of the high-intermediate English group is native-like.

Significant differences are also found between the Japanese groups and the control group ($F(3,80) = 8.740$, $p < .001$). Although the three Japanese groups do not differ significantly from each other, the low-intermediate and intermediate Japanese groups differ significantly from the native control group ($p < .001$ and $p = .005$ respectively). The judgement of the high-intermediate group is native-like.

The Korean groups and the control group differ significantly ($F(3,97 = 12.846$, $p < .001$). No significant difference is found between the three Korean groups, but the low-intermediate and intermediate groups differ significantly from the control group ($p < .001$). The judgement of the high-intermediate group is near native ($p = .043$). It can be concluded, therefore, that Korean-speaking learners' L2 Chinese grammar with regard to this type of compound causative is developing toward the target grammar.

One-way ANOVA tests were also conducted on the mean scores of this type of compound causative construction between groups from different L1s but at the same L2 Chinese proficiency levels. No significant difference is found between the low-intermediate groups ($F(2,65) = 1.104$, $p = .338$), the intermediate groups ($F(2,53) = 2.469$, $p = .094$) or the high-intermediate groups ($F(2,57) = 1.370$, $p = .262$).

Comparisons between results on Type A seem to suggest that L2 Chinese groups at the high-intermediate stage are able to achieve native or near-native representations of this type of compound causative construction, which may imply that the functional category AspP involved in this construction can be properly projected in L2 Chinese grammars and that L2 Chinese learners are able to acquire the syntactic structure of compound causative constructions with the increase in their L2 Chinese proficiency.

As on Type A, one-way ANOVA and pair-wise Scheffé tests were conducted on the mean scores of the other types of compound causatives between the English groups, the Japanese groups and the Korean groups respectively, with the native group as a control. To save space, results of the tests are given in Appendix 8. Let us now find out how L2 Chinese learners judge the other types of compound causatives.

Type B contains a transitive $V_1$ ( e. g. *ma* ' scold ') and an unergative $V_2$ ( e. g. *ku* ' cry ') as shown in (7B). In terms of mean scores, none of the L2 Chinese groups accepts (mean score $\geqslant +1$) this type of compound causative (see Table 14 in Appendix 7 for descriptive statistics). Instead, the high-intermediate English group, the intermediate Japanese group, the high-intermediate and intermediate Korean groups tend to reject it (mean score ranging between 0 and -1). One-way ANOVA and pair-wise Scheffé tests indicate that none of the L2 Chinese groups has native-like judgement on this structure.

Type C contains an unergative $V_1$ ( e. g. *ku* ' cry ') and an adjective $V_2$ ( e. g. *shi* ' wet ') as shown in (7C). Pair-wise comparisons indicate that the intermediate English group's judgement of this type of compound causative is native-like, but there are significant differences between judgements of other L2 Chinese groups and judgment of the control group (see Appendix 8).

Type D contains an unergative $V_1$ ( e. g. *ku* ' cry ') and a psych verb $V_2$ ( e. g. *fan* ' bore ') as exemplified in (7D). As seen in Table 7.6, it is the least acceptable type of compound causative in terms of consistent subjects. With regard to mean scores, the three English groups, the three Korean groups and the intermediate Japanese group show degrees of rejection of it. None of the L2 Chinese groups has native-like judgement on it.

Type E and Type F contain a transitive $V_1$ and a psych verb $V_2$.

They differ in that $NP_2$ is inanimate in Type E but animate in Type F. The intermediate (mean score = 1.17) and high-intermediate (mean score = 1.38) Japanese groups accept Type E and the other L2 groups, except for the low-intermediate Korean group, tend to accept it (mean score ranging between 0 and +1) (see Table 17 in Appendix 7). The high-intermediate English and Japanese groups and the intermediate Japanese group have native-like judgements on it (see Appendix 8). With regard to Type F, the three English groups show degrees of rejection, while the Japanese and Korean groups show degrees of acceptance (see Table 18 in Appendix 7). The judgments of the three Japanese groups are native-like, but the judgments of the other L2 groups are all non-native-like (see Appendix 8).

Generally speaking, of the six types of compound causative under examination, Type A is the most acceptable while Type D is the least acceptable. As stated in Chapter 3, Chinese compound causatives have the same underlying structure as illustrated in (39) of Chapter 3. Then why do L2 learners show variations in judging different types of compound causative? I will address this problem in § 7.4.

### 7.2.2 Results of the comprehension test

In the AJ test, six types of compound causative constructions were tested. Among them, Type F has ambiguous readings. To find out whether L2 Chinese learners can acquire the semantic structure of this type of compound causative, we used it in the comprehension test. An example of the construction is repeated in (9) for the convenience of discussion.

(9) Compound causative construction used in the comprehension test
   (Type F in the AJ test)
   Zhangsan zhui-*lei*    le    Lisi.
   Zhangsan chase-tire ASP Lisi

■ Results and discussion: resultative and compound causative constructions ■

 (i) 'Zhangsan chased Lisi and got tired as a result.'(Option B)
 (ii) 'Zhangsan chased Lisi and Lisi got tired as a result.' (Option C)
 (iii) 'Zhangsan chased Lisi and either Zhangsan or Lisi got tired as a result.' (Option D)

As pointed out in § 5.4.2.3, five options from A to E are provided for each sentence in the comprehension test. If a learner chooses Option A or Option E, it indicates that he treats the structure as either ungrammatical or incomprehensible. Choosing Options B, C or D indicates that the learner takes the sentence as grammatical and understands it in a certain way: Option B stands for reading (i); Option C stands for reading(ii); Option D stands for reading (iii). The structure is presented in three ways: a) in sentences without a context; b) in a pictorial context biased toward Option B (i.e. reading (i)); c) in a pictorial context biased toward Option C (i.e. reading (ii)).

 To find out how the structure is interpreted, I counted the number of interpretations for each option (B, C and D) and the number of subjects who consistently choose the same option (B, C or D) on the three tokens of the structure. The percentage of interpretations for each option (B, C or D) out of the total number of interpreted tokens is given in Table 7.7. The percentage of consistent subjects out of those who show a certain way of understanding (by choosing B, C or D on the three tokens) is given in Table 7.8. The three readings as shown in (9) are all possible interpretations of the structure. The percentage of Option B is shaded and the percentage of Option C is italicised.

· 243 ·

Table 7.7 The compound causative construction in the comprehension test: frequency (in percentage) of each of the interpretations

| Subject groups | | In sentences without a context | | | In context biased toward Option B | | | In context biased toward Option C | | |
|---|---|---|---|---|---|---|---|---|---|---|
| | | B % | C % | D % | B % | C % | D % | B % | C % | D % |
| English | LI | 44 | 47 | 9 | 55 | 40 | 5 | 21 | 75 | 4 |
| | IN | 24 | 42 | 33 | 38 | 59 | 3 | 23 | 70 | 7 |
| | HI | 32 | 63 | 5 | 45 | 52 | 3 | 32 | 62 | 6 |
| Japanese | LI | 92 | 8 | 0 | 93 | 7 | 0 | 82 | 15 | 3 |
| | IN | 89 | 5 | 5 | 83 | 14 | 3 | 93 | 7 | 0 |
| | HI | 53 | 43 | 4 | 73 | 27 | 0 | 52 | 46 | 2 |
| Korean | LI | 36 | 46 | 18 | 68 | 22 | 10 | 52 | 38 | 10 |
| | IN | 67 | 31 | 2 | 64 | 26 | 10 | 57 | 35 | 8 |
| | HI | 47 | 53 | 0 | 63 | 33 | 5 | 63 | 38 | 0 |
| Native control | | 7 | 45 | 49 | 51 | 27 | 22 | 5 | 77 | 18 |

Table 7.8 The compound causative construction in the comprehension test: percentage of subjects who consistently chose the same option (B, C or D) on the three tokens of the construction

| Subject groups | | In sentences without a context | | | In context biased toward Option B | | | In context biased toward Option C | | |
|---|---|---|---|---|---|---|---|---|---|---|
| | | B % | C % | D % | B % | C % | D % | B % | C % | D % |
| English | LI | 7 | 14 | 0 | 5 | 5 | 0 | 0 | 40 | 0 |
| | IN | 14 | 57 | 0 | 11 | 33 | 0 | 11 | 33 | 0 |
| | HI | 9 | 27 | 0 | 14 | 29 | 0 | 0 | 30 | 0 |
| Japanese | LI | 88 | 0 | 0 | 80 | 0 | 0 | 88 | 0 | 0 |
| | IN | 80 | 0 | 0 | 67 | 0 | 0 | 100 | 0 | 0 |
| | HI | 27 | 27 | 0 | 25 | 8 | 0 | 18 | 27 | 0 |
| Korean | LI | 17 | 8 | 0 | 38 | 0 | 0 | 25 | 6 | 0 |
| | IN | 33 | 33 | 0 | 33 | 0 | 0 | 25 | 0 | 0 |
| | HI | 13 | 25 | 0 | 36 | 18 | 0 | 20 | 20 | 0 |
| Native control | | 0 | 16 | 32 | 25 | 0 | 17 | 0 | 53 | 7 |

As shown in Table 7.7, a large proportion of tokens taken as grammatical and comprehensible are interpreted as C (i.e. the reading

## 7 Results and discussion: resultative and compound causative constructions

that 'Zhangsan chased Lisi and Lisi got tired as a result') or D (i. e. the reading that 'Zhangsan chased Lisi and either Zhangsan or Lisi got tired as a result') by native Chinese speakers when the compound causative construction is presented without a context. When it is presented in a context biased toward Option B (i. e. the reading that 'Zhangsan chased Lisi and got tired as a result'), more than half of the tokens (51%) are interpreted by native subjects as the context suggests. When it is presented in a context biased toward Option C (i. e. the reading that 'Zhangsan chased Lisi and Lisi got tired as a result'), more than three quarters (77%) of the tokens are interpreted as the context suggests. When the structure occurs in either of the pictorial contexts, about 20 percent (22% and 18%) of the tokens are interpreted as ambiguous by native speakers although both contexts favour unambiguous readings (see (26) and (27) of Chapter 5). The ambiguity of the compound causative construction is more clearly seen in the percentage of consistent native subjects shown in Table 7. 8. When the structure is presented without a context, nearly one third (32%) of the native subjects consistently interpret it as ambiguous. When it occurs in a biased context, some native subjects still choose the ambiguous reading.

In the English groups, more tokens are interpreted as C, while Option D is the least favoured in most cases, whether the structure occurs in a context or whatever context it occurs in, as shown in Table 7. 7. The tendency is more revealing with regard to the percentage of consistent subjects shown in Table 7. 8. None of the English subjects consistently interprets the structure as ambiguous.

In the Japanese groups, more than half of the tokens are interpreted as B in all circumstances and, as in the case of English groups, Option D is the least favoured. As seen in Table 7. 8, none of the Japanese subjects consistently chooses D in any of the situations and only at the high-intermediate stage do some Japanese subjects consistently interpret the compound causative construction as C.

In the Korean groups, an overwhelming majority of tokens are interpreted as B and C when they are presented without a context. When presented in a context, more than half of the tokens are interpreted as B whether the context is biased toward it or not. As shown in Table 7.8, consistent Korean subjects for Option B outnumber those for Option C when a context is provided, but none of the Korean subjects interprets the compound causative construction as ambiguous whether a context is provided or not.

To sum up, while native Chinese speakers seem to prefer to interpret the compound causative construction as C or D, most L2 Chinese learners interpret it as B or C. None of the subjects in any of the L2 Chinese groups consistently interprets the construction as ambiguous (i.e. as Option D), as shown in Table 7.8.

Results of the comprehension test seem to indicate that L2 Chinese learners have problems with the interpretation of compound causatives. They can project AspP in their L2 Chinese grammars, as we have seen in § 7.2.1.2, but they seem uncertain about which argument is assigned a θ-role by the result predicate. Since Options B, C and D are all possible interpretations of the compound causative, contexts are expected to play an important role in learners' comprehension of the construction, as found in the native control group (see Tables 7.7 and 7.8). However, the influence of contexts on L2 learners' comprehension is not as much as that on native Chinese speakers' comprehension of the construction, especially with respect to the percentage of consistent subjects (see Table 7.8). In addition, none of the L2 learners consistently chooses the ambiguous reading (i.e. Option D) no matter how the construction is presented. This implies that L2 learners have problems with θ-role assignment by the result predicate.

## 7 Results and discussion: resultative and compound causative constructions

Is there any effect of L1 transfer in L2 learners' comprehension of the Chinese compound causative construction? Let us have a closer look at the test results.

We know that English does not have compound causative constructions, but it allows resultative constructions that observe DOR according to which the result element can only be predicated of the object (Levin and Rappaport Hovav 1995; Simpson 1983; see §3.1.1). If English-speaking learners apply DOR to Chinese compound causative constructions, the result element $V_2$ (e.g. *lei* 'tire' in (9)) will be predicated of the object (e.g. *Lisi* in (9)), resulting in reading (ii) (i.e. Option C). English speakers do show a preference for Option C, as seen in Tables 7.7 and 7.8, especially with regard to consistent subjects. This can be taken as an effect of L1 transfer.

As mentioned in § 3.3, Japanese compound causatives do not allow ambiguous readings and both $V_1$ and $V_2$ are predicated of the sentence subject obligatorily, as shown in (10) (repeated from (57) of Chapter 3):

(10) a. *John-ga Mary-o naguri-shinu-ta.
John-NOM Mary-ACC hit-die-PST
b. John-ga Mary-o naguri-korosu-ta.
John-NOM Mary-ACC hit-kill-PST
'John hit Mary and as a result killed her.'

If L1 transfer happens in Japanese speakers' L2 Chinese, the result element $V_2$ (e.g. *lei* 'tire' in (9)) will be more likely to assign a θ-role to $NP_1$ (e.g. *Zhangsan* in (9)) than to $NP_2$ (e.g. *Lisi* in (9)), resulting in reading (i) (i.e. Option B). This is the case as shown in Tables 7.7 and 7.8: Option B dominates Japanese speakers' interpretations in all circumstances and only at the high-intermediate stage do some Japanese subjects consistently interpret the construction as Option C. Since no inferential statistics was conducted, we do not know whether differences between Japanese speakers and English- and Korean-speaking learners in interpreting the compound causative are significant. However, Tables 7.7 and 7.8 do show that Japanese-speaking learners prefer Option B to Options C and D.

If we take English and Japanese speakers' interpretations of the Chinese compound causative construction as an effect of L1 transfer, then such effect is not seen in the Korean groups. The result predicate of Korean compound causatives assigns a θ-role to the object, i.e. $NP_2$, which is marked accusative case, as shown in (11) (repeated from (59b) of Chapter 3):

(11) John-i    Bill-ul    sswa-a-cwuk-i-ess-ta.
     John-NOM Bill-ACC shoot-die-CAUS-PAST-DEC
     'John shot Bill dead.'

Results of the comprehension test indicate that when the Chinese compound causative construction is presented without a context, Korean-speaking learners are more likely to interpret it as C at the low-intermediate and high-intermediate stages but prefer B at the intermediate stage. When it is presented in contexts, they are more likely to interpret it as B whatever context it occurs in. The inconsistency can be attributed to their uncertainty about this type of compound causative (i.e. Type F in the AJ test). As seen from the AJ test results (see Table 18 in Appendix 7), Korean speakers' representations of this type of compound causative seem to be fossilized (see Table 3 in Appendix 8). Their uncertainty about this construction may be rooted in the difference between the underlying structure of Korean compound causatives and that of Chinese compound causatives (see §3.5). Both Chinese and Korean contain functional categories in compound causative constructions: in Korean it is a causative $v$ (marked with -$i$) which selects VP as complement, whereas in Chinese it is Asp (with a phonetically unrealised head) which selects a result XP as complement. If L1 transfer happens, Korean-speaking learners need to readjust the position of the functional category in their L1 (i. e. the $v$) to accommodate Chinese data. This may cause uncertainty and bring about inconsistency in their judgments of the Chinese compound causative construction.

### 7.2.3 Summary

In § 7.2.1 and § 7.2.2, results of the AJ test and the comprehension test on Chinese compound causative constructions were reported. Results of the AJ test suggest that L2 Chinese learners can acquire the syntactic structure of compound causatives as all the high-intermediate L2 Chinese groups accept Type A of the compound causative and have native-like (in the case of English and Japanese speakers) or near-native-like (in the case of Korean speakers) judgments on this structure. Results on Type E reveal L1 transfer in Japanese-speaking learners' L2 Chinese compound causatives. The comprehension test seems to indicate that L2 Chinese learners cannot interpret the compound causative construction as native Chinese speakers do and that learners' L1s may play a role in their interpretation of this construction. It seems that L1 transfer happens but only in certain aspects and that functional categories like AspP involved in Chinese compound causatives can be properly projected in L2 Chinese grammars.

## 7.3 Comparisons between results on the resultative construction, the compound causative construction and the V-NP-XP structure

As stated in Chapter 3, both resultative constructions and compound causative constructions in Chinese involve the functional category AspP. Given that AspP is headed by a phonetically realized marker *de* in resultatives but a phonetically unrealized marker in compound causatives, it was hypothesized that L2 Chinese learners would have less difficulty acquiring the resultative construction than the compound causative construction due to the prominence of the head *de* in the former. It was also hypothesized that English- and Japanese-speaking learners would probably start from the V-NP-XP structure ( e. g. *Tom cried the handkerchief soggy* or *Tom pounded the metal flat*), which is available in their L1s ( ignoring the difference between English and Japanese in the headedness parameter of VP ) but disallowed in Chinese.

Let us now find out whether the hypotheses are borne out. Comparisons were made between Type A of the resultative construction in (1A) (repeated in (12a)), Type C of the compound causative construction in (7C) (repeated in (12b)) and the V-NP-XP structure as in (12c).

(12) a. Resultative construction (Type A in the AJ test)
   Zhangsan ku de shoujuan    dou shi le.
   Zhangsan cry *de* handkerchief even wet ASP
   'Zhangsan cried the handkerchief soggy.'
   b. Compound causative construction (Type C in the AJ test)
   Zhangsan ku-*shi*  le  shoujuan.
   Zhangsan cry-wet ASP handkerchief
   'Zhangsan cried the handkerchief soggy.'
   c. *The V-NP-XP structure
   *Zhangsan ku shoujuan    shi le.
   Zhangsan cry handkerchief wet ASP
   'Zhangsan cried the handkerchief soggy.'

# 7 Results and discussion: resultative and compound causative constructions

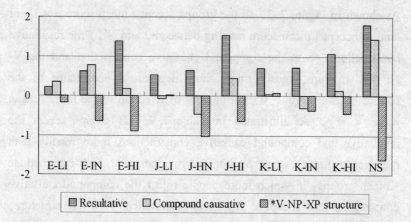

*Figure 7.3 Comparisons between the resultative construction, the compound causative construction and the V-NP-XP structure: mean scores in the AJ test*

The mean scores of these structures are illustrated in Figure 7.3. The percentage of subjects who consistently accept or reject the three tokens of each structure is given in Table 7.9. The percentage of acceptance is shaded.

*Table 7.9 Percentage of subjects who consistently accepted or rejected the three tokens of the resultative construction, the compound causative construction and the V-NP-XP structure in the AJ test*

| Subject groups | | Resultative | | Compound causative | | *V-NP-XP structure | |
|---|---|---|---|---|---|---|---|
| | | Accept % | Reject % | Accept % | Reject % | Accept % | Reject % |
| English | LI | 12 | 8 | 23 | 8 | 8 | 12 |
| | IN | 38 | 8 | 31 | 8 | 0 | 31 |
| | HI | 88 | 6 | 31 | 19 | 6 | 50 |
| Japanese | LI | 20 | 7 | 0 | 7 | 20 | 7 |
| | IN | 39 | 6 | 0 | 7 | 0 | 39 |
| | HI | 74 | 0 | 30 | 0 | 4 | 39 |
| Korean | LI | 37 | 0 | 15 | 15 | 15 | 4 |
| | IN | 40 | 4 | 4 | 28 | 12 | 39 |
| | HI | 48 | 0 | 10 | 19 | 5 | 29 |
| Native control | | 89 | 0 | 75 | 0 | 0 | 96 |

As shown in Figure 7.3, all the groups accept (mean score $\geq$ +1) or tend to accept (mean score ranging between 0 and +1) the resultative construction. As to the compound causative construction and the V-NP-XP structure, most groups show degrees of acceptance of the former (mean score > 0) but degrees of rejection of the latter (mean score < 0). As illustrated in Table 7.9, L2 groups accept the resultative and compound causative constructions more readily than they reject them except for the intermediate and high-intermediate Korean groups, in which more people reject the compound causative construction than accept it. On the ungrammatical V-NP-XP structure, most groups show more rejection than acceptance. This seems to suggest that at the developmental stages under examination the functional AspP involved in resultatives and compound causatives has started to emerge in L2 learners' Chinese grammars as we have seen in the learners' judgments in the AJ test (see § 7.1.1 and § 7.2.1) and that L2 learners have realized that Chinese does not allow the V-NP-XP structure.

To find out whether English- and Japanese-speaking learners accept the V-NP-XP structure more than Korean-speaking learners, one-way ANOVA tests were conducted on the mean scores in judging the V-NP-XP structure between L2 groups from different L1s but at the same Chinese proficiency levels. No significant difference is found between the low-intermediate groups ($F(2,65) = 0.630, p = .536$), the intermediate groups ($F(2,53) = 2.600, p = .084$) or the high-intermediate groups ($F(2,57) = 0.957, p = .390$). Given that the V-NP-XP structure is allowed in English and Japanese but not allowed in Korean, the results reveal no effect of L1 transfer.[2]

Let us now find out whether the three structures are treated differently. As shown in the examples in (12), lexical items are controlled in the three types of construction so that any significant difference in the results of comparison between the resultative and the V-NP-XP structure can be reduced to the projection of the functional category AspP and that any significant difference between judgement of the resultative and judgement of the compound causative may be attributed to the morphological (un)realization of the head of the AspP. Paired-samples T tests were conducted on the mean scores of each structure within each group. The results are presented in Table 7.10. As shown in the Table, learner groups treat the resultative construction and the V-NP-XP structure differently except for the low-intermediate Japanese group. This seems to suggest that most L2 Chinese groups have knowledge of the status of *de* as delimiting an unbounded activity and heading the result component of a cause-effect relation. In other words, they realize that *de* is a way of realizing causativity in Chinese and that it occurs in Chinese resultatives obligatorily.

Table 7.10 Results of paired-samples T tests between the mean scores on the resultative construction, the compound causative construction and the V-NP-XP structure within each subject group in the AJ test

| Subject groups | | df | Resultative vs. *V-NP-XP | | Compound causative vs. resultative | |
| --- | --- | --- | --- | --- | --- | --- |
| | | | t | p | t | p |
| English | LI | 25 | 2.131* | .043 | 0.471 | .642 |
| | IN | 12 | 3.472* | .005 | 0.102 | .920 |
| | HI | 15 | 7.277** | .000 | -3.336* | .005 |
| Japanese | LI | 14 | 1.448 | .170 | -2.918* | .011 |
| | IN | 17 | 5.207** | .000 | -3.620* | .002 |
| | HI | 20 | 9.432** | .000 | -5.375** | .000 |
| Korean | LI | 26 | 2.533* | .018 | -2.328* | .028 |
| | IN | 24 | 3.831* | .001 | -3.811* | .001 |
| | HI | 20 | 4.782** | .000 | -3.053* | .006 |
| Native control | | 27 | 36.004** | .000 | -3.421* | .002 |

$p^* < .05$, $p^{**} < .001$

Comparisons between mean scores on resultatives and mean scores on compound causatives reveal significant differences in most learner groups. The three Japanese groups, the three Korean groups and the high-intermediate English group accept the resultative construction more than the compound causative construction. The results confirm our hypothesis that learners have less difficulty acquiring the resultative construction than the compound causative construction. This seems to imply that functional categories with a phonetically realized head (e. g. *de* in the resultative construction) are easier to project than those with a phonetically null head.

### 7. 4  Discussion

The results of the AJ test and the comprehension test reported in this chapter have confirmed that a) the high-intermediate L2 Chinese groups can acquire the resultative construction; b) they are able to acquire Type A of the compound causative construction; and c) resultatives are acquired earlier than compound causatives. The results seem to lead to a conclusion that the functional category AspP involved in Chinese resultatives and compound causatives can be projected in L2 Chinese grammars whether such a functional category is available in the L1 or not.

#### 7. 4. 1  The acquisition of the resultative construction

According to the Minimal Trees Hypothesis (Vainikka and Young-Scholten 1994, 1996a, 1996b), L1 functional categories are not transferred and the development of L2 functional categories is triggered by overt morphological evidence in the L2. This hypothesis may have two implications. First, functional categories with overt morphology would be easier to acquire than those with covert morphology. Second, the projection of L2 functional categories is not influenced by the properties of functional categories in the L1. These implications seem to be confirmed by the test results reported in this chapter. First, the resultative construction, due to the overt morpheme *de* heading the construction, is acquired earlier than the compound causative construction, which is headed by a covert morpheme, as shown in § 7.3. Second, the lack of functional categories in resultatives in L1 English and Japanese does not put English- and Japanese-speaking learners of Chinese at a distinct disadvantage. The representations of resultatives in their L2 Chinese develop as their Chinese proficiency increases and become native-like when they are at the high-intermediate Chinese proficiency level (see § 7.1.1). In contrast, Korean-speaking learners' representation of Chinese resultatives is non-native-like although resultative AspP is present in Korean.

A possible reason for Korean-speaking learners' non-native-like representations of Chinese resultatives is that these learners do not identify resultatives in Chinese with resultatives in L1 Korean due to their difference in the surface structure. Resultatives in the two languages have the same underlying structure except for the headedness direction of VP, as shown in (13) (irrelevant nodes omitted). The resultative morpheme *de* heads Chinese resultatives, while the resultative suffix *-key* heads Korean resultatives. In both languages, a functional AspP is projected between the activity VP and the result XP.

(13) a. Chinese resultatives

$[_{VP}[_{V'} V_{activity} [_{AspP} [_{Asp'} de [_{XP} [_{X'} V_{result}]]]]]]$

b. Korean resultatives

$[_{VP} [_{AspP} [_{XP} [V_{result\ X'}] -key_{Asp'}] V_{activity\ V'}]]$

In the surface structure, *de* in Chinese resultatives is attached to the activity predicate $V_1$, while *-key* in Korean resultatives adjoins to the result predicate $V_2$. The difference in the surface structure between resultatives in the two languages is thus derived. It may mislead

Korean-speaking learners into believing that *de* in Chinese and *-key* in Korean have different functions. Consequently, these learners may be uncertain about Chinese resultative constructions and cannot achieve a native-like representation at the developmental stages under study.

### 7.4.2 The acquisition of the compound causative construction

As we have seen from § 7.2.1.2, different language groups vary in judging compound causatives. Let us first find out whether their judgments are native-like or not. The results of each L2 Chinese group in judging the six types of compound causatives are summarized in Table 7.11 (see Tables 13-18 in Appendix 7 for descriptive statistics and Appendix 8 for the results of one-way ANOVA and pairwise Scheffé tests).

*Table 7.11 Summary: L2 Chinese groups' judgments of the six types of compound causative construction in terms of mean scores and native-like judgments*

| Subject groups | | Type A | | Type B | | Type C | | Type D | | Type E | | Type F | |
|---|---|---|---|---|---|---|---|---|---|---|---|---|---|
| | | M | NJ | M | NJ | M | NJ | M | NJ | M | NJ | M | NJ |
| English | LI | | | | | | | | | | | | |
| | IN | √ | | | | | + | | | | | | |
| | HI | √ | + | | | | | | | | + | | |
| Japanese | LI | √ | | | | | | | | | | | + |
| | IN | √ | | | | | | | | √ | + | | + |
| | HI | √ | + | | | | | | | √ | + | | + |
| Korean | LI | | | | | | | | | | | | |
| | IN | | | | | | | | | | | | |
| | HI | √ | | | | | | | | | | | |

M = mean score; NJ = native-like judgement; "√" stands for acceptance in terms of the mean score ($\geq +1$); "+" stands for native-like judgment found in pairwise Scheffé tests.

As shown in Table 7.11, Type A of the compound causative is the most acceptable to L2 groups of the three L1s. The three Japanese groups, the intermediate and high-intermediate English groups and the high-intermediate Korean group accept it (mean score $\geq +1$); the high-intermediate English and Japanese groups have native-like judgments (the high-intermediate Korean group's judgment is near-native, see § 7.2.1.2). In contrast, Type B and Type D are the least acceptable. If we take the percentage of subjects who show consistent acceptance and rejection into account (see Table 7.6), Type D is more unacceptable than Type B. In terms of acceptability, the six types of compound causatives under study show a hierarchy, as shown in Table 7.12.

Table 7.12 The six types of compound causative construction under study: hierarchy of acceptability in terms of mean scores and native-like judgments

| Rank* | Type | $V_1$ | $V_2$ | θ-role $V_2$ assigns |
|---|---|---|---|---|
| 1 | Type A | Transitive | Unaccusative | Theme |
| 2 | Type E | Transitive | Psych verb | Experiencer |
| 3 | Type F | Transitive | Psych verb | Experiencer |
| 4 | Type C | Unergative | Adjective | Theme |
| 5 | Type B | Transitive | Unergative | Agent |
| 6 | Type D | Unergative | Psych verb | Experiencer |

* "1" stands for "the most acceptable" while "6" stands for the least acceptable.

Let us now examine why L2 Chinese learners judge different types of compound causatives differently.

### 7.4.2.1 L2 Chinese representations of compound causatives

On the basis of the semantic structure of causatives (Levin and Rappaport Hovav 1995: 94) in (14a) and the causative template (Baker 1988; Hale and Keyser 1993) in (14b), I propose two conditions in (15), under which L2 learners judge the acceptability of Chinese compound causatives.

(14) a. [[x DO SOMETHING] CAUSE [y BECOME STATE]]

b. [$_{VP_1}$ Agent [$_{V_1}$, CAUSE [$_{VP_2}$ Theme[$_{V_2}$, BECOME XP]]]]

(15) Condition 1: The argument of the result predicate (i.e. $V_2$) is coindexed with the internal argument of the activity predicate (i.e. $V_1$);

Condition 2: The result predicate (i.e. $V_2$) assigns a θ-role to an internal argument.

In order for L2 grammars to accept Chinese compound causatives, both conditions must be satisfied. To meet Condition 1, the activity predicate must be a transitive verb and the argument of $V_2$ must be coindexed with the internal (Theme) argument of $V_1$. To satisfy Condition 2, the argument of $V_2$ must be an internal argument. The structure illustrated in (16) meets both conditions (irrelevant modes omitted). We will use Type A, shown in (17), to illustrate the two conditions.

(16)

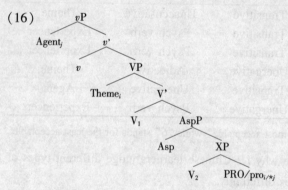

(17) a. Zhangsan da-*sui*  le  Lisi de huaping. (Type A)
Zhangsan hit-break ASP Lisi's  vase
'Zhangsan broke Lisi's vase'
b. [[*x* DO SOMETHING TO *y*]CAUSE[*y* BECOME STATE]]
c. [$_{vP}$Zhangsan$_j$[$_{VP}$Lisi de huaping$_i$[$_{V'}$ da [$_{AspP}$[$_{XP}$[$_{X'}$ sui PRO/pro$_{i/*j}$]]]]]]
Zhangsan  Lisi's vase     hit    break

As shown in (17a), the activity predicate of Type A is a transitive verb like *da* 'hit', which selects an external argument like *Zhangsan* and an internal argument like *Lisi de huaping* 'Lisi's vase'; the result predicate is an unaccusative verb like *sui* 'break', which selects an internal Theme argument occurring at the complement position of the result XP. As shown in the syntactic structure in (17c), the argument of the result predicate, i. e. the pro/PRO, is coindexed with the internal argument of $V_1$ *Lisi de huaping* 'Lisi's vase', generating a reading that "Zhangsan hit Lisi's vase, which broke as a result". Condition 1 is thus satisfied. The argument of $V_2$, i. e. the pro/PRO, is an internal argument and is assigned a Theme θ-role by $V_2$. Condition 2 is thus met. Type A has a semantic structure as in (17b).

Type A satisfies the two conditions and is therefore the most acceptable compound causative. We may call it the prototype of compound causative and the structure in (16) the prototypical structure of compound causatives. Since the compound causative generated from (16) is the most acceptable compound causative to L2 Chinese learners, the structure in (16) seems to be the structure of compound causatives in L2 Chinese grammars.

The fact that most L2 Chinese groups accept Type A indicates that the two conditions play an important role in L2 learners' judgment of compound causatives. It also indicates that L2 learners are able to acquire the syntactic structure of Chinese compound causatives and that the functional AspP involved in compound causatives can be properly projected. If they show any variation in judging different types of compound causative, a possible reason will be that the type of compound causative can or cannot be accommodated by the L2 compound causative structure shown in (16).

Now let us find out how the most acceptable compound causative, i. e. Type A, differs from the least acceptable type of compound causative, i. e. Type D (see Table 7.6 in this chapter and Table 16 in Appendix 7). Type D is exemplified in (18a) for the convenience of discussion. It has a semantic structure as in (18b) and a syntactic structure as in (18c) (irrelevant nodes omitted):

(18) a. Zhangsan ku-*fan* le Lisi. (Type D)
Zhangsan cry-bore ASP Lisi
'Zhangsan cried and got Lisi bored as a result.'
b. [ [ $x$ DO SOMETHING ] CAUSE [ $y$ BECOME STATE ] ]
c. [ $_{vP}$Zhangsan$_j$ [ $_{VP}$ [ $_{V'}$ku [ $_{AspP}$Lisi$_i$ [ $_{Asp'}$ [ $_{XP}$PRO/pro$_{i/*j}$ [ $_{X'}$ fan ]]]]]]]
Zhangsan　　　cry　　Lisi　　　　　　　　　　　　bore
d. [ $_{vP}$Zhangsan$_j$ [ $_{VP}$ [ $_{V'}$ku [ $_{AspP}$Lisi$_i$ [ $_{Asp'}$ [ $_{XP}$ [ $_{X'}$ fan PRO/pro$_i$ ]]]]]]]
Zhangsan　　　cry　　Lisi　　　　　　bore

As shown in (18c), as an unergative verb, $V_1$ (i.e. *ku* 'cry') can only select an Agent argument, namely $NP_1$ (i.e. *Zhangsan*); $NP_2$ (i.e. *Lisi*) occurs at Spec-AspP as an Event Measurer (see Slabakova 2001; Tenny 1994; Travis 2003); the Experiencer pro/PRO that the psych verb $V_2$ (i.e. *fan* 'bore') selects is an external argument, which occurs at Spec-XP, coindexed with $NP_2$ (see Pesetsky 1995 for the thematic hierarchy concerning psych verbs; also see § 2.2.2). As can be seen from (18c), Type D satisfies neither of the two conditions: $V_1$ does not select an internal argument, so Condition 1 is not satisfied; $V_2$ assigns a θ-role of Experiencer to an external argument, so Condition 2 is not met. It is therefore not acceptable to L2 groups of the three L1s. Another possibility is that the psych verb $V_2$ (i.e. *fan* 'bore') selects an internal Theme argument in accordance with the thematic hierarchy, which is coindexed with $NP_2$ (i.e. *Lisi*) at Spec-AspP, as shown in (18d). In this case, Condition 2 is met, but Condition 1 is not. Therefore, it is not accepted by L2 grammars. L2 grammars cannot accommodate this type of compound causative because it does not fit into the structure for compound causatives in L2 grammars shown in (16).

As shown in (19a), Type B contains a transitive $V_1$ (i.e. *ma* 'scold'), which selects an Agent argument (i. e. *Zhangsan*) and a Theme argument (i. e. *Lisi*), and an unergative $V_2$ (i. e. *ku* 'cry'), which selects an external argument. The external argument pro/PRO of $V_2$ (i. e. *ku* 'cry') is coindexed with the Theme argument of $V_1$ (i. e. *Lisi*), generating a reading as shown in the translation. It has a semantic structure as in (19b) and a syntactic structure as in (19c) (see § 3.2.2.2 for detailed discussion of the syntactic derivation).

(19) a. Zhangsan ma-*ku*   le   Lisi.   (Type B)
   Zhangsan scold-cry ASP Lisi
   'Zhangsan scolded Lisi and Lisi cried.'
  b. [ [ $x$DO SOMETHING TO $y$ ] CAUSE [ $y$DO SOMETHING ] ]
  c. [$_{vP}$Zhangsan$_j$ [$_{VP}$Lisi$_i$ [$_{V'}$ ma [$_{AspP}$ [$_{Asp'}$ [$_{XP}$PRO/pro$_{i/*j}$ [$_{X'}$ ku ] ] ] ] ] ] ]
    Zhangsan      Lisi      scold                                    cry

In Type B, the argument of $V_2$ is coindexed with the internal argument of $V_1$, thus Condition 1 is met. However, Condition 2 is not satisfied because $V_2$ assigns a θ-role to the external argument rather than to the internal one. Because of this, this type of compound causative cannot be accommodated by the structure shown in (16). It is among the least acceptable types of compound causative, as shown in Table 7.11.

Type C is illustrated in (20). In (20a), $V_1$ is an unergative verb (i. e. *ku* 'cry'), which selects an external Agent argument only, therefore Condition 1 is not satisfied; $V_2$ is an adjective (i. e. *shi* 'wet'), which selects a Theme argument. In this case, however, the Theme is not the internal argument but the external argument of $V_2$. Thus Condition 2 is not met. It is shown in Table 7.11 that Type C is not accepted by any of the L2 groups in terms of the mean scores, but the intermediate English group has native-like judgment of it. This will be explained in § 7.4.2.2.

(20) a. Zhangsan ku-*shi* le shoujuan. (Type C)
　　　　Zhangsan cry-wet ASP handkerchief
　　　　'Zhangsan cried the handkerchief soggy.'
　　b. [[$x$ DO SOMETHING] CAUSE [$y$ BECOME STATE]]
　　c. [$_{vP}$Zhangsan$_j$ [$_{VP}$[$_{V'}$ku [$_{AspP}$shoujuan$_i$ [$_{Asp'}$[$_{XP}$PRO/pro$_{i/*j}$[$_{X'}$ shi]]]]]]]]
　　　　Zhangsan　　　cry　　handkerchief　　　　　　　　wet

In Type E, as shown in (21c), NP$_2$ (i.e. *na shou ge* 'that song') is the internal argument of the transitive V$_1$ (i.e. *ting* 'listen'); the psych verb V$_2$ (i.e. *fan* 'bore') selects an external argument, which is a pro/PRO at Spec-XP. This pro/PRO is coindexed not with the Theme argument of V$_1$ (i.e. *na shou ge* 'that song'), but with the Agent argument of V$_1$ (i.e. *Zhangsan*). Therefore, this type of compound causative has a semantic structure as shown in (21b). It satisfies neither of the conditions and should be one of the least acceptable types of compound causative. However, the intermediate and high-intermediate Japanese groups accept and have native-like judgments on it. In addition to the two Japanese groups, the high-intermediate English group has native-like judgment on it. In terms of mean scores and native-like judgments, it is the second most acceptable type of compound causative. This will be explained in § 7.4.2.2.

(21) a. Zhangsan ting-*fan* le na shou ge. (Type E)
　　　　Zhangsan listen-bore ASP that CL song
　　　　'Zhangsan listened to that song (time and again) and got bored.'
　　b. [[$x$DO SOMETHING TO $y$] CAUSE [$_{x/*y}$BECOME STATE]]
　　c. [$_{vP}$Zhangsan$_j$ [$_{VP}$na shou ge$_i$ [$_{V'}$ting [$_{AspP}$[$_{XP}$PRO/pro$_{j/*i}$[$_{X'}$ fan]]]]]]
　　　　Zhangsan　　that CL song　listen　　　　　　　　　　bore

(22) a. Zhangsan zhui-*lei* le Lisi. (Type F)
　　　　Zhangsan chase-tire ASP Lisi
　　　　(i) 'Zhangsan chased Lisi and got tired as a result.'

## 7 Results and discussion: resultative and compound causative constructions

(ii) 'Zhangsan chased Lisi and Lisi got tired as a result.'
b. $[\,[\,x\text{DO SOMETHING TO}y\,]\text{CAUSE}[\,_{x/y}\text{BECOME STATE}\,]\,]$
c. $[\,_{vP}\text{Zhangsan}_j[\,_{VP}\text{Lisi}_i[\,_{V'}\text{zhui}\,[\,_{AspP}[\,_{Asp'}[\,_{XP}\text{PRO/pro}_{i/j}[\,_{X'}\text{lei}\,]\,]\,]\,]\,]\,]\,]$
 Zhangsan  Lisi  chase                              tire

A shown in (22), Type F contains a transitive $V_1$ (i.e. *zhui* 'chase') and a psych verb $V_2$ (i.e. *lei* 'tire'), as in Type E. The two types differ in that in Type F the external argument of $V_2$, which is a pro/PRO at Spec-XP, can be coindexed with both $NP_1$ (i.e. *Zhangsan*) and $NP_2$ (i.e. *Lisi*), while in Type E it can only be coindexed with $NP_1$. Type F satisfies neither of the conditions when it is interpreted as reading (i). It satisfies Condition 1 in the case of reading (ii). The results in Table 7.11 indicate that none of the English and Korean groups accepts or has native-like judgments on it, but the three Japanese groups' judgments are native-like. Japanese speakers' judgments of this type of compound causative can be explained in terms of L1 transfer, as we will see in § 7.4.2.2.

The fact that L2 Chinese learners have native or near-native representations of certain types of compound causatives may indicate that they can acquire the syntactic structure of Chinese compound causatives and project the functional AspP in their L2 Chinese grammars. If the above analysis of different types of compound causative in terms of the two conditions we postulated is on the right track, we may now argue that L2 Chinese learners judge different types of compound causative differently not because they are unable to acquire the syntactic structure, but because their L2 Chinese grammars cannot accommodate certain ways of θ-role assignment. An implication is that L2 syntactic structure may develop independently of L2 thematic structure. L2 learners are able to achieve native-like syntactic representations while they have problems assigning certain θ-role to certain argument in their L2 Chinese grammars.

## 7.4.2.2 L1 transfer

As we know from Chapter 3, English allows resultatives but disallows compound causatives, whereas Japanese and Korean allow both. Chinese resultatives and compound causatives contain a functional AspP. Such an AspP is also present in Korean resultatives, but it is not available in English or Japanese resultatives, nor in Japanese or Korean compound causatives. Given different properties of resultatives and compound causatives in the four languages, a question arises: is there L1 effect in L2 learners' judgments of the compound causatives under study?

Type A is the most acceptable to all L2 groups while Types B and D are the least acceptable. L1 effect can be ruled out in the judgments of these types of compound causative at the developmental stages under study because L2 Chinese grammars of different L1s do not show any variation. Let us now examine L2 learners' judgments on Types C, E and F, in which variations exist.

If L1 transfer happened, Japanese- and Korean-speaking learners would accept Type C more than English-speaking learners because compound causative is allowed in Japanese and Korean but disallowed in English. The results indicate otherwise. The intermediate English group has native-like judgment on it, but none of the Japanese or Korean groups accepts it or has native-like judgment on it. It appears that L1 transfer could be ruled out, but such a conclusion may be premature if we examine this type of compound causative in detail. Type C, as shown in (20), contains an unergative $V_1$ like *ku* 'cry' and an adjective $V_2$ like *shi* 'wet', which form a compound causative like *ku-shi* 'cry-wet'. However, this type of structure (verb-adjective) is not allowed in Japanese or Korean compound causatives (see § 3.3 and § 3.4). As a result, Japanese- and Korean-speaking learners will not accept it if L1 transfer happens. That is to say, these learners' non-acceptance of this structure may be a sign of L1 transfer rather than the opposite.

How can English-speaking learners achieve a native-like judgment on Type C? English allows resultatives like 'John cried the handkerchief soggy', as we can see from § 3.1. The difference in the underlying structure between the English resultative and the Chinese compound causative is illustrated in (23):

(23) a. English resultative:

$[_{VP}[_{V'}\text{cry}[_{XP}\text{ the handkerchief}[_{X'}\text{soggy}]]]]$

b. Chinese resultative:

$[_{VP}[_{V'}\text{ku}[_{AspP}[_{Asp'}[_{XP}\text{shoujuan }[_{X'}\text{shi}]]]]]]$
cry　　　　　handkerchief wet

According to Tang (1997), Chinese compound causatives and English resultatives have a parametric difference: the former contain a functional category which triggers movement, but the latter do not (see § 3.2.1.3). If the functional AspP can be projected in the L2 Chinese grammar and verb raising is involved in the derivation, a structure as (23b) can be generated in English-speaking learners' L2 Chinese.

As seen from Table 7.11, Japanese-speaking learners accept Type E and Type F. This can be attributed to L1 transfer. In Japanese compound causatives, as shown in (10), repeated in (24), both $V_1$ (i.e. *naguri* 'hit' in (24b)) and $V_2$ (i.e. *korosu* 'kill' in (24b)) are predicated of $NP_1$ obligatorily. Otherwise, an ill-formed sentence would result, as shown in (24a). This is the case in Type E of the Chinese compound causative, as shown in (21), in which both the transitive $V_1$ (i. e. *ting* 'listen') and the psych verb $V_2$ (i. e. *fan* 'bore') are predicated of $NP_1$ (i. e. *Zhangsan*), generating a reading that "Zhangsan listened to the song time and again and got bored". In Type F, as shown in (22), the transitive $V_1$ (i. e. *zhui* 'chase') and the psych verb $V_2$ (i. e. *lei* 'tire') can also be predicated of $NP_1$ (i. e. *Zhangsan*), generating a reading that "Zhangsan chased Lisi and got tired". Thus, Japanese-speaking learners' native-like judgments on the two types of compound causatives can be taken as a sign of L1 transfer. The results of the AJ test match the results of the comprehension test. In both cases, Japanese-speaking learners interpret Type F in such a way that both $V_1$ and $V_2$ are predicated of $NP_1$.

(24) a. *John-ga    Mary-o    naguri-shinu-ta.
        John-NOM Mary-ACC hit-die-PAST
    b.  John-ga    Mary-o    naguri-korosu-ta.
        John-NOM Mary-ACC hit-kill-PAST
       'John hit Mary and as a result killed her.'

If Japanese-speaking learners' acceptance of Type E is treated as an effect of L1 transfer, how can we explain the high-intermediate English group's native-like judgment on Type E as compound causative is not allowed in English? A possible reason is that English-speaking learners may treat $NP_2$ (i. e. *na shou ge* 'that song' in (21)) as the Theme of the psych verb $V_2$ (i. e. *fan* 'bore' in (21)), in accordance with the thematic hierarchy concerning psych verbs proposed by Pesetsky (1995) (see § 2.2.2 for related discussion). Therefore, the underlying structure of this type of compound causative in English-speaking learners' L2 Chinese is as illustrated in (25):

(25) [$_{vP}$Zhangsan$_j$ [$_{VP}$ na shou ge$_i$ [$_{V'}$ ting [$_{AspP}$ [$_{Asp'}$ [$_{XP}$ [$_{X'}$ fan pro/PRO$_i$ ]]]]]]]
     Zhangsan    that CL song listen                    bore

## 7 Results and discussion: resultative and compound causative constructions

If this is the case, the structure of Type E satisfies both conditions we postulated in (15) and can be accommodated by the L2 structure shown in (16).

Korean allows compound causatives. Why is L1 effect not observed in Korean-speaking learners' judgments of Chinese compound causatives? Korean compound causatives and Chinese compound causatives have different underlying structures, as shown in (26) ((26a) repeated from (11)):

(26) a. Korean compound causatives:

$[_{vP}[_{VP}[_{XP}[V_{activity\ X'}]\ V_{result\ V'}]-i_{v'}]]$

John-i　　　Bill-ul　　sswa-a-cwuk-i-ess-ta.
John-NOM Bill-ACC shoot-die-CAUS-PAST-DEC
'John shot Bill dead.'

b. Chinese compound causatives:

$[_{vP}[_{v'}[_{VP}[_{V'}\ V_{activity}[_{AspP}[_{XP}V_{result}]]]]]]$

John sha-si　le　Bill.
John kill-die ASP Bill
'John killed Bill.'

In Chinese compound causatives causativity is realized through the functional category AspP, whereas in Korean compound causatives it is represented by the causative marker -i heading the upper $v$P. They are both functional categories, but different in three aspects. First, they have different positions: AspP in Chinese compound causatives occurs between the VP headed by the activity predicate and the XP headed by the result predicate, but $v$P in Korean compound causatives occurs beyond the XP and the VP. Second, AspP in Chinese has a covert head, but $v$P in Korean has an overt head -i marked on the result predicate. Third, the functional Asp induces movement in Chinese, but the $v$ in Korean does not.

Since Chinese and Korean have different representations of

compound causatives, L1 transfer can only impede Korean speakers' L2 acquisition of Chinese compound causatives. In the study, I do not have direct evidence that L1 transfer happens in the Korean groups in terms of Chinese compound causatives. However, from their non-native judgments on the six types of compound causative, I assume that it does.

To conclude, the results reported in this chapter indicate that L2 Chinese learners can acquire the syntactic structure of Chinese resultatives and are more likely to interpret these resultatives in the target way. While they can also acquire the syntactic structure of compound causatives, their L2 grammars cannot accommodate compound causatives if $NP_2$ is not the internal argument of $V_1$ or if $V_2$ assigns a θ-role to an external argument. It is argued that a compound causative is easier to acquire in L2 Chinese if the result predicate assigns a Theme θ-role to the internal argument and if this internal argument is coindexed with the internal argument of $V_1$.

## Notes

[1] As shown in Table 7.2 and Table 7.3, the percentages of choices of Options B, C and D add up to 100%, but the percentages of consistent subjects for the three options may not. The reason is that the occurrences of each option were counted on the basis of individual tokens, whereas consistent subjects were counted on the basis of three tokens. If a subject chooses B twice and C once on the three tokens of the construction, he is not counted as a consistent subject but the three tokens were all counted as occurrences of certain interpretations.

[2] The conclusion that the V-NP-XP structure is not transferred from learners' L1 English or Japanese into L2 Chinese should be treated tentatively. A reason is that one type of the V-NP-XP structure, which involves an unergative verb like *ku* 'cry' in (12c), was used in the test, while structures involving transitive verbs were not used. A possible consequence is that L2 learners show degrees of rejection to sentences like (12c) not because of the V-NP-XP structure involved but because of the unergative verbs used.

# Representations of causativity in L2 Chinese: summary, implication and conclusion

导言

本章是对全书、特别是实证研究部分的总结。概括了第六章和第七章的试验结果之后,作者把试验结果放在第二语言习得研究的大框架中讨论了迁移、功能范畴和僵化现象三个方面。

(1)迁移问题。作者认为,前人的研究多持"非黑即白"的观点,这些观点在试验中并没有得到证实。试验结果显示,第一语言迁移现象有些地方发生,有些地方没有发生,因此不是绝对的。作者认为,前人有关第一语言迁移的论述在迁移的时间问题上表述不清,大多数观点认为第一语言迁移发生在处于初态的中介语中,然而对"初态"的定义却没有清晰的界定,这样即使大家都在使用"初态"这个术语,但其含义却不同。

(2)功能范畴。作者认为,第一语言无而第二语言有的功能范畴(如汉语结果补语和复合使动结构中的"体短语")能够在中介语中具有适当表征,目标语中存在的大量的正面证据,刺激参数重设,使中介语语法具有目标语语法的参数。

(3)僵化问题。作者认为,除前人指出的造成僵化现象的诸多原因外,中介语语法不能正确指派论元角色,也是僵化现象产生的原因。此外,目标语缺乏第一语言具有的形态变化,也导致学习者在格和论元角色的识别上出现困难。还有一个原因是,汉语中一些动词仍然保留使动用法的一些遗迹,对学习者可能产生误导。鉴于复合使动结构有多种构成形式而且不同形式的结构习得顺序有差异,作者建议在教学及教材编写中应该考虑这些因素。

# Representations of causativity in L2 Chinese: summary, implication and conclusion

In this chapter I will summarize findings of the present study and explore their implications to second language acquisition and future research. Section 8.1 is a summary of the results of the empirical study. Section 8.2 is a general discussion of some theoretical issues in second language acquisition. Suggestions for future research are presented in § 8.3. The present study is concluded in § 8.4.

## 8.1 Summary of the empirical study

As mentioned in Chapter 1, the present study explores causativity in the native Chinese grammar and English-, Japanese-, and Korean-speaking learners' L2 Chinese grammars. In Chapter 2 and Chapter 3, we studied properties of unaccusative verbs, psych verbs, resultative constructions and compound causative constructions in Chinese, English, Japanese and Korean. I proposed a VP shell for English unaccusative verbs and OE verbs, but a single VP for these verbs in Chinese, Japanese and Korean. With regard to Chinese resultatives and compound causatives, I argued that they involve a functional AspP that occurs between the activity predicate and the result predicate. English has resultatives, while Japanese and Korean have both resultatives and compound causatives. However, AspP is only present in Korean resultatives. It is absent in English and Japanese resultatives and is unavailable in Korean and Japanese compound causatives.

To examine representations of causativity in English-, Japanese- and Korean-speaking learners' L2 Chinese grammars, an empirical study was conducted. We briefly reviewed SLA studies in Chapter 4 and proposed research questions and hypotheses of the present study in Chapter 5. The focus of the present study is causativity in L2 Chinese. Due to different properties of the verbs and constructions under study, we hoped to find out, through representations of causativity in L2 Chinese, whether L1 transfer happens and whether the functional AspP can be projected in L2 Chinese resultatives and compound causatives. The empirical study consists of three tasks, an AJ test, a production test and a comprehension test.

Results of the tests on L2 acquisition of unaccusative verbs and psych verbs were reported in Chapter 6. They indicate that L2 Chinese learners show degrees of rejection to causative psych verbs (i. e. OE verbs) and most L2 groups have native-like representations of psych verbs. This suggests that a single VP is projected for psych verbs in L2 Chinese syntax. The result that L2 Chinese learners accept analytical causative construction but reject the OE-verb structure suggests that they are aware that psych verbs cannot project a VP shell in Chinese.

In contrast to results on psych verbs, causative errors in relation to unaccusative verbs are found to be very common in L2 Chinese grammars irrespective of learners' L1s. These verbs seem to have a representation shown in (1) in L2 Chinese grammars, which is different from representations in the native Chinese grammar, as shown in (2a) and (2b). In the native Chinese grammar, the Theme NP, when it is definite, raises to the subject position to be case-marked, as in (2a); when it is indefinite, the indefinite part (e. g. *yi tiao tui* 'one leg' in (2b)) can remain in situ and is assigned partitive case, while the set to which the indefinite part belongs to (e. g. *Zhangsan* at the speficier position of the Theme NP in (2b)) raises to the subject position, as in (2b). In both cases, no verb raising is involved. In contrast, in the L2 Chinese grammar shown in (1), unaccusative verbs project a VP shell and verb raising is involved in the derivation. It should be noted that the verb *duan* 'break' in (2b) is an unaccusative verb although it can assign partitive case to the following indefinite NP.

(1) [$_{vP}$Agent[$_{v'}$ $v_i$ [$_{VP}$Theme[$_{V'}$ $t_i$ ]]]]

(2) a. [$_{IP}$Theme[$_{I'}$ [$_{VP}$$t_i$[$_{V'}$ V [$_{NP}$ $t_i$ ]]]]]

 b. [$_{IP}$Zhangsan$_i$[$_{I'}$ [$_{VP}$$t_i$[$_{V'}$ duan le[$_{NP}$$t_i$[$_{N'}$ yi tiao tui ]]]]]].
    Zhangsan             break ASP      one CL leg

'Zhangsan broke a leg.'

The results indicate that the representation of unaccusative verbs in L2 Chinese is similar to that of transitive verbs and this non-native representation seems likely to be fossilized in Japanese and Korean speakers' L2 Chinese grammars.

Results of the tests on L2 acquisition of Chinese resultatives and compound causatives were reported in Chapter 7. They indicate that L2 Chinese learners, except for the Korean groups, are able to acquire resultative constructions at least at the high-intermediate stage and that they are more likely to interpret Chinese resultatives in the target way than otherwise. This seems to imply that the functional category AspP involved in this construction can be projected in L2 Chinese grammars.

The test results on Chinese compound causatives indicate that, of the six types of compound causatives tested, Type A (i.e. the compound causative with a transitive $V_1$ and an unaccusative $V_2$) is the most acceptable and is the only compound causative on which L2 Chinese learners of the three L1s are able to achieve a native or near-native representation at the high-intermediate stage. I argued that the syntactic structure of compound causatives can be acquired by L2 Chinese learners and that the functional AspP involved in the construction can be projected in L2 Chinese grammars. Comparisons between results on different types of compound causatives indicate that L2 Chinese grammars can only accommodate compound causatives that satisfy two conditions, which are: 1) the argument of the result predicate is coindexed with the internal argument of the activity predicate; and 2) the result predicate assigns a θ-role to an internal argument. Type A of the compound causative satisfies the two conditions and is thus the most acceptable compound causative, while Type D, which contains an unergative $V_1$ and a psych verb $V_2$, satisfies neither of the conditions and is thus the least acceptable compound causative. None of the other four types of compound causatives satisfies both conditions, so they are less acceptable (ignoring L1 effect in Japanese-speaking learners' judgments of Type E and Type F). It is also found out that learners' L1 thematic structure may play a role in their judgments and interpretation of Chinese compound resultatives. In other words, while they are able to acquire the syntactic structure of Chinese compound causatives, the thematic structure of these compound causatives may be that of L1s.

## 8.2　General discussion: theoretical issues in SLA revisited

In Chapter 4 and Chapter 5, I addressed several problems in second language acquisition in general and reviewed L2 studies of causativity in particular. In this section, I will revisit some of the issues in relation to the findings in my empirical study.

### 8.2.1　L1 transfer

As we learned in Chapter 4, there are different proposals regarding the effect of L1 in L2 grammars. The full-transfer hypotheses (e. g. Schwartz and Sprouse 1994, 1996) claim that both lexical and functional categories in L1 are transferred into L2 and form the initial state of L2 grammar. The partial-transfer hypotheses (e. g. Eubank 1994a, 1994b, 1996; Vainikka and Young-Scholten 1994, 1996a, 1996b) argue that L1 lexical categories are transferred into L2 while L1 functional categories are not. The no-transfer hypotheses (e. g. Epstein et al 1996; Platzack 1996) claim that neither lexical nor functional categories are transferred and that L1 acquisition and L2 acquisition start from UG directly. Despite their differences, all these hypotheses have a clear-cut definition of what can or cannot be transferred.

None of these proposals is confirmed consistently by findings in the present study: while L1 effect is seen in some places, it is not observed in others. On psych verbs, English-speaking learners seem to transfer the VP-shell structure in the L1 into L2 Chinese at an early stage and Japanese-speaking learners seem to transfer the single VP structure in the L1 into L2 Chinese. As a result, their judgments on the OE-verb structure are different from each other at the low-intermediate stage (see § 6.1.1.2). However, English-speaking learners' judgment of the incorrect OE-verb structure and Korean-speaking learners' judgment of this structure do not differ significantly in spite of the fact that OE verbs are allowed in English but disallowed in Korean. This seems to reveal no L1 effect. However, L1 transfer may well happen in English-Chinese and Korean-Chinese interlanguages at early stages although I did not find evidence of L1 transfer at the developmental stages under study. It is possible that L1 transfer occurs before my empirical study started. If this is the case, similar representations of psych verbs in English- and Korean-speaking learners' L2 Chinese grammars at the intermediate stages cannot be treated as evidence that L1 transfer does not happen.

Results of the tests on unaccusative verbs indicate that L2 Chinese learners all accept the incorrect alternating unaccusative structures irrespective of their L1s. English-speaking learners' acceptance of these structures could be taken as a sign of L1 transfer. If Japanese- and Korean-speaking learners transferred the syntactic structure of unaccusative verbs in the L1s to L2 Chinese, they would reject these structures more readily than accept them. However, they fail to reject these alternating unaccusative structures and find it difficult to distinguish between unaccusative verbs and transitive verbs.

Chinese and Korean resultatives contain the functional AspP, while English and Japanese resultatives do not, as stated in Chapter 3. If the functional AspP in Korean transferred into L2 Chinese, Korean-speaking learners would acquire Chinese resultatives earlier than English- and Japanese-speaking learners. However, the hypothesis was not confirmed by the results. Unexpectedly, English and Japanese speakers seem to have native-like representations of Chinese resultatives at the high-intermediate stage, while Korean speakers do not.

Both Japanese and Korean have compound causatives while English does not. If L1 transfer happened, Japanese- and Korean-speaking learners would acquire Chinese compound causatives earlier than English-speaking learners. This is not the case. As we have seen from § 7.2, learners from the three L1s do not show much variation in their judgments of the six types of compound causatives as a whole. L2 learners from different L1s accept Type A the most and Types B and D the least (see § 7.4.2.1). Therefore, no effect of L1 transfer is found in the judgments of these three types of compound causative. However, on the other types, L1 effect can be observed (see § 7.4.2.2).

On the whole, results of the empirical study seem to suggest that L1 transfer happens in some L2 Chinese structures, but its effect is not seen in all the L2 structures. Therefore, neither the no-transfer hypotheses (e. g. Epstein et al 1996; Platzack 1996) nor the full-transfer hypotheses (e. g. Clahsen and Hong 1995; Schwartz and Sprouse 1994, 1996) are confirmed. In the case of Japanese- and Korean-speaking learners, the empirical study suggests that the single VP that unaccusative verbs project in their L1s does not transfer into L2 Chinese grammar, therefore the partial-transfer hypotheses (e. g. Eubank 1994a, 1994b, 1996), which claim that L1 lexical categories transfer into L2, are not supported either.

Why is L1 transfer observed in some structures but not in others? This can be explained in terms of the timing at which L1 transfer takes place and the well-foundedness of the hypotheses proposed. All the hypotheses about transfer claim that L1 transfer happens in the initial state of L2 grammars if it happens at all. The problem is "how initial is the initial state" (Yuan 2002, personal communication). Is it an early stage of L2 acquisition when learners have been exposed to L2 input for some time but their L2 proficiency is still low? Or is it the moment when learners are exposed to L2 input of a structure for the first time? It seems that the former situation is treated as the initial state in many SLA studies. Thus the initial state as claimed in the proposals above may be a form of grammar after some restructuring has taken place. According to Hawkins (2001a), restructuring toward the L2 may be very rapid, depending on the evidence available and the nature of the transferred property in question. Thus it may be difficult to detect initial transfer empirically if low-level subjects are examined. Conclusions about L1 transfer on the basis of L2 data of such low-proficiency learners may be unreliable.

The second problem concerns the well-foundedness of the hypotheses proposed. It was hypothesized that Korean-speaking learners would not have much difficulty in acquiring Chinese resultatives because both languages contain a functional AspP in the resultatives (see § 3.2.2.1 and § 3.4). The hypothesis was not borne out (see § 7.1.1). Although a functional AspP is projected between VP headed by the activity predicate and XP headed by the result predicate in resultatives of both languages, the structures of resultatives in the two languages are different in two aspects. First, movement is involved in Chinese resultatives, but not in Korean resultatives, as shown in (3) and (4). In Chinese, the head of the AspP (i.e. *de*) raises and attaches to the activity predicate, whereas in Korean, the head (i.e. -*key*) remains in situ and does not raise. Second, in the surface structure, the resultative morpheme is marked on the activity predicate in Chinese resultatives but on the result predicate in Korean resultatives.

(3) Chinese resultatives
    a. Zhangsan ku de shoujuan    dou shi le
        Zhangsan cry *de* handkerchief even wet ASP
        'Zhangsan cried the handkerchief soggy.'
    b. [$_{VP}$ [$_{V'}$ V$_{activity}$ [$_{AspP}$ [$_{Asp'}$ *de* [$_{XP}$ [$_{X'}$ V$_{result}$ ]]]]]]

(4) Korean resultatives
    a. Ku-nun (casin-uy) sonswuken-i ces-key wul-ess-ta.
        he-TOP self-GEN handkerchief-NOM soggy-*key* cry-PAST-DEC
        'He cried the handkerchief soggy.'
    b. [$_{VP}$ [$_{AspP}$ [$_{XP}$ [V$_{result\ X'}$ ] -*key*$_{Asp'}$ ] V$_{activity\ V'}$ ]]

When hypotheses were proposed, I did not take into account the movement involved and the structural difference that exists between Chinese and Korean resultatives. Because my hypotheses are not well-founded, L1 transfer which is expected to happen is not observed in the data.

## 8.2.2 Functional categories

As mentioned in § 4.1.3, there is little agreement among SLA researchers on whether functional categories can be projected in L2 grammar: some argue that they can (e.g. Grondin and White 1996; Lakshmanan and Selinker 1994), while others claim that they are impaired in the interlanguage representations (e.g. Beck 1997; 1998; Eubank and Grace 1998) or that L2 grammar is restricted to the functional categories and features that are exemplified in the L1 (Smith and Tsimpli 1995; Hawkins and Chan 1997; Hawkins 2001a).

As mentioned in Chapter 3, the functional AspP is an *ad hoc* category proposed for Chinese resultatives and compound causatives in the present study although it could be projected in languages such as English, Japanese and Korean for constructions other than those for expressing causativity. The empirical study demonstrates that English- and Japanese-speaking learners can project a native-like functional category AspP in their L2 Chinese resultatives although this functional category is not involved in resultatives in their L1s. Regarding compound causatives, the L2 Chinese groups of the three L1s have native or near-native representations of Type A of the compound causative at the high-intermediate stage, which indicates that the functional AspP in Chinese compound causatives can be projected in L2 Chinese in spite of its unavailability in the L1s. The data from the present study support the claim that functional categories can be properly projected in L2 grammar whether they are available in the L1 or not (cf. Slabakova 2003); L2 learners whose L1 does not have certain functional category are not in a disadvantageous position with regard to the acquisition of this functional category in L2.

How can the functional AspP be projected in L2 Chinese resultatives and compound causatives? An important factor is the robust, unambiguous positive evidence. According to Li and Thompson (1976b), single verbs in Chinese have gradually lost their causative ability, and verb compounds, which include the V-*de* compound (i. e. resultatives) and $V_1$-$V_2$ compounds (i. e. compound causatives), are used obligatorily to express causativity. These compounds are used in all kinds of genres and consequently L2 Chinese learners are able to have frequent contact with them.

### 8.2.3 Fossilization

SLA researchers propose different causes for fossilization (see Han 2004 for a general review). In SLA studies within the generative framework, fossilization is claimed to be caused by lack of access of UG (Schachter 1996), failure of parameter resetting (Eubank 1995), L1 influence (Kellerman 1989; Selinker and Lakshmanan 1993), quality of input (Gass and Lakshmanan 1991), lack of sensitivity to input (Long 2003 or failed functional features (Hawkins and Chan 1997).

In the present study, fossilization is observed in Japanese- and Korean-speaking learners' representations of Chinese unaccusative verbs which are incorrectly used as transitive verbs (see § 6.2.1). Of the possible reasons for fossilization listed above, L1 influence and quality of L2 input are likely to be two causes of fossilization in Japanese- and Korean-speaking learners' L2 Chinese concerning unaccusatives.

Japanese and Korean have verbal inflections and case markers while Chinese has neither. As a result, L2 Chinese learners of the two L1s cannot rely on affixes or case markers to represent grammatical relations in L2 Chinese. In this case, they may turn to word order and assign different grammatical functions to words at different positions. They may treat the subject of an incorrect alternating unaccusative sentence as Agent and the object as Theme. Previous studies (e.g. Montrul 2001a) found that errors with argument structure alternations are related to the way alternations are morphologically expressed in L1 and L2: L2 learners are more likely to acquire the alternation if the causative or anticausative morpheme has a covert form in L1 but is phonetically realized in L2; they may have more difficulty with the alternation if causative or anticausative morpheme has an overt form in L1 but a covert form in L2. The present study has similar findings: Japanese- and Korean-speaking learners make causative errors with Chinese unaccusative verbs because grammatical relations are represented overtly in their L1 Japanese and Korean while the target language Chinese does not have verbal inflections or case markers.

In addition to lack of morphological markings in the L2, misleading evidence may also be a cause of fossilization. Chinese unaccusative verbs are able to assign partitive case. Due to lack of case markers, partitive-case-marked NPs may be taken as accusative-case-marked. Lack of disconfirming evidence may mislead Japanese and Korean speakers into projecting a VP shell rather than a single VP for Chinese unaccusative verbs. The results of the present study suggest that morphological markings absent in the target language but available in the L1s and lack of vigorous and unambiguous evidence are causes of fossilization.

In the present study, L2 Chinese learners judge different types of compound causatives differently. They accept certain types of compound causatives but their L2 grammars seem to be fossilised on some types of compound causative like Type D. I argued that fossilization on some types of compound causative could be attributed to L2 learners' difficulty with certain θ-role assignment by the result predicate. If such an analysis is on the right track, the fact that L2 grammars cannot accommodate certain types of structures may also be a cause of fossilization.

## 8.3 Implications for future research

The present study involves L2 Chinese learners from three L1s, of which one is an Indo-European language (i. e. English) and two are non-Indo-European languages (i. e. Japanese and Korean). Comparisons are made both between L2 groups from the same L1s but at different Chinese proficiency levels and between L2 groups at the same Chinese proficiency levels but from different L1s.

In spite of the scope of the present study, the findings should be treated tentatively. In the first place, all the L2 subjects in the empirical study are intermediate learners. Since no beginners were involved, we know little about the initial-state L2 Chinese grammar concerning causativity in L2 Chinese. Even though we may infer what the initial-state L2 Chinese grammar is like from L2 learners' performance at the intermediate stages, we do not have direct knowledge of how causativity is represented at the initial stage. Moreover, due to practical constraints, I was unable to investigate all L2 Chinese causative structures. In terms of compound causatives, for example, only agentive types (i. e. those in which the sentence subject is Agent, see Cheng et al 1997) were examined. Other types as in (5) were not covered.

(5) a. Yi ping jiu zui-*dao* le san ge ren.
　　　one CL wine drunk-fall ASP three CL people
　　　'One bottle of wine caused three people to get drunk.'
　　b. Malasong bisai pao-*po* le wo de yundong xie.
　　　Marathon competition run-break ASP my sports shoe
　　　'The Marathon wore out my sports shoes.'

Theta-role assignment in compound causatives as in (5) is different from that in compound causatives examined in the present study. Therefore, the two conditions that I claimed to be responsible for the difference in L2 learners' judgments of different types of compound causatives (see § 7.4.2.1) may be challenged when they are used in the constructions in (5).

To obtain a full picture of L2 Chinese causative structures, future research on causativity in L2 Chinese can be carried out in the following directions. First, beginning learners should be involved to examine the initial-state L2 Chinese grammars concerning causativity. Second, more research should be conducted on the fossilized representations of unaccusative verbs in Japanese- and Korean-speaking learners of Chinese. To test the findings of the present study, subjects from other L1s with rich morphological markings should be included. Thirdly, in-depth and wide-scope studies should be conducted on each type of verb and construction examined in the present study, in particular unaccusative verbs and compound causative constructions.

## 8.4 Conclusion

The present study examines representations of causativity in L2 Chinese grammars. It is found that L1 transfer happens in some L2 structures, but not in all the structures under examination and that functional projections can be properly projected in L2 grammars. It is also found that fossilization may result from lack of morphological markings in L2, misleading evidence in L2 and learners' difficulty with certain θ-role assignment. It is suggested that L2 learners' comprehension of an L2 structure may be influenced by the L1 thematic structure even though they can acquire a native-like syntactic representation of the L2 structure.

# References

Adger, D. 2003. *Core Syntax: A Minimalist Approach*. Oxford: Oxford University Press.

Adjemian, C. 1976. On the nature of interlanguage systems. *Language Learning*, Vol. 26, pp. 297-320.

Allen, S. 1996. *Aspects of Argument Structure in Inuktitut*. Phidelphia, PA: John Benjamins.

Andersen, R. 1983. Transfer to somewhere. In S. Gass and L. Selinker (eds.), *Language Transfer in Language Learning*, pp. 177-201. Rowley, MA: Newbury House.

Baker, M. 1988. *Incorporation: A Theory of Grammatical Function Changing*. Chicago: The University of Chicago Press.

Baltin, M. R. 1998. A nonargument for small clauses as constituents. *Linguistic Inquiry*, Vol. 29, 513-515.

Basilico, D. 2003. The topic of small clauses. *Linguistic Inquiry*, Vol. 34, pp. 1-35.

Beck, M. -L. 1997. Regular verbs, past tense and frequency: tracking down one potential source of NS/NNS syntactic competence differences. *Second Language Research*, Vol. 13, pp. 93-115.

Beck, M. -L. 1998. L2 acquisition and obligatory head movement: English-speaking learners of German and the Local Impairment Hypothesis. *Studies in Second Language Acquisition*, Vol. 20, pp. 311-348.

Belletti, A. 1988. The case of unaccusatives. *Linguistic Inquiry*, Vol. 19, pp. 1-34.

Belletti, A. and L. Rizzi. 1988. Psych-verbs and θ-theory. *Natural Language and Linguistic Theory*, Vol. 6, pp. 291-352.

Bender, E. 2000. The syntax of Mandarin BA: reconsidering the verbal analysis. *Journal of East Asian Linguistics*, Vol. 9, pp. 105-145.

Bennett, S. 1994. Interpretation of English reflexives by adolescent speakers of

Serbo-Croatian. *Second Language Research*, Vol. 10, pp. 125-156.

Berwick, R. C. 1985. *The Acquisition of Syntactic Knowledge*. Cambridge, MA: MIT Press.

Bialystok, E. 1994. Analysis and control in the development of second language proficiency. *Studies in Second Language Acquisition*, Vol. 16, 157-168.

Birdsong, D. 1989. *Metalinguistic Performance and Interlinguistic Competence*. Berlin: Springer.

Birdsong, D. 1992. Ultimate attainment in second language acquisition. *Language*, Vol. 68, pp. 706-755.

Blake, B. J. 2001. *Case* (Second Edition). Cambridge: Cambridge University Press.

Bley-Vroman, R. 1986. Hypothesis testing in second-language acquisition theory. *Language Learning*, Vol. 36, pp. 353-376.

Bley-Vroman, R. 1989. What is the logical problem of foreign language learning? In S. Gass and J. Schachter (eds.), *Linguistic Perspectives on Second Language Acquisition*, pp. 41-68. Cambridge: Cambridge University Press.

Bley-Vroman, R. 1990. The logical problem of foreign language learning. *Linguistic Analysis*, Vol. 20, pp. 3-49.

Boulouffe, J. 1986. Intake as the locus of equilibration in language learning. *Language Learning*, Vol. 36, pp. 245-275.

Bowerman, M. 1990. Mapping thematic roles onto syntactic functions: are children helped by innate linking rules? *Linguistics*, Vol. 28, pp. 1253-1289.

Bowers, J. 1993. The syntax of predication. *Linguistic Inquiry*, Vol. 24, pp. 591-656.

Bowers, J. 2002. Transitivity. *Linguistic Inquiry*, Vol. 33, pp. 183-224.

Bryman, A. and D. Cramer. 1999. *Quantitative Data Analysis with SPSS Release 8 for Windows: A Guide for Social Scientists*. London: Routledge.

Burzio, L. 1986. *Italian Syntax: A Government-Binding Approach*. Dordrecht: Reidel.

Cabrera, M. and M. L. Zubizarreta. 2003. On the acquisition of Spanish causative structures by L1 speakers of English. In J. M. Liceras, H. Zobl and H. Goodluck (eds.), *Proceedings of the 6$^{th}$ Generative Approaches to Second Language Acquisition Conference* (*GASLA* 2002), pp. 23-33. Somerville, MA: Cascadilla Press.

Carrier, J. and J. H. Randall. 1992. The argument structure and syntactic structure of resultatives. *Linguistic Inquiry*, *Vol.* 23, *pp.* 173-234.

Carroll, S. E. 2001. *Input and Evidence: The Raw Material of Second Language Acquisition*. Amsterdam: John Benjamins.

Carroll, S. and M. Swain. 1993. Explicit and implicit negative feedback: an empirical study of the learning of linguistic generalizations. *Studies in Second Language Acquisition*, *Vol.* 15, *pp.* 357-386.

Chao, Y. -R. 1968. *A Grammar of Spoken Chinese*. Berkeley and Los Angeles: University of California Press.

Chaudron, C. 1985. Intake: on models and methods for discovering learners' processing of input. *Studies in Second Language Acquisition*, *Vol.* 7, *pp.* 1-14.

Chen, D. 1995. UTAH: Chinese psych verbs and beyond. In J. Camacho and L. Choueiri (eds.), *Proceedings of the 6th North American Conference on Chinese Linguistics*, *pp.* 15-29. Graduate Students in Linguistics, University of Southern California.

Cheng, L. -S. 1995. On *dou*-quantification. *Journal of East Asian Linguistics*, *Vol.* 4, *pp.* 197-234.

Cheng, L. -S., C. -T. Huang, Y. -H. Li and C. -C. Tang. 1997. Causative compounds across Chinese dialects: a study of Cantonese, Mandarin and Taiwanese. In C. Tseng (ed.), *Chinese Languages and Linguistics 4: Typological Studies of Languages in China*, *pp.* 199-224. Taipei: Academia Sinica.

Chikamatsu, N. 1996. The effects of L1 orthography on L2 word recognition: a study of American and Chinese learners of Japanese. *Studies in Second Language Acquisition*, *Vol.* 18, *pp.* 403-32.

Chomsky, N. 1980. *Rules and Representations*. New York: Columbia University Press.

Chomsky, N. 1981. *Lectures on Government and Binding*. Dordrecht: Foris.

Chomsky, N. 1982. *Some Concepts and Consequences of the Theory of Government and Binding*. Cambridge, MA: MIT Press.

Chomsky, N. 1986. *Knowledge of Language: Its Nature, Origin and Use*. New York: Praeger.

Chomsky, N. 1995. *The Minimalist Program*. Cambridge, MA: MIT Press.

Chu, C. C. 1973. The passive construction: Chinese and English. *Journal of*

*Chinese Linguistics*, Vol. 1, *pp.* 437-470.

Chu, C. C. 1976. Some semantic aspects of action verbs. *Lingua*, Vol. 40, *pp.* 43-54.

Clahsen, H. 1990. The comparative study of first and second language development. *Studies in Second Language Acquisition*, Vol. 12, *pp.* 135-153.

Clahsen, H. and P. Muysken. 1986. The availability of Universal Grammar to adult and child learners: a study of the acquisition of German word order. *Second Language Research*, Vol. 2, *pp.* 93-119.

Clahsen, H. and U. Hong. 1995. Agreement and null subjects in German L2 development: new evidence from reaction-time experiments. *Second Language Research*, Vol. 11, *pp.* 57-87.

Comrie, B. 1976. The syntax of causative constructions: cross-language similarities and divergences. In M. Shibatani (ed.), *The Grammar of Causative Constructions* (*Syntax and Semantics*, Vol. 6), *pp.* 261-312. New York: Academic Press.

Comrie, B. 1985. Causative verb formation and other verb-deriving morphology. In T. Shopen (ed.), *Grammatical Categories and the Lexicon* (*Language Typology and Syntactic Description*, Vol. 3), *pp.* 309-348. Cambridge: Cambridge University Press.

Comrie, B. 1989. *Language Universals and Linguistic Typology: Syntax and Morphology* (Second Edition). Oxford: Blackwell.

Corder, S. P. 1967. The significance of learners' errors. *International Review of Applied Linguistics*, Vol. 5, *pp.* 161-170.

Corver, N. 2003. Perfect projections. In R. van Hout, A. Hulk, F. Kuiken and R. Towell (eds.), *The Lexicon-Syntax Interface in Second Language Acquisition*, *pp.* 45-68. Amsterdam: John Benjamins.

Croft, W. 1998. Event structure in argument linking. In M. Butt and W. Geuder (eds.), *The Projection of Arguments: Lexical and Compositional Factors*, *pp.* 21-63. Stanford: CSLI Publications.

Crookes, G. 1991. Second language speech production research: a methodologically oriented review. *Studies in Second Language Acquisition*, Vol. 13, *pp.* 113-132.

Davies, A. 1984. Introduction. In A. Davies, C. Criper, and A. P. R. Howatt (eds.), *Interlanguage*, ix-xv. Edinburgh: Edinburgh University Press.

Dowty, D. 1979. *Word Meaning and Montague Grammar: The Semantics of Verbs and Times in Generative Semantics and in Montague's PTQ*. Dordrecht: Reidel.

Dowty, D. 1991. Thematic proto-roles and argument selection. *Language*, Vol. 67, pp. 547-619.

Ellis, R. 1985. *Understanding Second Language Acquisition*. Oxford: Oxford University Press.

Ellis, R. 1991. Grammaticality judgments and second language acquisition. *Studies in Second Language Acquisition*, Vol. 13, pp. 161-186.

Embick, D. 2004. On the structure of resultative participles in English. *Linguistic Inquiry*, Vol. 35, pp. 355-392.

Epstein, S., S. Flynn and G. Martohardjono. 1996. Second language acquisition: theoretical and experimental issues in contemporary research. *Behavioral and Brain Sciences*, Vol. 19, pp. 677-758.

Eubank, L. 1993/1994. On the transfer of parametric values in L2 development. *Language Acquisition*, Vol. 3, pp. 183-208.

Eubank, L. 1994a. Optionality and the initial state in L2 development. In T. Hoekstra and B. D. Schwartz (eds.), *Language Acquisition Studies in Generative Grammar: Papers in Honour of Kenneth Wexler From the 1991 GLOW Workshops*, pp. 369-388. Amsterdam: John Benjamins.

Eubank, L. 1994b. Towards an explanation for the late acquisition of agreement in L2 English. *Second Language Research*, Vol. 10, pp. 84-93.

Eubank, L. 1995. Generative research on second language acquisition. *Annual Review of Applied Linguistics*, Vol. 15, pp. 93-107.

Eubank, L. 1996. Negation in early German-English interlanguage: more valueless features in the L2 initial state. *Second Language Research*, Vol. 12, pp. 73-106.

Eubank, L. and S. Grace. 1998. V-to-I and inflection in non-native grammars. In M. -L. Beck (ed.), *Morphology and Its Interfaces in L2 Knowledge*, pp. 69-88. Amsterdam: John Benjamins.

Flynn, S. 1986. Production vs. comprehension: differences in underlying competence. *Studies in Second Language Acquisition*, Vol. 8, pp. 135-164.

Flynn, S. 1987. Contrast and construction in a parameter-setting model of second language acquisition. *Language Learning*, Vol. 37, pp. 19-62.

Flynn, S. 1996. A parameter-setting approach to second language acquisition. In W. Ritchie and T. Bhatia (eds.), *Handbook of Language Acquisition*, pp. 121-158. San Diego: Academic Press.

Fodor, J. D. and S. Crain. 1987. Simplicity and generality of rules in language acquisition. In B. MacWhinney (ed.), *Mechanisms of Language Acquisition*, pp. 35-63. Hillsdale, NJ: Lawrence Erlbaum.

Fotos, S. S. 1991. The close test as an integrative measure of EFL proficiency: a substitute for essays on college entrance examinations? *Language Learning*, Vol. 41, pp. 313-336.

Franceschina, F. 2001. Morphological or syntactic deficits in near-native speakers? An assessment of some current proposals. *Second Language Research*, Vol. 17, pp. 213-247.

Fukui, N. 1988. Deriving the differences between English and Japanese: a case study in parametric syntax. *English Linguistics*, Vol. 5, pp. 249-270.

Fukui, N. 1993. Parameters and optionality. *Linguistic Inquiry*, Vol. 24, pp. 399-420.

Fukui, N. 2001. Phrase structure. In M. Baltin and C. Collins (eds.), *The Handbook of Contemporary Syntactic Theory*, pp. 374-406. Malden, MA: Blackwell.

Fukui, N. and Y. Takano. 1998. Symmetry in syntax: Merge and Demerge. *Journal of East Asian Linguistics*, Vol. 7, pp. 27-86.

Gao, Q. 1997. Resultative verb compounds and ba-construction in Chinese. *Journal of Chinese Linguistics*, Vol. 25, pp. 84-130.

Gasde, H. -D. and W. Paul. 1996. Functional categories, topic prominence and complex sentences in Mandarin Chinese. *Linguistics*, Vol. 34, pp. 263-294.

Gass, S. M. 1984. A review of interlanguage syntax: Language transfer and language universals. *Language Learning*, Vol. 34, pp. 115-131.

Gass, S. M. and U. Lakshmanan. 1991. Accounting for interlanguage subject pronouns. *Second Language Research*, Vol. 7, pp. 181-203.

Goddard, C. 1998. *Semantic Analysis: A Practical Introduction*. Oxford: Oxford University Press.

Goldberg, A. E. 1995. *Constructions: A Construction Grammar Approach to Argument Structure*. Chicago: University of Chicago Press.

Goldberg, A. E. 2001. Patient argument of causative verbs can be omitted: the role of information structure in argument distribution. *Language Sciences*, Vol. 23, pp. 503-524.

Goodall, G. 1987. On the argument structure and L-marking with Mandarin Chinese BA. In J. McDonough and B. Plunker (eds.), *Proceedings of the North East Linguistic Society*, Vol. 17, pp. 232-242. Amherst: University of Massachusetts.

Goodall, G. 1989. Evidence for an asymmetry in argument structure. *Linguistic Inquiry*, Vol. 20, pp. 669-674.

Goodall, G. 1990. X-bar-internal word order in Mandarin Chinese. *Linguistics*, Vol. 28, pp. 241-261.

Goodall, G. 1999. Accusative case in passives. *Linguistics*, Vol. 37, pp. 1-12.

Goodluck, H. 1991. *Language Acquisition: A Linguistic Introduction*. Oxford: Blackwell.

Green, D. W. 2003. Neural basis of lexicon and grammar in L2 acquisition: the convergence hypothesis. In R. van Hout, A. Hulk, F. Kuiken and R. Towell (eds.), *The Lexicon-Syntax Interface in Second Language Acquisition*, pp. 197-218. Amsterdam: John Benjamins.

Gregg, K. R. 1996. The logical and developmental problems of second language acquisition. In W. Ritchie and T. Bhatia (eds.), *Handbook of Second Language Acquisition*, pp. 49-81. San Diego: Academic Press.

Grimshaw, J. 1990. *Argument Structure*. Cambridge, MA: MIT Press.

Grondin, N. and L. White. 1996. Functional categories in child L2 acquisition of French. *Language Acquisition*, Vol. 5, pp. 1-34.

Guasti, M. T. 1997. Romance causatives. In L. Haegeman (ed.), *The New Comparative Syntax*, pp. 124-144. London: Longman.

Haegeman, L. 1994. *Introduction to Government and Binding Theory* (Second Edition). Oxford: Blackwell.

Hale, K. and S. J. Keyser. 1993. On argument structure and the lexical expression of syntactic relations. In K. Hale and S. J. Keyser (eds.), *The View from Building 20: Essays in Linguistics in Honour of Sylvain Bromberger*, pp. 53-109. Cambridge, MA: MIT Press.

Hale, K. and J. Keyser. 2002. *Prolegomenon to a Theory of Argument Structure*. Cambridge, MA: MIT Press.

Han, Z. 2004. *Fossilization in Adult Second Language Acquisition*. Clevedon:

Multilingual Matters.
Harada, N. 1999. On certain differences between English and Japanese verbs. In F. D. Gobbo and H. Hoshi (eds.), *UCI Working Papers in Linguistics*, Vol. 5, pp. 57-76. Irvine Linguistics Students Association.
Harada, N. 2000. A parametric approach to intransitive verbs. In R. Daly and A. Riehl (eds.), *Proceedings of ESCOL ' 99*, pp. 84-94. University of Connecticut.
Harada, N. 2002. *Licensing PF-Visible Formal Features: A Linear Algorithm and Case-Related Phenomena in PF*. PhD Dissertation. University of California, Irvine.
Haspelmath, M. 1993. More on the typology of inchoative/causative verb alternations. In B. Comrie and M. Polinsky (eds.), *Causatives and Transitivity*, pp. 87-120. Amsterdam: John Benjamins.
Hawkins, R. 2001a. *Second Language Syntax: A Generative Introduction*. Oxford: Blackwell.
Hawkins, R. 2001b. The theoretical significance of Universal Grammar in second language acquisition. *Second Language Research*, Vol. 17, pp. 345-367.
Hawkins, R. and C. Y.-H. Chan. 1997. The partial availability of Universal Grammar in second language acquisition: the 'failed functional features hypothesis'. *Second Language Research*, Vol. 13, pp. 187-226.
Hawkins, R. and S. Liszka. 2003. Locating the source of defective past tense marking in advanced L2 English speakers. In R. van Hout, A. Hulk, F. Kuiken and R. Towell (eds.), *The Lexicon-Syntax Interface in Second Language Acquisition*, pp. 21-44. Amsterdam: John Benjamins.
Haznedar, B. 2003. Missing surface inflection in adult and child L2 acquisition. In J. M. Liceras, H. Zobl and H. Goodluck (eds.), *Proceedings of the 6th Generative Approaches to Second Language Acquisition Conference (GASLA 2002)*, pp. 140-149. Somerville, MA: Cascadilla Press.
Hedgcock, J. 1993. Well-formed vs. ill-formed strings in L2 metalingual tasks: specifying features of grammaticality judgments. *Second Language Research*, Vol. 9, pp. 1-21.
Helms-Park, R. 2001. Evidence of lexical transfer in learner syntax: the acquåisition of English causatives by speakers of Hindi-Urdu and Vietnamese. *Studies in Second Language Acquisition*, Vol. 23, pp. 71-102.

Herschensohn, J. 2000. *The Second Time Around: Minimalism and L2 Acquisition*. Amsterdam: John Benjamins.

Herschensohn, J. 2001. Missing inflection in second language French: accidental infinitives and other verbal deficits. *Second Language Research*, Vol. 17, pp. 273-305.

Higginbotham, J. 1985. On semantics. *Linguistic Inquiry*, Vol. 16, pp. 547-593.

Hilles, S. 1991. Access to Universal Grammar in second language acquisition. In L. Eubank (ed.), *Point Counterpoint: Universal Grammar in the Second Language*, pp. 305-338. Amsterdam: John Benjamins.

Hirakawa, M. 1995. L2 acquisition of English unaccusative constructions. In D MacLaughlin and S. McEwen (eds.), *Proceedings of the 19$^{th}$ Boston University Conference on Language Development*, pp. 291-302. Sommerville, MA: Cascadilla Press.

Hirakawa, M. 1999. L2 acquisition of Japanese unaccusative verbs by speakers of English and Chinese. In K. Kanno (ed.), *The Acquisition of Japanese as a Second Language*, pp. 291-302. Somerville, MA: Cascadilla Press.

Hochberg, J. 1986. Children's judgments of transitivity errors. *Journal of Child Language*, Vol. 13, pp. 317-334.

Hoekstra, T. 1988. Small clause results. *Lingua*, Vol. 74, pp. 101-139.

Hoekstra, T. 1992. Aspectual and theta theory. In I. M. Roca (ed.), *Thematic Structure: Its Role in Grammar*, pp. 145-174. Berlin: Foris.

Hornstein, N. and D. Lightfoot. 1981. Introduction. In N. Hornstein and D. Lightfoot (eds.), *Explanation in Linguistics: The Logical Problem of Language Acquisition*. London: Longman.

Huang, C.-T. J. 1984. On the distribution and reference of empty pronouns. *Linguistic Inquiry*, Vol. 15, pp. 531-574.

Huang, C.-T. J. 1988. *Wo pao de kuai* and Chinese phrase structure. *Language*, Vol. 64, pp. 274-311.

Huang, C.-T. J. 1989. Pro-drop in Chinese: a generalized control theory. In O. Jaeggli and K. Safir (eds.), *The Null Subject Parameter*, pp. 185-214. Dordrecht: Kluwer.

Huang, C.-T. J. 1992. Complex predicates in Control. In R. K. Larson, S. Iatridou, U. Lahiri and J. Higginbotham (eds.), *Control and Grammar*, pp. 109-147. Dordrecht: Kluwer.

Huang, S. -F. 1974. Mandarin causatives. *Journal of Chinese Linguistics*, Vol. 2, pp. 354-369.

Hulstijn, J. H. 1997. Second language acquisition research in the laboratory: possibilities and limitations. *Studies in Second Language Acquisition*, Vol. 19, pp. 131-143.

Inagaki, S. 2001. Motion verbs with goal PPs in the L2 acquisition of English and Japanese. *Studies in Second Language Acquisition*, Vol. 23, pp. 153-170.

Inagaki, S. 2002. Japanese learners' acquisition of English manner-of-motion verbs with location/directional PPs. *Second Language Research*, Vol. 18, pp. 3-27.

Ionin, T. and K. Wexler. 2002. Why is 'is' easier than '-s'?: acquisition of tense/agreement morphology by child second language learners of English. *Second Language Research*, Vol. 18, pp. 95-136.

Jackendoff, R. 1990. *Semantic Structure*. Cambridge, MA: MIT Press.

Jiang, ZiXin. 1990. A constraint on topic in Chinese. *Journal of Chinese Linguistics*, Vol. 18, pp. 231-260.

Jin, H. G. 1994. Topic-prominence and subject-prominence in L2 acquisition: evidence of English-to-Chinese typological transfer. *Language Learning*, Vol. 44, pp. 101-122.

Johnson, K. 1991. Object position. *Natural Language and Linguistic Theory*, Vol. 9, pp. 577-636.

Jordens, P. 1996. Input and instruction in second language acquisition. In P. Jordens and J. Lalleman (eds.), *Investigating Second Language Acquisition*, pp. 407-449. Berlin: Mouton de Gruyter.

Ju, M. 2000. Overpassivization errors by second language learners: The effects of conceptualizable agents in discourse. *Studies in Second Language Acquisition*, Vol. 22, pp85-111.

Juffs, A. 1996a. *Learnability and the Lexicon: Theories and Second Language Acquisition Research*. Amsterdam: John Benjamins.

Juffs, A. 1996b. Semantics-syntax correspondences in second language acquisition. *Second Language ResearchAmsterdam* 12, pp177-221.

Juffs, A. 2000. An overview of the second language acquisition of links between verb semantics and morpho-syntax. In J. Archibald (ed.), *Second Language Acquisition and Linguistic Theory*, pp. 187-227. Oxford:

Blackwell.

Juffs, A. and M. Harrington. 1995. Parsing effects in second language sentence processing: subject and object asymmetries in wh- extraction. *Studies in Second Language Acquisition*, Vol. 17, pp. 483-516.

Juffs, A. and M. Harrington. 1996. Garden path sentences and error data in second language sentence processing. *Language Learning*, Vol. 46, pp. 283-326.

Kellerman, E. 1977. Toward a characterization of the strategies of transfer in second language learning. *Interlanguage Studies Bulletin*, Vol. 2, pp. 58-145.

Kellerman, E. 1979. Transfer and non-transfer: where we are now? *Studies in Second Language Acquisition*, Vol. 2, pp. 37-57.

Kellerman, E. 1983. Now you see it, now you don't. In S. Gass and L. Selinker (eds.), *Language Transfer in Language Learning*, pp. 112-134. Rowley, MA: Newbury House.

Kellerman, E. 1989. The imperfect conditional: fossilization, cross-linguistic influence and natural tendencies in a foreign language setting. In K. Hyltenstam and L. Obler (eds.), *Bilingualism Across Life Span*, pp. 87-115. Cambridge: Cambridge University Press.

Kellerman, E. 1995. Crosslinguistic influence: transfer to nowhere? *Annual Review of Applied Linguistics*, Vol. 15, pp. 125-150.

Kim, J.-B. 1999. Constraints on the formation of Korean and English resultatives. In P. Tamanji, M. Hirotani and N. Hall (eds.), *Proceedings of the North East Linguistic Society*, Vol. 29, pp. 137-151. Amherst: University of Massachusetts.

Kim, M. 1999. *A Cross-linguistic Perspective on the Acquisition of Locative Verbs*. PhD Dissertation. University of Delaware.

Kiparsky, P. 1998. Partitive case and aspect. In M. Butt and W. Geuder (eds.), *The Projection of Arguments: Lexical and Compositional Factors*, pp. 265-307. Stanford: CSLI Publications.

Klein, E. and G. Martohardjono. 1999. Investigating second language grammars: some conceptual and methodological issues in generative SLA research. In E. Klein and G. Martohardjono (eds.), *The Development of Second Language Grammars: A Generative Approach*, pp. 3-34. Amsterdam: John Benjamins.

Laesch, K. B. and A. van Kleeck. 1987. The cloze test as an alternative measure of language proficiency of children considered for exit from bilingual education. *Language Learning*, Vol. 37, pp. 171-189.

Lakshmanan, U. 1993/1994. The boy for the cookie: some evidence for the nonviolation of the case filter in child second language acquisition. *Language Acquisition*, Vol. 3, pp. 55-91.

Lakshmanan, U. and L. Selinker. 1994. The status of CP and the tensed complementizer that in the development of L2 grammars of English. *Second Language Research*, Vol. 10, pp. 25-48.

Lakshmanan, U. and L. Selinker. 2001. Analysing interlanguage: how do we know what learners know? *Second Language Research*, Vol. 17, pp. 394-420.

Lardiere, D. 1998a. Case and tense in the "fossilized" steady-state. *Second Language Research*, Vol. 14, pp. 1-26.

Lardiere, D. 1998b. Dissociating syntax from morphology in a divergent L2 end-state grammar. *Second Language Research*, Vol. 14, pp. 359-375.

Lardiere, D. 2000. Mapping features to forms in second language acquisition. In J. Archibald (ed.), *Second Language Acquisition and Linguistic Theory*. pp. 102-129. Oxford: Blackwell.

Larson, R. 1988. On the double object construction. *Linguistic Inquiry*, Vol. 19, pp. 335-392.

Lasnik, H. 1992. Case and expletives: notes toward a parametric account. *Linguistic Inquiry*, Vol. 23, pp. 381-405.

Lemmens, M. 1998. *Lexical Perspectives on Transitivity and Ergativity*. Amsterdam: John Benjamins.

Leow, R. P. 1993. To simplify or not to simplify: a look at intake. *Studies in Second Language Acquisition*, Vol. 15, pp. 333-355.

Levin, B. 1993. *English Verb Classes and Alternations*. Chicago: The University of Chicago Press.

Levin, B. and M. Rappaport Hovav. 1995. *Unaccusativity: At the Syntax-Lexical Semantics Interface*. Cambridge, MA: MIT Press.

Li, C. N. and S. A. Thompson. 1976a. Subject and topic: a new typology of language. In C. N. Li (ed.), *Subject and Topic*, pp. 457-489. New York: Academic Press.

Li, C. N. and S. A. Thompson. 1976b. Development of the causative in

Mandarin Chinese: interaction of diachronic processes in syntax. In M. Shibatani (ed.), *The Grammar of Causative Constructions* (*Syntax and Semantics*, Vol. 6), pp. 477-492. New York: Academic Press.

Li, C. N. and S. A. Thompson. 1981. *Mandarin Chinese: A Functional Reference Grammar*. Berkley and Los Angeles: University of California Press.

Li, J. 1995. Dou and wh-Questions in Mandarin Chinese. *Journal of East Asian Linguistics*, Vol. 4, pp. 313-323.

Li, Y. -F. 1990. On V-V compounds in Chinese. *Natural Language and Linguistic Theory*, Vol. 8, pp. 177-207.

Li, Y. -F. 1993. Structural head and aspectuality. *Language*, Vol. 69, pp. 480-504.

Li, Y. -F. 1995. The thematic hierarchy and causativity. *Natural Language and Linguistic Theory*, Vol. 13, pp. 255-282.

Li, Y. -F. 1998. Chinese resultative constructions and the Uniformity of Theta Assignment Hypothesis. In J. Packard (ed.), *New Approaches to Chinese Word Formation*, pp. 285-310. Berlin: Mouton de Gruyter.

Li, Y. -H. A. 1990. *Order and Constituency in Mandarin Chinese*. Dordrecht: Kluwer.

Lightfoot, D. 1991. *How to Set Parameters: Arguments from Language Change*. Cambridge, MA: MIT Press.

Lin, H. -L. 1999. Aspect licensing and verb incorporation. In C. Sun (ed.), *Proceedings of the 10$^{th}$ North American Conference on Chinese Linguistics*, pp. 205-220. Graduate Students in Linguistics, University of Southern California.

Liu, L. C. -S. 1997. Light verb and accusative-ing gerund in Taiwanese. In L. C. -S. Liu and K. Takeda (eds.), *UCI Working Papers in Linguistics*, Vol. 3, pp. 99-123. Irvine Linguistic Students Association.

Liu, Z. 2003. Ye tan jiegou zhuci *de* de laiyuan ji V *de* C shubu jiegou de xingcheng (Some problems in the article the origin of complement marker de and verb-complement construction'). *Zhongguo Yuwen* 2003(4), pp. 379-381.

Long, M. H. 2003. Stabilization and fossilization in interlanguage development. In C. J. Doughty and M. H. Long (eds.), *The Handbook of Second*

Language Acquisition, pp. 487-536. Oxford: Blackwell.

López, L. 2001. On the (non)complementarity of θ-theory and checking theory. Linguistics Inquiry, Vol. 32, pp. 694-716.

Lyons, J. 1977. Semantics (Vol. 2). Cambridge: Cambridge University Press.

Mandell, P. B. 1999. On the reliability of grammaticality judgment tests in second language acquisition research. Second Language Research, Vol. 15, pp. 73-99.

Matsumoto, Y. 1996a. Complex Predicates in Japanese: A Syntactic and Semantic Study of the Notion 'Word'. Stanford: CSLI Publications.

Matsumoto, Y. 1996b. A syntactic account of light verb phenomena in Japanese. Journal of East Asian Linguistics, Vol. 5, pp. 107-149.

Mazurkewich, I. 1984. Dative questions and markedness. In F. Eckman, L. Bell, and D. Nelson (eds.), Universals of Second Language Acquisition, pp. 119-131. Rowley, MA: Newbury House.

Meisel, J. M. 1991. Principles of Universal Grammar and strategies of language learning: some similarities and differences between first and second language acquisition. In L. Eubank (ed.), Point Counterpoint: Universal Grammar in the Second Language, pp. 231-276. Amsterdam: John Benjamins.

Meisel, J. M. 1997. The acquisition of the syntax of negation in French and German: contrasting first and second language development. Second Language Research, Vol. 13, 187-226.

Miyagawa, S. 1984. Blocking and Japanese causatives. Lingua, Vol. 64, pp. 177-207.

Miyagawa, S. 1989. Structure and Case Marking in Japanese (Syntax and Semantics, Vol. 22). San Diego: Academic Press.

Montrul, S. 1999. Causative errors with unaccusative verbs in L2 Spanish. Second Language Research, Vol. 15, pp. 191-219.

Montrul, S. 2000. Transitivity alternations in second language acquisition: toward a modular view of transfer. Studies in Second Language Acquisition, Vol. 22, 229-274.

Montrul, S. 2001a. First-language-constrained variability in the second-language acquisition of argument-structure-changing morphology with causative verbs. Second Language Research, Vol. 17, 144-194.

Montrul, S. 2001b. The acquisition of causative/inchoative verbs in L2 Turkish. *Language Acquisition*, Vol. 9, pp. 1-58.

Montrul, S. 2001c. Causatives and transitivity in L2 English. *Language Learning*, Vol. 51, pp. 51-106.

Morikawa, H. 1991. Acquisition of causatives in Japanese. *Papers and Reports on Child Language Development*, Vol. 30, pp. 80-87.

Nagata, H. 1988. The relativity of linguistic intuitions: the effect of repetition on grammaticality judgments. *Journal of Psycholinguistic Research*, Vol. 17, pp. 1-17.

Nishiyama, K. 1998. V-V compounds as serialization. *Journal of East Asian Linguistics*, Vol. 7, pp. 175-217.

Odlin, T. 1989. *Language Transfer*. Cambridge: Cambridge University Press.

Odlin, T. 2003. Cross-linguistic influence. In C. J. Doughty and M. H. Long ( eds. ), *The Handbook of Second Language Acquisition*, pp. 436-86. Oxford: Blackwell.

Parsons, T. 1990. *Events in the Semantics of English: A Study in Subatomic Semantics*. Cambridge, MA: MIT Press

Perlmutter, D. M. 1978. Impersonal passives and the unaccusative hypothesis. In *Proceedings of the 4th Annual Meeting of the Berkeley Linguistics Society*, pp. 157-189. University of California, Berkeley: Berkeley Linguistic Society.

Pesetsky, D. 1995. *Zero Syntax: Experiencers and Cascades*. Cambridge, MA: MIT Press.

Pienemann, M. and G. Håkansson. 1999. A unified approach toward the development of Swedish as L2: a processability account. *Studies in Second Language Acquisition*, Vol. 21, pp. 383-420.

Pierce, A. 1992. *Language Acquisition and Syntactic Theory: A Comparative Analysis of French and English Child Grammars*. Dordrecht: Kluwer.

Pinker, S. 1989. *Learnability and Cognition: the Acquisition of Argument Structure*. Cambridge, MA: MIT Press.

Platzack, C. 1996. The initial hypothesis of syntax: a minimalist perspective on language acquisition and attrition. In H. Clahsen ( ed. ), *Generative Perspectives on Language Acquisition*, pp. 369-414. Amsterdam: John Benjamins.

Prévost, P. and L. White. 2000. Missing surface inflection or impairment in second language acquisition? Evidence from tense and agreement. *Second Language Research*, Vol. 16, pp. 103-133.

Pustejovsky, J. 1991. The syntax of event structure. *Cognition*, Vol. 41, pp. 47-81.

Radford, A. 1990. *Syntactic Theory and the Acquisition of English Syntax*. Oxford: Blackwell.

Radford, A. 1997. *Syntactic Theory and the Structure of English*. Cambridge: Cambridge University Press.

Rapoport, T. R. 1999. Structure, aspect and the predicate. *Language*, Vol. 75, pp. 653-77.

Rappaport Hovav, M., and B. Levin. 2001. An event structure account of English resultatives. *Language*, Vol. 77, pp. 766-797.

Ren, X. 1991. The post-verbal constituent in Chinese passive forms. *Journal of Chinese Linguistics*, Vol. 19, pp. 221-242.

Ritter, E. and S. T. Rosen. 1998. Delimiting events in syntax. In M. Butt and W. Geuder (eds.), *The Projection of Arguments: Lexical and Compositional Factors*, pp. 135-164. Stanford: CSLI Publications.

Robertson, D. 2000. Variability in the use of the English article system by Chinese learners of English. *Second Language Research*, Vol. 16, pp. 135-172.

Rutherford, W. E. 1989. Preemption and the learning of L2 grammars. *Studies in Second Language Acquisition*, Vol. 11, pp. 441-457.

Saito, M. 1992. Long-distance scrambling in Japanese. *Journal of East Asian Linguistics*, Vol. 1, pp. 69-118.

Sasaki, Y. 1994. Paths of processing strategy transfers in learning Japanese and English as foreign languages: a competition model approach. *Studies in Second Language Acquisition*, Vol. 16, pp. 43-72.

Sato, Y. 2003. Japanese learners' linking problems with English psych verbs. *Reading Working Papers in Linguistics*, Vol. 7, pp. 125-144.

Schachter, J. 1988. Second language acquisition and its relationship to Universal Grammar. *Applied Linguistics*, Vol. 9, pp. 219-235.

Schachter, J. 1990. On the issue of completeness in second language acquisition. *Second Language Research*, Vol. 6, pp. 93-124.

Schachter, J. 1996. Learning and triggering in adult L2 acquisition. In G. Brown, K. Malmkaer and J. Williams ( eds. ), *Performance and Competence in Second Language Acquisition*, pp. 70-88. Cambridge: Cambridge University Press.

Schachter, J. and V. Yip. 1990. Grammaticality judgments: why does anyone object to subject extraction? *Studies in Second Language Acquisition*, Vol. 12, pp. 379-392.

Schwartz, B. D. 1993. On explicit and negative data effecting and affecting competence and linguistic behavior. *Studies in Second Language Acquisition*, Vol. 15, pp. 147-163.

Schwartz, B. D. 1998. On two hypotheses of "transfer" in L2A: Minimal trees and absolute L1 influence. In S. Flynn, G. Martohardjono and W. O'Neil ( eds. ), *The Generative Study of Second Language Acquisition*, pp. 35-59. Hillsdale, NJ: Erlbaum.

Schwartz, B. D. and R. A. Sprouse. 1994. Word order and nominative case in nonnative language acquisition: a longitudinal study of ( L1 Turkish) German interlanguage. In T. Hoekstra and B. D. Schwartz ( eds. ), *Language Acquisition Studies in Generative Grammar: Papers in Honour of Kenneth Wexler From the 1991 GLOW Workshops*, pp. 317-368. Amsterdam: John Benjamins.

Schwartz, B. D. and R. A. Sprouse 1996. L2 Cognitive State and the Full Transfer/Full Access Model. *Second Language Research*, Vol. 12, pp. 40-72.

Selinker, L. 1972. Interlanguage. *International Review of Applied Linguistics*, Vol. 10, pp. 209-231.

Selinker, L. 1996. On the notion of "IL competence" in early SLA research: an aid to understanding some baffling current issues. In G. Brown, K. Malmkaer and J. Williams ( eds. ), *Performance and Competence in Second Language Acquisition*, pp. 92-113. Cambridge: Cambridge University Press.

Selinker, L. and J. T. Lamendella. 1978. Two perspectives on fossilization in interlanguage learning. *Interlanguage Studies Bulletin*, Vol. 3, pp. 143-191.

Selinker, L. and U. Lakshmanan. 1993. Language transfer and fossilization: the Multiple Effects Principle. In S. M. Gass and L. Selinker ( eds. ), *Language Transfer in Language Learning*, pp. 197-216. Amsterdam: John

Benjamins.

Sharwood Smith, M. 1993. Input enhancement in instructed SLA: theoretical bases. *Studies in Second Language Acquisition*, Vol. 15, pp. 165-179.

Sharwood Smith, M. and E. Kellerman. 1986. Crosslinguistic influence in second language acquisition: an introduction. In E. Kellerman and M. Sharwood Smith (eds.), *Crosslinguistic Influence in Second Language Acquisition*, pp. 1-9. New York: Pergamon Press.

Shi, D. 1997. Issues on Chinese passives. *Journal of Chinese Linguistics*, Vol. 25, pp. 41-70.

Shi, D. 2000. Topic and topic-comment constructions in Mandarin Chinese. *Language*, Vol. 76, pp. 383-408.

Shibatani, M. 1976a. The grammar of causative constructions: a conspectus. In M. Shibatani (ed.), *The Grammar of Causative Constructions (Syntax and Semantics*, Vol. 6), pp. 1-40. New York: Academic Press.

Shibatani, M. 1976b. Causativization. In M. Shibatani (ed.), *Japanese Generative Grammar (Syntax and Semantics*, Vol. 5), pp. 239-294. New York: Academic Press.

Simpson, J. 1983. Resultatives. In L. Levin, M. Rappaport Hovav, and A. Zaenen (eds.), *Papers in Lexical-Functional Grammar*, pp. 143-157. Bloomington: Indiana University Linguistics Club.

Singleton, D. 1987. Mother and other tongue influence on learner French: a case study. *Studies in Second Language Acquisition*, Vol. 9, pp. 327-346.

Slabakova, R. 2000. L1 transfer revisited: the L2 acquisition of telicity marking in English by Spanish and Bulgarian native speakers. *Linguistics*, Vol. 38, pp. 739-770.

Slabakova, R. 2001. *Telicity in the Second Language*. Amsterdam: John Benjamins.

Slabakova, R. 2003. Semantic evidence for functional categories in interlanguage grammars. *Second Language Research*, Vol. 19, pp. 42-75.

Smith, C. S. 1997. *The Parameter of Aspect* (Second Edition). Dordrecht: Kluwer.

Smith, N. and I. -M. Tsimpli 1995. *The Mind of A Savant*. Oxford: Blackwell.

Sohn, H. -M. 1994. *Korean*. London: Routledge.

Song, J. J. 1996. *Causatives and Causation: A Universal-Typological*

Perspective. London: Longman.

Sorace, A. 1993. Incomplete vs. divergent representations of unaccusativity in non-native grammars of Italian. *Second Language Research*, Vol. 9, pp. 22-47.

Sorace, A. 1995. Acquiring linking rules and argument structures in a second language: the unaccusative/unergative distinction. In L. Eubank, L. Selinker, and M. Sharwood Smith (eds.), *The Current State of Interlanguage*, pp. 153-175. Amsterdam: John Benjamins.

Sorace, A. 2004. Gradience at the lexicon-syntax interface: evidence from auxiliary selection and implications for unaccusativity. In A. Alexiadou, E. Anagnostopoulou, and M. Everaert (eds.), *The Unaccusativity Puzzle: Explorations of the Syntax-Lexicon Interface*, pp. 243-268. Oxford: Oxford University Press.

Sugioka, Y. 1985. *Interaction of Derivational Morphology and Syntax in Japanese and English*. New York: Garland.

Sybesma, R. 1992. *Causatives and Accomplishments: the Case of Chinese ba*. Dordrecht: Holland Institute of Generative Linguistics.

Sybesma, R. 1997. Why Chinese verb-le is a resultative predicate. *Journal of East Asian Linguistics*, Vol. 6, pp. 215-262.

Tai, J. H. -Y. 1984. Verbs and times in Chinese: Vendler's four categories. In D. Testen, V. Mishra and J. Drogo (eds.), *Papers From the Parasession on Lexical Semantics*. Chicago Linguistic Society.

Takano, Y. 2004. Coordination of verbs and two types of verbal inflection. *Linguistic Inquiry*, Vol. 35, pp. 168-178.

Talmy, L. 1985. Lexicalization patterns: semantic structure in lexical patterns. In T. Shopen (ed.), *Grammatical Categories and the Lexicon (Language Typology and Syntactic Description*, Vol. 3), pp. 57-149. Cambridge: Cambridge University Press.

Tang, S. -W. 1997. The parametric approach to the resultative construction in Chinese and English. In L. C. -S. Liu and K. Takeda (eds.), *UCI Working Papers in Linguistics*, Vol. 3, pp. 203-226. Irvine Linguistics Students Association.

Tang, S. -W. 2001. A complementation approach to Chinese passives and its consequences. *Linguistics*, Vol. 39, pp. 257-295.

Tenny, C. L. 1994. *Aspectual Roles and the Syntax-Semantics Interface.* Dordrecht: Kluwer.

Thomas, M. 1989. The interpretation of English reflexive pronouns by non-native speakers. *Studies in Second Language Acquisition*, Vol. 11, pp. 281-303.

Thomas, M. 1991. Universal Grammar and the interpretation of reflexives in a second language. *Language*, Vol. 67, pp. 211-239.

Thompson, S. A. 1973. Transitivity and some problems with the ba construction in Mandarin Chinese. *Journal of Chinese Linguistics*, Vol. 1, pp. 208-221.

Ting, J. 1998. Deriving the bei-construction in Mandarin Chinese. *Journal of East Asian Linguistics*, Vol. 7, pp. 319-354.

Toth, P. D. 2000. The interaction of instruction and learner-internal factors in the acquisition of L2 morphosyntax. *Studies in Second Language Acquisition*, Vol. 22, pp. 169-208.

Towell, R. R. Hawkins and N. Bazergui. 1993. Systematic and nonsystematic variability in advanced language learning. *Studies in Second Language Acquisition*, Vol. 15, pp. 439-460.

Trahey, M. 1996. Positive evidence in second language acquisition: some long-term effects. *Second Language Research*, Vol. 12, pp. 111-139.

Trahey, M. and L. White. 1993. Positive evidence and preemption in the second language classroom. *Studies in Second Language Acquisition*, Vol. 15, pp. 181-204.

Travis, L. 1991. Inner aspect and the structure of VP. *Cahiers de Linguistique de l' UQAM*, Vol. 1, pp. 132-146.

Travis, L. 2003. Lexical items and zero morphology. In J. M. Liceras, H. Zobl and H. Goodluck (eds.), *Proceedings of the 6$^{th}$ Generative Approaches to Second Language Acquisition Conference (GASLA 2002)*, pp. 315-330. Somerville, MA: Cascadilla Press.

Tsimpli, I. -M. and A. Roussou. 1991. Parameter resetting in L2? *UCL Working Papers in Linguistics*, Vol. 3, pp. 149-169.

Tsujimura, N. 1990. Unaccusative nouns and resultatives in Japanese. In H. Hoji (ed.), *Japanese/Korean Linguistics*, pp. 335-349. Stanford: CSLI Publications.

Ura, H. 1999. Checking theory and dative subject constructions in Japanese and Korean. *Journal of East Asian Linguistics*, Vol. 8, pp. 223-254.

Uziel, S. 1993. Resetting Universal Grammar parameters: evidence from second language acquisition of Subjacency and Empty Category Principle. *Second Language Research*, Vol. 9, pp. 49-83.

Vainikka, A. and J. Maling. 1996. Is partitive case inherent or structural? In J. Hoeksema (ed.), *Partitives: Studies on the Syntax and Semantics of Partitive and Related Constructions*, pp. 179-208. Berlin: Mouton de Gruyter.

Vainikka, A. and M. Young-Scholten. 1994. Direct access to X'-theory: evidence from Korean and Turkish adults learning German. In T. Hoekstra and B. D. Schwartz (eds.), *Language Acquisition Studies in Generative Grammar: Papers in Honour of Kenneth Wexler From the 1991 GLOW Workshops*, pp. 265-316. Amsterdam: John Benjamins.

Vainikka, A. and M. Young-Scholten. 1996a. The early stages of adult L2 syntax: additional evidence from Romance speakers. *Second Language Research*, Vol. 12, pp. 140-176.

Vainikka, A. and M. Young-Scholten. 1996b. Gradual development of L2 phrase structure. *Second Language Research*, Vol. 12, pp. 7-39.

van de Craats, I. 2003. L1 features in the L2 output. In R. van Hout, A. Hulk, F. Kuiken and R. Towell (eds.), *The Lexicon-Syntax Interface in Second Language Acquisition*, pp. 69-95. Amsterdam: John Benjamins.

van Hout, A. 2004. Unaccusativity as telicity checking. In A. Alexiadou, E. Anagnostopoulou and M. Everaert (eds.), *The Unaccusativity Puzzle: Explorations of the Syntax-Lexicon Interface*, pp. 60-83. Oxford: Oxford University Press.

Van Valin, R. D. and R. J. LaPolla. 1997. *Syntax: Structure, Meaning and Function*. Cambridge: Cambridge University Press.

van Voorst, J. 1992. The aspectual semantics of psychological verbs. *Linguistics and Philosophy*, Vol. 15, pp. 65-92.

VanPatten, B. 1990. Attending to form and content in the input: an experiment in consciousness. *Studies in Second Language Acquisition*, Vol. 12, pp. 287-301.

VanPatten, B. and T. Cadierno. 1993. Explicit instruction and input processing. *Studies in Second Language Acquisition*, Vol. 15, pp. 225-243.

Vendler, Z. 1967. *Linguistics in Philosophy*. Ithaca/New York: Cornell

University Press.

Verkuyl, H. J. 1972. *On the Compositional Nature of the Aspects*. Dordrecht: Reidel.

Wakabayashi, S. 2002. The acquisition of non-null subjects in English: a minimalist account. *Second Language Research*, Vol. 18, pp. 28-71.

Wanner, A. 2000. Intransitive verbs as case assigner. In H. Janβen (ed.), *Verbal Projections*, pp. 85-103. Tübingen: Max Niemeyer Verlag GmbH.

Washio, R. 1997. Resultatives, compositionality and language variation. *Journal of East Asian Linguistics*, Vol. 6, pp. 1-49.

Webelhuth, G. 1995. X-bar theory and case-theory. In G. Webelhuth (ed.), *Government and Binding Theory and the Minimalist Program*, pp. 15-95. Cambridge, MA: Blackwell.

Wechsler, S. and B. Noh. 2001. On resultative predicates and clauses: parallels between Korean and English. *Language Sciences*, Vol. 23, pp. 391-423.

Wexler, K. and M. R. Manzini. 1987. Parameters and learnability in Binding Theory. In T. Roeper and E. Williams (eds.), *Parameter Setting*, pp. 41-76. Dordrecht: Reidel.

White, L. 1985. The pro-drop parameter in adult second language acquisition. *Language Learning*, Vol. 35, pp. 47-62.

White, L. 1986. Implications of parametric variation for adult second language acquisition: an investigation of the 'pro-drop' parameter. In V. Cook (ed.), *Experimental Approaches to Second Language Acquisition*, pp. 55-72. Oxford: Pergamon Press.

White, L. 1989a. *Universal Grammar and Second Language Acquisition*. Amsterdam: John Benjamins.

White, L. 1989b. The adjacency condition on case assignment: do L2 learners observe the Subset Principle? In S. M. Gass and J. Schachter (eds.), *Linguistic Perspectives on Second Language Acquisition*, pp. 134-158. Cambridge: Cambridge University Press.

White, L. 1990. Second language acquisition and universal grammar. *Studies in Second Language Acquisition*, Vol. 12, pp. 121-133.

White, L. 1991. Argument structure in second language acquisition. *Journal of French Language Studies*, Vol. 1, pp. 189-207.

White, L. 1993. Universal grammar: is it just a new name for old problems? In S. M. Gass and L. Selinker (eds.), *Language Transfer in Language Learning*, pp. 217-232. Amsterdam: John Benjamins.

White, L. 1996. Clitics in L2 French. In H. Clahsen (ed.), *Generative Perspectives on Language Acquisition: Empirical Findings, Theoretical Considerations, Crosslinguistic Comparisons*, pp. 335-368. Amsterdam: John Benjamins.

White, L. 2000. Second language acquisition: from initial to final state. In J. Archibald (ed.), *Second Language Acquisition and Linguistic Theory*, pp. 130-155. Oxford: Blackwell.

White, L. 2003a. *Second Language Acquisition and Universal Grammar*. Cambridge: Cambridge University Press.

White, L. 2003b. Fossilization in steady state L2 grammars: persistent problems with inflectional morphology. *Bilingualism: Language and Cognition*, Vol. 6, pp. 129-141.

White, L. and F. Genesee. 1996. How native is near-native? The issue of ultimate attainment in adult second language acquisition. *Second Language Research*, Vol. 12, pp. 233-265.

White, L. S. Montrul, M. Hirakawa, D. Chen, J. B. de Garavito and C. Brown. 1998. Zero morphology and the T/SM restriction in the L2 acquisition of psych verbs. In M.-L. Beck (ed.), *Morphology and Its Interface in Second Language Knowledge*, pp. 257-282. Amsterdam: John Benjamins.

White, L. C. Brown, J. B. de Garavito, D. Chen, M. Hirakawa and S. Montrul. 1999. Psych verbs in second language acquisition. In E. Klein and G. Martohardjono (eds.), *The Development of Second Language Grammar: A Generative Approach*, pp. 171-196. Amsterdam: John Benjamins.

Williams, Edwin. 1980. Predication. *Linguistic Inquiry*, Vol. 11, pp. 203-238.

Wolfe-Quintero, K. 1992. Learnability and the acquisition of extraction in relative clauses in wh-questions. *Studies and Second Language Acquisition*, Vol. 14, pp. 39-70.

Wyngaerd, G. V. 2001. Measuring events. *Language*, Vol. 77, pp. 61-90.

Xu, L. and T. Langendoen. 1985. Topic structure in Chinese. *Language*, Vol. 61, pp. 1-27.

Yip, V. 1995. *Interlanguage and Learnability: From Chinese to English*. Amsterdam: John Benjamins.

Yu, N. 1995. Towards a definition of unacuusative verbs in Chinese. In J. Camacho and L. Choueiri (eds.), *Proceedings of the 6<sup>th</sup> North American Conference on Chinese Linguistics*, 339-53. Graduate Students in Linguistics, University of Southern California.

Yuan, B. -P. 1995. Acquisition of base-generated topics by English-speaking learners of Chinese. *Language Learning*, Vol. 45, pp. 567-603.

Yuan, B. -P. 1998. Interpretation of binding and orientation of the Chinese reflexive *ziji* by English and Japanese speakers. *Second Language Research*, Vol. 14, pp. 324-340.

Yuan, B. -P. 1999. Acquiring the unaccusative/unergative distinction in a second language: evidence from English-speaking learners of L2 Chinese. *Linguistics*, Vol. 37, pp. 275-296.

Yuan, B. -P. 2001. The status of thematic verbs in the second language acquisition of Chinese: against inevitability of thematic-verb raising in second language acquisition. *Second Language Research*, Vol. 17, pp. 248-272.

Yuan, B. -P. 2003. The syntax of clausal negation in French and English speakers' L2 Chinese. In J. M. Liceras, H. Zobl and H. Goodluck (eds.), *Proceedings of the 6th Generative Approaches to Second Language Acquisition Conference (GASLA 2002)*, pp. 352-360. Somerville, MA: Cascadilla Press.

Zhang, S. -Q. 1995. Semantic differentiation in the acquisition of English as a second language. *Language Learning*, Vol. 45, pp. 225-249.

Zhao, C. 2002. Jiegou zhuci *de* de laiyuan yu 'V *de* C' shubu jiegou de xingcheng ('The origin of the complement marker *de* and the verb-complement construction'). *Zhongguo Yuwen* 2002/2, pp. 123-129.

Zhu, D. -X. 1982. *Yufa Jiangyi* ('Lecture Notes on Grammar'). Beijing: The Commercial Press.

Zobl, H. 1980. The formal and developmental selectivity of L1 influence on L2 acquisition. *Language Learning*, Vol. 30, pp. 43-57.

Zobl, H. 1986. A functional approach to the attainability of typological targets in by Japanese learners of English. In J. Pankhurst, M. Sharwood Smith and P. van Buren (eds.), *Learnability and Second Languages: A Book of Readings*, pp. 116-131. Dordrecht: Foris.

Zobl, H. 1989. Modularity in adult L2 acquisition. *Language Learning*, Vol. 39, pp. 49-79.

Zobl, H. 1992. Sources of linguistic knowledge and uniformity of nonnative performance. *Studies in Second Language Acquisition*, Vol. 14, pp. 387-402.

Zou, K. 1993. The syntax of the Chinese BA construction. *Linguistics*, Vol. 31, pp. 715-736.

# Appendixes

## Appendix 1  General introductions and personal information

**General Introduction**

The test to be conducted consists of three parts: (1) your personal information; (2) a cloze test; (3) the body of the test.

Part One (personal information) contains some questions and you are required to answer the questions briefly. Part Two (cloze test) consists of two passages, each with 20 blanks. You are required to fill in each blank with one Chinese character or *pinyin* standing for that character. Part Three (body of the test) consists of three sections. Section A contains 12 groups of words and you are required to form one sentence with one group of words if possible. Section B contains 8 4 sentences. You are required to make judgment on the acceptability or grammaticality of each sentence. Section C contains 27 sentences, each followed by five options. You are required to choose the best option for the sentence.

The purpose of the experiment is to test your language intuition of Chinese. Please do all the test items one by one and not linger on one item for a long time. Please ensure that you do all the sentences and complete the test. Otherwise, your paper will be invalid, which will result in waste of time and money. **PLEASE DO NOT CONSULT DICTIONARIES OR OTHER PEOPLE**!

The test result is only used for my personal research project. Any information in the test will be strictly confidential.

**Personal Information**

This part is about your background information, in particular related to Chinese learning. Please fill in the blanks.

Age _____ Nationality _____ Native Language _____

How long had you studied Chinese before you came to China?

_____ year(s) _____ month(s)

How long have you lived in Mainland China?

_____ year(s) _____ month(s)

Have you been to Taiwan? Yes / No (please tick √)

If yes, how long were you there?

_____ year(s) _____ month(s) _____ week(s)

## Appendix 2 Cloze test

**Directions**: This part contains two passages with twenty blanks in each. Please fill in each blank with **ONE** Chinese character or **pinyin** that stands for the character. Possible new words are provided with explanations in brackets that follow.

Examples: 我们在校内,你帮我,我帮你。

OR: Wǒmen zài xiào nèi, nǐ bāng wǒ, wǒ bāng nǐ.

1. 有一____人在路上遇到(meet)一个神仙(fairy),这个神仙以前是他____朋友。他告____神仙,现在他的情况越____越不如从____,生活很困____。神仙听完____的话,用手一____路旁的一块小石头,那块石头立刻变____了金子,神仙把这块金子____了他。这个____得到金子,还不满意(satisfied)。神____又用手一指,把一块大石头____变成了金子,又给了____。这个人____是不满意。神仙＿＿＿他："怎么样你＿＿＿满意呢？"这个人回＿＿＿说："我想……我＿＿＿要你的＿＿＿。"

Yǒu yī ＿＿＿ rén zài lù shang yùdào ( meet ) yī gè shénxiān ( fairy ), zhè gè shénxiān yǐqián shì tā ＿＿＿ péngyou. Tā gào ＿＿＿ shénxiān, xiànzài tāde qíngkuàng yuè ＿＿＿ yuè bù rú cóng ＿＿＿, shēnghuó hěn kùn ＿＿＿. Shénxiān tīng wán ＿＿＿ de huà, yòng shǒu yī ＿＿＿ lù páng de yī kuài xiǎo shítou, nà kuài shítou lìkè biàn ＿＿＿ le jīnzi, shénxiān bǎ zhè kuài jīnzi ＿＿＿ le tā. Zhè gè ＿＿＿ dédào jīnzi, hái bù mǎnyì ( satisfied ). shén ＿＿＿ yòu yòng shǒu yī zhǐ, bǎ yī kuài dà shítou ＿＿＿ biànchéng le jīnzi, yòu gěi le ＿＿＿. Zhè gè rén ＿＿＿ shì bù mǎnyì. Shénxiān ＿＿＿ tā："Zěnme yàng nǐ ＿＿＿ mǎnyì ne?" Zhè gè rén huí ＿＿＿ shuō："Wǒ xiǎng……wǒ ＿＿＿ yào nǐde ＿＿＿。"

2. 我们＿＿＿师说，学一＿＿＿字，应该记这个字的部首 ( radicals of a Chinese character )，比＿＿＿说"湖"这个字有三＿＿＿水，＿＿＿定＿＿＿水有＿＿＿系；"林"这个＿＿＿是木字旁，跟树木有关系。这一点很＿＿＿意思，＿＿＿在我才明白＿＿＿什么"吃"跟"喝"＿＿＿是口字＿＿＿。我的一个朋友说："当＿＿＿了，要＿＿＿没有嘴，怎＿＿＿吃，怎么喝？"可是我心里＿＿＿："茶杯"的"杯"字为什么是＿＿＿字旁呢？我从＿＿＿没看＿＿＿木头做的杯子。

Wǒmen ＿＿＿ shī shuō, xué yī ＿＿＿ zì, yīnggāi jì zhè gè zì de bùshǒu ( radicals of a Chinese character ), bǐ ＿＿＿ shuō "hú" zhè gè zì yǒu sān ＿＿＿ shuǐ, ＿＿＿ dìng ＿＿＿ shuǐ yǒu ＿＿＿ xì;  "lín" zhè gè ＿＿＿ shì mù zì páng, gēn shùmù yǒu guānxì. Zhè yīdiǎn hěn ＿＿＿ yìsi, ＿＿＿ zài wǒ cái míngbái ＿＿＿ shénme "chī" gēn "hē" ＿＿＿ shì kǒu zì ＿＿＿. Wǒ de yī gè péngyou shuō："Dāng ＿＿＿ le, yào ＿＿＿ méiyǒu zuǐ, zěn ＿＿＿ chī, zěnme hē?" Kěshì wǒ xīnlǐ ＿＿＿："chábēi" de "bēi" zì wèishénme shì ＿＿＿ zì páng ne? Wǒ cóng ＿＿＿ méi kàn ＿＿＿ mùtou zuò de bēizi.

# Appendix 3　The production test

**Directions**: This part contains 12 groups of words. Possible new words are given in the brackets. Please form **ONE** grammatically correct Chinese sentence with each group of the words. You must use **ALL and ONLY** those words that are given. You can't use your own words or add more words. If you can't form a grammatical Chinese sentence with the given words, please cross ( × ) after the arrow.

Examples:
(1) 毕业后,美国,去了,张三
　　张三毕业后去了美国。
(2) 小鸟,明天,张三的,飞过
　　×

A grammatical sentence can be formed with the first group of words. With the second group, you cannot form a grammatical sentence no matter what combinations you make.

1. 油漆,往墙上,刷,张三(油漆 paint,墙 wall,刷 brush)

2. 很失望,使,老师,张三的成绩(失望 disappoint,成绩 score)

3. 把,李四的花瓶,张三,碎了(花瓶 vase,碎 break)

4. 水,张三,浇,往花上(浇 pour on…)

5. 生气,张三的话,妈妈,了(生气 angry, anger)

6. 张三,使,那个消息,很激动(消息 news,激动 excite)

7. 往杯子里,灌,张三,水(杯子 glass,灌 pour)

8. 李四的足球,把,张三,破了(足球 football,破 break)

9. 爸爸,了,失望,张三的成绩(失望 disappoint,成绩 score)

10. 张三,那个消息,了,激动(消息 news,激动 excite)

11. 张三的话,很生气,妈妈,使(生气 angry,anger)

12. 断了,把,张三,李四的尺子(断 break,尺子 ruler)

# Appendix 4  The acceptability judgment test

**Directions**: This part contains 84 Chinese sentences. After each sentence, there is a continuum scale indicating the degree of acceptability, as shown below. The number " –2" stands for "completely unacceptable", " –1" for "probably unacceptable", " +1" for "probably acceptable", and " +2" for "completely acceptable". If you don't know or are completely unsure about your judgment, please choose "0". Please make your judgment and tick (√) the number accordingly.

–2 ——— –1 ——— 0 ——— +1 ——— +2
completely    probably      I don't know    probably      completely
unacceptable  unacceptable                  acceptable    acceptable

Examples:

(1) 我每天早晨八点起床。

−2 ———— −1 ———— 0 ———— +1 ———— +2
                                            √

(2) 我八点早晨起床每天。

−2 ———— −1 ———— 0 ———— +1 ———— +2
       √

Example (1) is completely grammatical and acceptable. Therefore, you should tick "+2". Example (2) is completely unacceptable in terms of Chinese word order, so you should tick "−2".

Please make your judgment on the sentences one by one. Since it is a test on your Chinese language intuition, please do not linger too long on one sentence. Please make your judgment on one sentence independently of other sentences. In other words, please do not make reference to other sentences. In some sentences, the context is provided in the brackets. It mainly tells you where the sentence occurs. Please do not judge on the bracketed context.

1. 李四的花瓶碎了。(花瓶 vase, 碎 break)
   _____

2. 这个消息高兴了张三。(消息 news, 高兴 please)
   _____

3. (听到这个消息)张三高兴得又唱又跳。(消息 news, 高兴 please, 唱 sing, 跳 jump)
   _____

4. 张三扔了李四的尺子。(扔 throw, 尺子 ruler)
   _____

5. 张三看书了两个小时。(看书 read a book)
   _____

6. (在葬礼上)张三哭手绢都湿了。(葬礼 funeral, 手绢 handkerchief, 湿 wet)

   _____

7. 这个消息使张三高兴得又唱又跳。(消息 news, 高兴 please, 唱 sing, 跳 jump)

   _____

8. 张三把茶杯碎了。(茶杯 teacup, 碎 break)

   _____

9. 张三学烦了法语(想学中文)。(烦 bore, 法语 French)

   _____

10. 大风很多玻璃碎了。(玻璃 glass, 碎 break)

    _____

11. 张三骂哭了李四。(骂 scold)

    _____

12. 张三破了李四的足球。(破 break, 足球 football)

    _____

13. (听到这个消息)张三很高兴。(消息 news, 高兴 please)

    _____

14. 张三吃得烤鸭都腻了(不想再吃了)。(烤鸭 roast duck, 腻 bore)

    _____

15. 李四的尺子被张三扔了。(尺子 ruler, 扔 throw)

    _____

16. 张三吵烦了李四。(吵 quarrel, 烦 bore)

    _____

17. 张三偷了李四的足球。(偷 steal, 足球 football)

    _____

18. 这个消息把张三高兴了。(消息 news, 高兴 please)

    _____

19. （看球赛的时候）张三喊得嗓子都哑了。（球赛 ball game，嗓子 throat，哑 hoarse）

---

20. 李四的花瓶被张三碎了。（花瓶 vase，碎 break）

---

21. （听到这个消息）张三兴奋得睡不着觉。（消息 news，兴奋 excite，睡不着觉 can't go to sleep）

---

22. 张三吃饭了一个小时。

---

23. 这个消息使张三很生气。（消息 news，生气 angry）

---

24. 李四的足球破了。（足球 football，破 break）

---

25. 张三追烦了李四。（追 chase，烦 bore）

---

26. 张三惊讶了这个消息。（惊讶 surprise，消息 news）

---

27. 张三踢破了李四的足球。（踢 kick，破 break，足球 football）

---

28. （在葬礼上）张三哭湿了手绢。（葬礼 funeral，湿 wet，手绢 handkerchief）

---

29. 张三追李四得累了。（追 chase，累 tire）

---

30. （听完那个笑话）张三笑肚子都疼了。（笑话 joke，肚子 belly，疼 ache）

---

31. 这个消息惊讶了张三。（消息 news，惊讶 surprise）

---

32. 张三把嗓子破了。(嗓子 throat, 破 break)

33. 这个消息使张三兴奋得睡不着觉。(消息 news, 兴奋 excite, 睡不着觉 can't go to sleep)

34. 张三卖了李四的花瓶。(卖 sell, 花瓶 vase)

35. 这个消息使张三高兴又唱又跳。(消息 news, 高兴 please, 唱 sing, 跳 jump)

36. 张三听烦了那首歌(不想再听了)。(烦 bore)

37. 张三断了李四的尺子。(断 break, 尺子 ruler)

38. 大风很多树枝断了。(树枝 branches of a tree, 断 break)

39. 张三踢李四的足球破了。(踢 kick, 足球 football, 破 break)

40. 张三追累了李四。(追 chase, 累 tire)

41. 张三打哭了李四。

42. 李四的尺子被张三断了。(尺子 ruler, 断 break)

43. (听完那个笑话)张三笑得肚子都疼了。(笑话 joke, 肚子 belly, 疼 ache)

44. (听到这个消息)张三惊讶说不出话。(消息 news, 惊讶 surprise, 说不出话 can't speak)

45. 张三学得法语都烦了(想学中文)。(法语 French, 烦 bore)

46. 这个消息使张三很高兴。(消息 news, 高兴 please)

47. 李四的足球被张三偷了。(足球 football, 偷 steal)

48. 张三把皮带断了。(皮带 leather belt, 断 break)

49. 张三碎了李四的花瓶。(碎 break, 花瓶 vase)

50. 张三骑马了三个小时。(骑 ride, 马 horse)

51. 这个消息使张三惊讶得说不出话。(消息 news, 惊讶 surprise, 说不出话 can't speak)

52. (看球赛的时候)张三喊嗓子都哑了。(球赛 ball game, 嗓子 throat, 哑 hoarse)

53. 张三高兴了这个消息。(高兴 please, 消息 news)

54. 李四的尺子断了。(尺子 ruler, 断 break)

55. (听到这个消息)张三高兴又唱又跳。(消息 news, 高兴 please, 唱 sing, 跳 jump)

56. 张三打碎了李四的花瓶。(碎 break, 花瓶 vase)

57. 这个消息把张三生气了。(消息 news, 生气 angry)

58. 张三追李四得烦了。(追 chase, 烦 bore)

59. 张三哭烦了李四。(烦 bore)

60. (听到这个消息)张三很生气。(消息 news, 生气 angry)

61. 大风很多窗户破了。(窗户 window, 破 break)

62. (听到这个消息)张三惊讶得说不出话。(消息 news, 惊讶 surprise, 说不出话 can't speak)

63. 张三压李四的尺子断了。(压 crush, 尺子 ruler, 断 break)

64. 张三骂烦了李四。(骂 scold, 烦 bore)

65. 张三听得那首歌都烦了(不想再听了)。(烦 bore)

66. 这个消息使张三很惊讶。(消息 news, 惊讶 surprise)

67. 李四的足球被张三破了。(足球 football, 破 break)

68. 张三压断了李四的尺子。(压 crush, 断 break, 尺子 ruler)

69. (看球赛的时候)张三喊哑了嗓子。(球赛 ball game, 哑 hoarse, 嗓子 throat)

70. 张三骂李四得烦了。(骂 scold, 烦 bore)

71. （听到这个消息）张三兴奋睡不着觉。（消息 news，兴奋 excite，睡不着觉 can't go to sleep）

72. 李四的花瓶被张三卖了。（花瓶 vase，卖 sell）

73. 这个消息生气了张三。（消息 news，生气 anger）

74. 张三吃腻了烤鸭（不想再吃了）。（腻 bore，烤鸭 roast duck）

75. 这个消息使张三惊讶说不出话。（消息 news，惊讶 surprise，说不出话 can't speak）

76. 张三生气了这个消息。（生气 anger，消息 news）

77. （在葬礼上）张三哭得手绢都湿了。（葬礼 funeral，手绢 handkerchief，湿 wet）

78. 这个消息使张三兴奋睡不着觉。（消息 news，兴奋 excite，睡不着觉 can't go to sleep）

79. 张三打李四的花瓶碎了。（打 hit，花瓶 vase，碎 break）

80. 张三逗笑了李四。（逗 tease）

81. 这个消息把张三惊讶了。（消息 news，惊讶 surprise）

82. 张三走累了双腿。（累 tire）

83. (听完那个笑话)张三笑疼了肚子。(笑话 joke, 疼 ache, 肚子 belly)

84. (听到这个消息)张三很惊讶。(消息 news, 惊讶 surprise)

## Appendix 5  Pictures used in the comprehension test

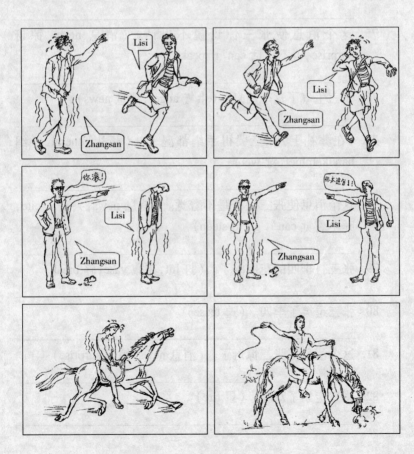

# Appendix 6 Testing items used in the experiment

**Part Ⅰ. The production test**

   A. Syntactic causatives with psych verbs:

      a. 张三,使,那个消息,很激动
         Zhangsan, *shi*, that CL news, very excite

      b. 很失望,使,老师,张三的成绩
         very disappoint, *shi*, teacher, Zhangsan's score

      c. 张三的话,很生气,妈妈,使
         what Zhangsan said, very anger, mum, *shi*

   B. Intransitive SE-verbs (no grammatical sentences can be formed)

      a. 张三,那个消息,了,激动
         Zhangsan, that CL news, ASP, excite

      b. 生气,张三的话,妈妈,了
         anger, what Zhangsan said, mum, ASP

      c. 老师,了,失望,张三的成绩
         teacher, ASP, disappoint, Zhangsan's score

   C. Alternating unaccusative verbs (no grammatical sentences can be formed)

      a. 把,李四的花瓶,张三,碎了
         *ba*, Lisi's vase, Zhangsan, break ASP

      b. 李四的足球,把,张三,破了
         Lisi's football, *ba*, Zhangsan, break ASP

      c. 断了,把,张三,李四的尺子
         break ASP, *ba*, Zhangsan, Lisi's ruler

## Part Ⅱ. The acceptability judgment test

*Psych verbs*

A. Intransitive SE-verbs：
    a.（听到这个消息,）张三很高兴。
       （hear this CL news）Zhangsan very please
    b.（听到这个消息,）张三很生气。
       （hear this CL news）Zhangsan very anger
    c.（听到这个消息,）张三很惊讶。
       （hear this CL news）Zhangsan very surprise

B. Syntactic causatives with psych verbs：
    a. 这个消息使张三很高兴。
       this CL news *shi* Zhangsan very please
    b. 这个消息使张三很生气。
       this CL news *shi* Zhangsan very anger
    c. 这个消息使张三很惊讶。
       this CL news *shi* Zhangsan very surprise

C. *SE-verbs as OE-verbs：
    a. 这个消息高兴了张三。
       this CL news please ASP Zhangsan
    b. 这个消息生气了张三。
       this CL news anger ASP Zhangsan
    c. 这个消息惊讶了张三。
       this CL news surprise ASP Zhangsan

*Unaccusative verbs*：

A. Theme raising to the subject position：
    a. 李四的花瓶碎了。
       Lisi's vase break ASP
    b. 李四的足球破了。
       Lisi's football break ASP

c. 李四的尺子断了。
   Lisi's ruler break ASP

B. As causative in active sentences：
   B1. *Experimental sentences：
   a. *张三碎了李四的花瓶。
      Zhangsan break ASP Lisi's vase
   b. *张三破了李四的足球。
      Zhangsan break ASP Lisi's football
   c. *张三断了李四的尺子。
      Zhangsan break ASP Lisi's ruler
   B2. Control sentences：
   a. 张三卖了李四的花瓶。
      Zhangsan sell ASP Lisi's vase
   b. 张三偷了李四的足球。
      Zhangsan steal ASP Lisi's football
   c. 张三扔了李四的尺子。
      Zhangsan throw away ASP Lisi's ruler

C. As causative in passive sentences：
   C1. *Experimental sentences：
   a. *李四的花瓶被张三碎了。
      Lisi's vase *bei* Zhangsan break ASP
   b. *李四的足球被张三破了。
      Lisi's football *bei* Zhangsan break ASP
   c. *李四的尺子被张三断了。
      Lisi's ruler *bei* Zhangsan break ASP
   C2. Control sentences：
   a. 李四的花瓶被张三卖了。
      Lisi's vase *bei* Zhangsan sell ASP
   b. 李四的足球被张三偷了。
      Lisi's football *bei* Zhangsan steal ASP

c. 李四的尺子被张三扔了。
Lisi's ruler *bei* Zhangsan throw away ASP

*Resultative constructions*:
A. With unergative $V_1$
 a. (在葬礼上)张三哭得手绢都湿了。
  (at funeral) Zhangsan cry de shoujuan even soggy ASP
 b. (看球赛的时候)张三喊得嗓子都哑了。
  (watch ball-game time) Zhangsan shout de throat even hoarse ASP
 c. (听了那个笑话)张三笑得肚子都疼了。
  (hear ASP that CL joke) Zhangsan laugh de belly even ache ASP
B. With psych verb $V_1$
 a. (听到这个消息)张三高兴得又唱又跳。
  (hear this CL news) Zhangsan please de both sing and dance
 b. (听到这个消息)张三兴奋得睡不着觉。
  (hear this CL news) Zhangsan excite de cannot go to sleep
 c. (听到这个消息)张三惊讶得说不出话。
  (hear this CL news) Zhangsan surprise de cannot talk
C. Causative morpheme shi + resultatives with psych verb $V_1$
 a. 这个消息使张三高兴得又唱又跳。
  this CL news shi Zhangsan please de both sing and dance
 b. 这个消息使张三兴奋得睡不着觉。
  this CL news shi Zhangsan excite de cannot go to sleep
 c. 这个消息使张三惊讶得说不出话。
  this CL news shi Zhangsan surprise de cannot talk

*Compound causative constructions*:
 Group 1. Transitive $V_1$

A. With unaccusative $V_2$
   a. 张三打碎了李四的花瓶。
      Zhangsan hit-break ASP Lisi's vase
   b. 张三踢破了李四的足球。
      Zhangsan kick-break ASP Lisi's football
   c. 张三压断了李四的尺子。
      Zhangsan press-break ASP Lisi's ruler

B. With unergative $V_2$
   a. 张三骂哭了李四。
      Zhangsan scold-cry ASP Lisi
   b. 张三逗笑了李四。
      Zhangsan tease-laugh ASP Lisi
   c. 张三打哭了李四。
      Zhangsan hit-cry ASP Lisi

*Group* 2. *Unergative* $V_1$

C. With adjective $V_2$
   a.（在葬礼上）张三哭湿了手绢。
      (at funeral) Zhangsan cry-soggy ASP handkerchief
   b.（看球赛的时候）张三喊哑了嗓子。
      (watch ball-game time) Zhangsan shout-hoarse ASP throat
   c.（听了那个笑话）张三笑疼了肚子。
      (hear that CL joke) Zhangsan laugh-ache ASP belly

D. With psych verb $V_2$
   a. 张三哭烦了李四。
      Zhangsan cry-bore ASP Lisi
   b. 张三走累了双腿。
      Zhangsan walk-tire ASP two legs
   c. 张三吵烦了李四。
      Zhangsan quarrel-bore ASP Lisi

Group 3. Transitive $V_1$, psych verb $V_2$
E. With inanimate $NP_2$
   a. 张三听烦了那首歌(不想再听了)。
      Zhangsan listen-bore ASP that CL song ( not want again listen ASP)
   b. 张三学烦了法语(想学中文)。
      Zhangsan study-bore ASP French ( want study Chinese)
   c. 张三吃腻了烤鸭(不想再吃了)。
      Zhangsan eat-bore ASP roast duck (not want again eat ASP)
F. With animate $NP_2$ ( ambiguous)
   a. 张三追累了李四。
      Zhangsan chase-tire ASP Lisi
   b. 张三骂烦了李四。
      Zhangsan scold-bore ASP Lisi
   c. 张三追烦了李四。
      Zhangsan chase-bore ASP Lisi

*The V-NP-XP structure ( for comparison)
   a. *(在葬礼上)张三哭手绢都湿了。
      (at funeral) Zhangsan cry shoujuan even soggy
   b. *(看球赛的时候)张三喊嗓子都哑了。
      (watch ball-game time) Zhangsan shout throat
   c. *(听了那个笑话)张三笑肚子都疼了。
      (hear ASP that CL joke) Zhangsan laugh belly even ache

## Part Ⅲ. The comprehension test
A. Compound causatives with ambiguous readings
   a. 张三追累了李四。
      Zhangsan chase-tire ASP Lisi
   b. 张三骂烦了李四。
      Zhangsan scold-bore ASP Lisi

c. 张三骑累了马。
　　　Zhangsan ride-tire ASP horse
B. Resultatives with single $V_1$
　　a. 张三追得李四都累了。
　　　Zhangsan chase de Lisi even tire ASP
　　b. 张三骂得李四都烦了。
　　　Zhangsan scold de Lisi even bore ASP
　　c. 张三骑得马都累了。
　　　Zhangsan ride de horse even tire ASP
C. Resultatives with reduplicated $V_1$
　　a. 张三追李四追得都累了。
　　　Zhangsan chase Lisi chase de even tire
　　b. 张三骂李四骂得都烦了。
　　　Zhangsan scold Lisi scold de even bore ASP
　　c. 张三骑马骑得都累了。
　　　Zhangsan ride horse ride de even tire ASP

# Appendix 7　Descriptive statistics

*Table 1. Intransitive SE verbs*

| Subject Groups | | N | Minimum | Maximum | Mean | Std. deviation |
|---|---|---|---|---|---|---|
| English | LI | 26 | -0.33 | 2.00 | 1.4746 | 0.6995 |
|  | IN | 13 | 0.67 | 2.00 | 1.7185 | 0.4045 |
|  | HI | 16 | 1.00 | 2.00 | 1.8584 | 0.2975 |
| Japanese | LI | 15 | -1.00 | 2.00 | 1.5787 | 0.7916 |
|  | IN | 18 | 0.67 | 2.00 | 1.7411 | 0.4358 |
|  | HI | 23 | -0.33 | 2.00 | 1.6530 | 0.7130 |
| Korean | LI | 27 | -1.00 | 2.00 | 1.3089 | 0.8624 |
|  | IN | 25 | -1.33 | 2.00 | 1.4800 | 0.8768 |
|  | HI | 21 | 0.00 | 2.00 | 1.6033 | 0.6025 |
| Native control | | 28 | 1.67 | 2.00 | 1.9881 | 0.0630 |

Table 2. Psych verbs used in the analytical causative construction

| Subject Groups | | N | Minimum | Maximum | Mean | Std. deviation |
|---|---|---|---|---|---|---|
| English | LI | 26 | 0.00 | 2.00 | 1.4619 | 0.6874 |
|  | IN | 13 | -1.00 | 2.00 | 1.3585 | 0.9766 |
|  | HI | 16 | -0.67 | 2.00 | 1.6875 | 0.6944 |
| Japanese | LI | 15 | 0.00 | 2.00 | 1.4233 | 0.6230 |
|  | IN | 18 | -0.67 | 2.00 | 1.3889 | 0.8272 |
|  | HI | 23 | -0.33 | 2.00 | 1.7248 | 0.5824 |
| Korean | LI | 27 | -1.00 | 2.00 | 1.0374 | 0.9671 |
|  | IN | 25 | -1.67 | 2.00 | 1.2936 | 1.0243 |
|  | HI | 21 | -0.67 | 2.00 | 1.6667 | 0.6588 |
| Native control | | 28 | 1.33 | 2.00 | 0.9405 | 0.1827 |

Table 3. *Psych verbs used as OE verbs

| Subject Groups | | N | Minimum | Maximum | Mean | Std. deviation |
|---|---|---|---|---|---|---|
| English | LI | 26 | -2.00 | 1.00 | -0.5512 | 0.8952 |
|  | IN | 13 | -2.00 | 0.00 | -1.1031 | 0.6580 |
|  | HI | 16 | -2.00 | 0.33 | -1.3338 | 0.9185 |
| Japanese | LI | 15 | -2.00 | -0.67 | -1.3127 | 0.5552 |
|  | IN | 18 | -2.00 | 0.67 | -1.2961 | 0.8473 |
|  | HI | 23 | -2.00 | 1.00 | -1.3491 | 0.8004 |
| Korean | LI | 27 | -2.00 | 2.00 | -0.6663 | 1.0254 |
|  | IN | 25 | -2.00 | 0.67 | -1.0664 | 0.9574 |
|  | HI | 21 | -2.00 | 1.33 | -0.9371 | 1.0570 |
| Native control | | 28 | -2.00 | -0.67 | -1.7381 | 0.4477 |

Table 4. Unaccusative verbs with the Theme argument as the sentence subject

| Subject Groups | | N | Minimum | Maximum | Mean | Std. deviation |
|---|---|---|---|---|---|---|
| English | LI | 26 | -0.33 | 2.00 | 1.1031 | 0.6306 |
|  | IN | 13 | -1.67 | 2.00 | 1.3585 | 0.9766 |
|  | HI | 16 | -1.00 | 2.00 | 1.1250 | 0.8848 |
| Japanese | LI | 15 | -0.67 | 2.00 | 1.1120 | 0.8427 |
|  | IN | 18 | -0.33 | 2.00 | 0.9072 | 0.7031 |
|  | HI | 23 | -1.67 | 2.00 | 1.1883 | 1.1055 |

| Subject Groups | | N | Minimum | Maximum | Mean | Std. deviation |
|---|---|---|---|---|---|---|
| Korean | LI | 27 | -1.67 | 2.00 | 0.7533 | 1.0612 |
| | IN | 25 | -2.00 | 2.00 | 0.5600 | 1.1669 |
| | HI | 21 | -1.00 | 2.00 | 0.7300 | 1.0730 |
| Native control | | 28 | 0.67 | 2.00 | 1.9289 | 0.2614 |

*Table 5.* * *Unaccusative verbs as alternating verbs in the active form*

| Subject Groups | | N | Minimum | Maximum | Mean | Std. deviation |
|---|---|---|---|---|---|---|
| English | LI | 26 | -1.67 | 2.00 | 0.6158 | 1.0699 |
| | IN | 13 | -1.00 | 2.00 | 0.5646 | 1.0835 |
| | HI | 16 | -2.00 | 2.00 | -0.3744 | 1.3099 |
| Japanese | LI | 15 | -0.67 | 2.00 | 1.1120 | 0.8427 |
| | IN | 18 | -2.00 | 2.00 | 0.8333 | 1.3153 |
| | HI | 23 | -2.00 | 2.00 | 0.8839 | 1.1315 |
| Korean | LI | 27 | -1.33 | 2.00 | 0.7778 | 1.1332 |
| | IN | 25 | -2.00 | 2.00 | 0.8540 | 1.0548 |
| | HI | 21 | -0.67 | 2.00 | 1.0476 | 0.8258 |
| Native control | | 28 | -2.00 | 1.00 | -1.1317 | 0.7928 |

*Table 6.* * *Unaccusative verbs as alternating verbs in the passive form*

| Subject Groups | | N | Minimum | Maximum | Mean | Std. deviation |
|---|---|---|---|---|---|---|
| English | LI | 26 | -1.33 | 2.00 | 1.0131 | 0.9355 |
| | IN | 13 | -1.67 | 2.00 | 0.9492 | 1.2315 |
| | HI | 16 | -2.00 | 2.00 | 0.2713 | 1.2945 |
| Japanese | LI | 15 | -2.00 | 2.00 | 0.7787 | 1.4116 |
| | IN | 18 | -2.00 | 2.00 | 1.2411 | 1.2041 |
| | HI | 23 | -2.00 | 2.00 | 1.3339 | 1.0784 |
| Korean | LI | 27 | -1.67 | 2.00 | 0.8519 | 1.1713 |
| | IN | 25 | -1.33 | 2.00 | 1.0412 | 0.9728 |
| | HI | 21 | 0.00 | 2.00 | 1.0795 | 0.7295 |
| Native control | | 28 | -2.00 | -0.33 | -1.2979 | 0.5907 |

Table 7. Transitive verbs in the active form

| Subject Groups | | N | Minimum | Maximum | Mean | Std. deviation |
|---|---|---|---|---|---|---|
| English | LI | 26 | -1.33 | 2.00 | 1.0000 | 0.8481 |
|  | IN | 13 | 0.33 | 2.00 | 1.2823 | 0.5747 |
|  | HI | 16 | 0.33 | 2.00 | 1.3331 | 0.6442 |
| Japanese | LI | 15 | -0.33 | 2.00 | 1.2447 | 0.8768 |
|  | IN | 18 | -0.67 | 2.00 | 1.3150 | 0.9253 |
|  | HI | 23 | 0.33 | 2.00 | 1.7543 | 0.4943 |
| Korean | LI | 27 | -1.00 | 2.00 | 0.9378 | 0.8575 |
|  | IN | 25 | -1.33 | 2.00 | 0.8272 | 1.1102 |
|  | HI | 21 | -0.67 | 2.00 | 1.3019 | 0.7222 |
| Native control | | 28 | 1.67 | 2.00 | 1.9293 | 0.1379 |

Table 8. Transitive verbs in the passive form

| Subject Groups | | N | Minimum | Maximum | Mean | Std. deviation |
|---|---|---|---|---|---|---|
| English | LI | 26 | -2.00 | 2.00 | 0.9227 | 1.0889 |
|  | IN | 13 | -2.00 | 2.00 | 1.1285 | 1.1427 |
|  | HI | 16 | -0.33 | 2.00 | 1.6463 | 0.3942 |
| Japanese | LI | 15 | -1.00 | 2.00 | 0.7787 | 1.4116 |
|  | IN | 18 | -1.00 | 2.00 | 1.4817 | 0.8106 |
|  | HI | 23 | -1.00 | 2.00 | 1.3630 | 0.8465 |
| Korean | LI | 27 | -1.33 | 2.00 | 0.5559 | 0.9916 |
|  | IN | 25 | -0.33 | 2.00 | 1.0412 | 0.9728 |
|  | HI | 21 | -1.00 | 2.00 | 1.0005 | 0.8092 |
| Native control | | 28 | 1.67 | 2.00 | 1.9764 | 0.0866 |

Table 9. Resultative construction: Type A

| Subject Groups | | N | Minimum | Maximum | Mean | Std. deviation |
|---|---|---|---|---|---|---|
| English | LI | 26 | -2.00 | 2.00 | 0.2177 | 0.9340 |
|  | IN | 13 | -2.00 | 2.00 | 0.6162 | 1.1131 |
|  | HI | 16 | -2.00 | 2.00 | 1.3756 | 1.0944 |
| Japanese | LI | 15 | -1.33 | 2.00 | 0.5333 | 1.0065 |
|  | IN | 18 | -1.33 | 2.00 | 0.6489 | 1.1578 |
|  | HI | 23 | -0.67 | 2.00 | 1.5370 | 0.6872 |

| Subject Groups | | N | Minimum | Maximum | Mean | Std. deviation |
|---|---|---|---|---|---|---|
| | LI | 27 | -1.00 | 2.00 | 0.6922 | 0.9911 |
| Korean | IN | 25 | -1.33 | 2.00 | 0.7200 | 1.0917 |
| | HI | 21 | -0.67 | 2.00 | 1.0633 | 0.8734 |
| Native control | | 28 | 0.67 | 2.00 | 1.7982 | 0.3880 |

Table 10. Resultative construction: Type B

| Subject Groups | | N | Minimum | Maximum | Mean | Std. deviation |
|---|---|---|---|---|---|---|
| | LI | 26 | -1.00 | 2.00 | 0.6277 | 0.7797 |
| English | IN | 13 | -1.00 | 2.00 | 1.2562 | 1.0112 |
| | HI | 16 | 0.33 | 2.00 | 1.5837 | 0.5100 |
| | LI | 15 | -0.33 | 2.00 | 0.8453 | 0.6996 |
| Japanese | IN | 18 | -1.33 | 2.00 | 1.1672 | 0.9646 |
| | HI | 23 | 0.33 | 2.00 | 1.6813 | 0.4769 |
| | LI | 27 | -0.67 | 2.00 | 1.0374 | 0.8185 |
| Korean | IN | 25 | -2.00 | 2.00 | 0.9608 | 1.1553 |
| | HI | 21 | -0.33 | 2.00 | 1.1905 | 0.8662 |
| Native control | | 28 | 1.67 | 2.00 | 1.9882 | 0.0634 |

Table 11. Resultative construction: Type C

| Subject Groups | | N | Minimum | Maximum | Mean | Std. deviation |
|---|---|---|---|---|---|---|
| | LI | 26 | -1.00 | 2.00 | 0.8204 | 0.8960 |
| English | IN | 13 | 0.33 | 2.00 | 1.4362 | 0.6435 |
| | HI | 16 | 0.33 | 2.00 | 1.6463 | 0.4947 |
| | LI | 15 | -1.67 | 2.00 | 1.1553 | 1.0079 |
| Japanese | IN | 18 | -1.33 | 2.00 | 0.7789 | 1.1196 |
| | HI | 23 | 0.67 | 2.00 | 1.7683 | 0.3818 |
| | LI | 27 | -0.67 | 2.00 | 1.1000 | 0.9371 |
| Korean | IN | 25 | -1.67 | 2.00 | 0.9332 | 1.0639 |
| | HI | 21 | -0.33 | 2.00 | 1.4924 | 0.6633 |
| Native control | | 28 | 1.33 | 2.00 | 1.9289 | 0.1659 |

Table 12. *The V-NP-XP structure*

| Subject Groups | | N | Minimum | Maximum | Mean | Std. deviation |
|---|---|---|---|---|---|---|
| English | LI | 26 | -1.67 | 1.33 | -0.1804 | 0.8124 |
|  | IN | 13 | -1.67 | 0.33 | -0.6415 | 0.6732 |
|  | HI | 16 | -2.00 | 1.33 | -0.8963 | 0.9408 |
| Japanese | LI | 15 | -1.67 | 1.00 | 0.0220 | 0.8024 |
|  | IN | 18 | -2.00 | 0.33 | -1.0178 | 0.7277 |
|  | HI | 23 | -2.00 | 1.00 | -0.6374 | 0.9535 |
| Korean | LI | 27 | -2.00 | 2.00 | 0.0744 | 0.9212 |
|  | IN | 25 | -2.00 | 2.00 | -0.3732 | 1.1156 |
|  | HI | 21 | -2.00 | 1.33 | -0.4438 | 1.0504 |
| Native control | | 28 | -2.00 | -0.33 | -1.6075 | 0.3971 |

Table 13. *Compound causative construction: Type A*

| Subject Groups | | N | Minimum | Maximum | Mean | Std. deviation |
|---|---|---|---|---|---|---|
| English | LI | 26 | -1.00 | 2.00 | 0.6538 | 0.9362 |
|  | IN | 13 | 0.33 | 2.00 | 1.4100 | 0.6271 |
|  | HI | 16 | 1.00 | 2.00 | 1.6463 | 0.3942 |
| Japanese | LI | 15 | .00 | 2.00 | 1.0673 | 0.7374 |
|  | IN | 18 | -0.67 | 2.00 | 1.2978 | 0.7751 |
|  | HI | 23 | -0.67 | 2.00 | 1.5074 | 0.7908 |
| Korean | LI | 27 | -1.33 | 2.00 | 0.5559 | 0.9916 |
|  | IN | 25 | -1.33 | 2.00 | 0.7996 | 1.1228 |
|  | HI | 21 | -0.67 | 2.00 | 1.2538 | 0.8686 |
| Native control | | 28 | 2.00 | 2.00 | 2.0000 | 0.0000 |

Table 14. *Compound causative construction: Type B*

| Subject Groups | | N | Minimum | Maximum | Mean | Std. deviation |
|---|---|---|---|---|---|---|
| English | LI | 26 | -1.67 | 1.67 | 0.1788 | 0.9632 |
|  | IN | 13 | -1.00 | 1.33 | 0.3585 | 0.7259 |
|  | HI | 16 | -2.00 | 1.33 | -0.6050 | 0.8950 |
| Japanese | LI | 15 | -1.33 | 2.00 | 0.5107 | 0.9502 |
|  | IN | 18 | -1.33 | 0.67 | -0.2211 | 0.6661 |
|  | HI | 23 | -2.00 | 2.00 | 0.4935 | 1.2950 |

| Subject Groups | | N | Minimum | Maximum | Mean | Std. deviation |
|---|---|---|---|---|---|---|
| Korean | LI | 27 | -1.67 | 2.00 | -0.1733 | 0.9404 |
| | IN | 25 | -2.00 | 2.00 | -0.1868 | 1.0231 |
| | HI | 21 | -1.00 | 2.00 | 0.2695 | 0.8798 |
| Native control | | 28 | 0.67 | 2.00 | 1.7861 | 0.3762 |

*Table 15. Compound causative construction: Type C*

| Subject Groups | | N | Minimum | Maximum | Mean | Std. deviation |
|---|---|---|---|---|---|---|
| English | LI | 26 | -2.00 | 2.00 | 0.3473 | 0.9592 |
| | IN | 13 | -1.33 | 2.00 | 0.6662 | 0.9619 |
| | HI | 16 | -2.00 | 2.00 | 0.1669 | 1.2408 |
| Japanese | LI | 15 | -1.67 | 1.33 | -0.0680 | 0.8847 |
| | IN | 18 | -1.33 | 0.33 | -0.4633 | 0.5721 |
| | HI | 23 | -1.00 | 2.00 | 0.4491 | 0.8860 |
| Korean | LI | 27 | -2.00 | 2.00 | 0.0370 | 1.1953 |
| | IN | 25 | -2.00 | 1.33 | -0.3204 | 0.9837 |
| | HI | 21 | -2.00 | 2.00 | 0.1424 | 1.0249 |
| Native control | | 28 | 0.33 | 2.00 | 1.4414 | 0.5300 |

*Table 16. Compound causative construction: Type D*

| Subject Groups | | N | Minimum | Maximum | Mean | Std. deviation |
|---|---|---|---|---|---|---|
| English | LI | 26 | -2.00 | 1.33 | -0.5115 | 0.9244 |
| | IN | 13 | -2.00 | 0.67 | -0.6908 | 0.9869 |
| | HI | 16 | -2.00 | 1.33 | -0.7500 | 0.9462 |
| Japanese | LI | 15 | -2.00 | 1.67 | 0.1340 | 0.8980 |
| | IN | 18 | -2.00 | 1.33 | -0.3144 | 0.9733 |
| | HI | 23 | -1.33 | 2.00 | 0.2178 | 1.0716 |
| Korean | LI | 27 | -2.00 | 2.00 | -0.1733 | 0.9404 |
| | IN | 25 | -2.00 | 0.67 | -0.6668 | 0.8215 |
| | HI | 21 | -2.00 | 2.00 | -0.0476 | 1.0659 |
| Native control | | 28 | -0.67 | 2.00 | 1.0354 | 0.6873 |

Table 17. Compound causative construction: Type E

| Subject Groups | | N | Minimum | Maximum | Mean | Std. deviation |
|---|---|---|---|---|---|---|
| English | LI | 26 | -1.00 | 2.00 | 0.3973 | 0.9388 |
| | IN | 13 | -1.67 | 1.67 | 0.0769 | 0.9641 |
| | HI | 16 | -1.33 | 2.00 | 0.9162 | 1.0287 |
| Japanese | LI | 15 | -1.00 | 2.00 | 0.6900 | 0.9134 |
| | IN | 18 | -1.00 | 2.00 | 1.1667 | 0.7518 |
| | HI | 23 | -0.33 | 2.00 | 1.3765 | 0.7737 |
| Korean | LI | 27 | -2.00 | 2.00 | -0.0496 | 0.9602 |
| | IN | 25 | -1.67 | 2.00 | 0.2264 | 1.0878 |
| | HI | 21 | -1.33 | 2.00 | 0.6505 | 1.1327 |
| Native control | | 28 | 0.33 | 2.00 | 1.6432 | 0.4882 |

Table 18. Compound causative construction: Type F

| Subject Groups | | N | Minimum | Maximum | Mean | Std. deviation |
|---|---|---|---|---|---|---|
| English | LI | 26 | -1.67 | 1.33 | -0.0773 | 0.8024 |
| | IN | 13 | -2.00 | 1.67 | -0.0761 | 0.9258 |
| | HI | 16 | -2.00 | 1.67 | -0.6044 | 1.0124 |
| Japanese | LI | 15 | -1.33 | 2.00 | 0.6667 | 0.9681 |
| | IN | 18 | -1.00 | 1.67 | 0.2783 | 0.7701 |
| | HI | 23 | -1.33 | 2.00 | 0.6522 | 1.1399 |
| Korean | LI | 27 | -1.33 | 2.00 | 0.2222 | 0.8519 |
| | IN | 25 | -2.00 | 2.00 | 0.1332 | 1.0450 |
| | HI | 21 | -2.00 | 2.00 | 0.1271 | 1.1763 |
| Native control | | 28 | -1.00 | 2.00 | 1.0596 | 0.8069 |

# Appendix 8  Pair-wise comparisons between judgments on compound causatives in the AJ test

*Table 1. Compound causatives: one-way ANOVA and mean differences between the English groups and the control group in pair-wise Scheffé tests*

| Groups | Group 1. Transitive $V_1$ | | Group 2. Unergative $V_1$ | | Group 3. Trans. $V_1$ + psych $V_2$ | |
|---|---|---|---|---|---|---|
| | Type A | Type B | Type C | Type D | Type E | Type F |
| HI vs. IN | 0.24 | -0.96* | -0.50 | -0.06 | 0.84 | -0.53 |
| HI vs. LI | 0.99** | -0.78* | -0.18 | -0.24 | 0.52 | -0.53 |
| IN vs. LI | 0.76* | 0.18 | 0.32 | -0.18 | -0.32 | 0.00 |
| NS vs. HI | 0.35 | 2.39** | 1.27** | 1.79** | 0.73 | 1.66** |
| NS vs. IN | 0.59* | 1.43** | 0.78 | 1.73** | 1.57** | 1.14* |
| NS vs. LI | 1.35** | 1.61** | 1.09* | 1.55** | 1.25** | 1.14** |
| $F(3, 79)$ | 23.187** | 39.477** | 9.393** | 22.978** | 14.596** | 15.104** |

*$p < 0.05$; **$p < 0.001$

*Table 2. Compound causatives: one-way ANOVA and mean differences between the Japanese groups and the control group in pair-wise Scheffé tests*

| Groups | Group 1. Transitive $V_1$ | | Group 2. Unergative $V_1$ | | Group 3. Trans. $V_1$ + psych $V_2$ | |
|---|---|---|---|---|---|---|
| | Type A | Type B | Type C | Type D | Type E | Type F |
| HI vs. IN | 0.21 | 0.71 | 0.91* | 0.53 | 0.21 | 0.37 |
| HI vs. LI | 0.44 | -0.02 | 0.52 | 0.08 | 0.69* | -0.01 |
| IN vs. LI | 0.23 | -0.73 | -0.40 | -0.45 | 0.48 | -0.39 |
| NS vs. HI | 0.49 | 1.29** | 0.99** | 0.82* | 0.27 | 0.41 |
| NS vs. IN | 0.70* | 2.01** | 1.90** | 1.35* | 0.48 | 0.78 |
| NS vs. LI | 0.93** | 1.28** | 1.51** | 0.90* | 0.95* | 0.39 |
| $F(3, 80)$ | 8.740** | 21.612** | 29.912** | 9.046** | 6.087* | 2.646 |

*$p < 0.05$; **$p < 0.001$

Table 3. Compound causatives: one-way ANOVA and mean differences between the Korean groups and the control group in pair-wise Scheffé tests

| Groups | Group 1. Transitive $V_1$ | | Group 2. Unergative $V_1$ | | Group 3. Trans. $V_1$ + psych $V_2$ | |
|---|---|---|---|---|---|---|
| | Type A | Type B | Type C | Type D | Type E | Type F |
| HI vs. IN | 0.45 | 0.46 | 0.46 | 0.62 | 0.42 | -0.01 |
| HI vs. LI | 0.61 | 0.32 | 0.11 | 0.13 | 0.32 | -0.09 |
| IN vs. LI | 0.16 | -0.14 | -0.36 | -0.49 | -0.11 | -0.09 |
| NS vs. HI | 0.75* | 1.52** | 1.30** | 1.08* | 0.99* | 0.93* |
| NS vs. IN | 1.20** | 1.97** | 1.76** | 1.70** | 1.42** | 0.93* |
| NS vs. LI | 1.36** | 1.84** | 1.40** | 1.21** | 1.31** | 0.84* |
| $F(3, 97)$ | 12.846** | 31.847** | 17.492** | 17.994** | 13.105** | 5.857* |

*$p < 0.05$; **$p < 0.001$

Table 4. Compound causatives: one-way ANOVA and mean differences between the three low-intermediate groups in pair-wise Scheffé tests

| Groups | Group 1. Transitive $V_1$ | | Group 2. Unergative $V_1$ | | Group 3. Trans. $V_1$ + psych $V_2$ | |
|---|---|---|---|---|---|---|
| | Type A | Type B | Type C | Type D | Type E | Type F |
| ES vs. JS | -0.41 | -0.33 | -0.29 | 0.42 | -0.65 | -0.74* |
| ES vs. KS | 0.01 | 0.23 | 0.06 | 0.31 | -0.34 | -0.30 |
| JS vs. KS | 0.43 | 0.56 | 0.36 | -0.11 | 0.31 | 0.44 |
| $F(2, 65)$ | 1.104 | 1.652 | 0.936 | 2.414 | 0.733 | 3.566* |

*$p < 0.05$; **$p < 0.001$

Table 5. Compound causatives: one-way ANOVA and mean differences between the three intermediate groups in pair-wise Scheffé tests

| Groups | Group 1. Transitive $V_1$ | | Group 2. Unergative $V_1$ | | Group 3. Trans. $V_1$ + psych $V_2$ | |
|---|---|---|---|---|---|---|
| | Type A | Type B | Type C | Type D | Type E | Type F |
| ES vs. JS | 0.11 | 0.58 | 1.13* | -0.38 | -1.09* | -0.35 |
| ES vs. KS | 0.61 | 0.55 | 0.99* | -0.02 | -0.15 | -0.21 |
| JS vs. KS | 0.50 | -0.03 | -0.14 | 0.35 | 0.94* | 0.15 |
| $F(2, 53)$ | 2.469 | 2.133 | 7.403* | 0.959 | 6.574* | 0.540 |

*$p < 0.05$; **$p < 0.001$

Table 6. Compound causatives: one-way ANOVA and mean differences between the three high-intermediate groups in pair-wise Scheffé tests

| Groups | Group 1. Transitive $V_1$ | | Group 2. Unergative $V_1$ | | Group 3. Trans. $V_1$ + psych $V_2$ | |
|---|---|---|---|---|---|---|
| | Type A | Type B | Type C | Type D | Type E | Type F |
| ES vs. JS | 0.14 | -1.10* | -0.28 | -0.97 | -0.46 | -1.26* |
| ES vs. KS | 0.39 | -0.87 | 0.02 | -0.70 | 0.27 | -0.73 |
| JS vs. KS | 0.25 | 0.22 | 0.31 | 0.27 | 0.73 | 0.53 |
| $F(2, 57)$ | 1.370 | 5.350* | 0.580 | 4.211* | 3.094 | 5.928* |

*$p < 0.05$; **$p < 0.001$